Tennyson
Interviews and Recollections

Other Interviews and Recollections volumes available on

BRENDAN BEHAN (*two volumes*) *edited by E. H. Mikhail*
DICKENS (*two volumes*) *edited by Philip Collins*
HENRY JAMES *edited by Norman Page*
KIPLING *edited by Harold Orel*
D. H. LAWRENCE (*two volumes*) *edited by Norman Page*
KARL MARX *edited by David McLellan*
THACKERAY (*two volumes*) *edited by Philip Collins*
H. G. WELLS *edited by J. R. Hammond*

Further titles in preparation

Also by Norman Page

THE LANGUAGE OF JANE AUSTEN
SPEECH IN THE ENGLISH NOVEL
THOMAS HARDY
THOMAS HARDY: The Writer and his Background (*editor*)
WILKIE COLLINS: The Critical Heritage (*editor*)
NABOKOV: The Critical Heritage (*editor*)
A DICKENS COMPANION
D. H. LAWRENCE: Interviews and Recollection (*editor*)
HENRY JAMES: Interviews and Recollections (*editor*)
E. M. FORSTER'S POSTHUMOUS FICTION
A KIPLING COMPANION
THOMAS HARDY ANNUAL (*editor*)
A. E. HOUSMAN: A Critical Biography

TENNYSON

Interviews and Recollections

Edited by

Norman Page

Professor of English
University of Alberta

MACMILLAN

First edition 1983
Reprinted 1985

Published by
THE MACMILLAN PRESS LTD
Houndmills, Basingstoke, Hampshire RG21 2XS
and London
Companies and representatives
throughout the world

Printed in Hong Kong

ISBN 0-333-28740-1 (*hardcover*)
ISBN 0-333-38658-2 (*paperback*)

Contents

Acknowledgement

The editor and publishers are grateful to Hallam Tennyson for granting permission to reproduce 'Memories of my Grandfather' by Sir Charles Tennyson.

Introduction

Tennyson was the last great English poet to enjoy the kind of public attention nowadays reserved for royalty and members of the entertainment industry—though 'enjoy' is hardly the right word, for he intensely disliked finding himself the object of vulgar curiosity, and could even be mildly paranoiac on the subject of invaders of his carefully contrived privacy: on one occasion sensitiveness conspired with short-sightedness to produce a ludicrous situation, the historian Lecky recalling Tennyson's 'alarm at a flock of sheep which he took for tourists'. But the irritation and resentment were usually well founded, and Lecky also notes that 'true privacy... became impossible to him, and troops of tourists, newspaper writers and interviewers were constantly occupied with his doings'.[1] His indignation extended to the intrusions of literary scholars and biographers: he believed that a writer may give his work to the public without also making it a present of his private life, and he obviously hated and feared the idea of posthumous prying. The stern injunction 'No trespassing' applied alike to his personality, his home life, his friendships and his workshop. A late sonnet, 'Poets and their Bibliographies', deplores what his friend William Allingham called the 'raking together and publishing the fragments of a deceased Poet'. An earlier poem, 'To ——, After Reading a Life and Letters', ironically summarises the demands catered for by opportunistic biographers almost before their subject is cold in his grave:

> 'Proclaim the faults he would not show:
> Break lock and seal: betray the trust:
> Keep nothing sacred: 'tis but just
> The many-headed beast should know.'

It was a theme to which Tennyson's conversation frequently turned in his later years, most tersely in the phrase 'After death the ghouls!'

Yet it would have been astonishing if a figure and personality so striking and so fascinating had not caught the attention of 'the many-headed beast'; and fortunately for us, if not for Tennyson, that figure and personality also impelled many of those who encountered him, briefly or otherwise, to put on record their impressions or their memories. He was, wrote Margot Asquith, 'a magnificent creature to look at. He had everything: height, figure, carriage, feature, and expression.'[2] Unusually tall, powerfully built (he once picked up a donkey and carried it across the lawn), 'Hercules as well as Apollo' as his friend Brookfield remarked, with a swarthy, gipsy-like complexion giving him a very un-English appearance, he looked in his youth every inch the romantic poet, and in his old age every inch the Bard who had become a national institution. He was, indeed, the last poet who could be referred to by his contemporaries, unfacetiously and unironically, as 'the Bard'. Extreme myopia was a social handicap but did not prevent him from registering minute details at close range: he once saw the moon reflected in a nightingale's eye. As if to compensate for his myopia, his hearing was exceptionally acute (he 'could hear the shriek of a bat'). He possessed considerable histrionic powers and, like Dickens, was a celebrated and to some extent a compulsive reader of his own work, though unlike Dickens he never did so for money; he exploited the resources of his powerful voice like a singer, and his vocal powers, combined with strong traces of a Lincolnshire accent and eccentric pronunciation of some common words, added up to a very distinctive performance. A reading by Tennyson was a memorable experience, and to other accounts presented in this volume may be added that of Edward FitzGerald:

Mouthing out his hollow oes and aes, deep-chested music, this is something as A. T. reads, with a broad north country vowel, except the u in such words as 'mute', 'brute', which he pronounces like the thin French 'u'. His voice, very deep and deep-chested, but rather murmuring than mouthing, like the sound of a far sea or of a pine-wood . . .[3]

and another by F. T. Palgrave:

casual hearers have found Tennyson's method too little varied or emphatic, his voice and delivery monotonous. Yet those who knew the speaker could easily see causes which explained and justified his method. Tennyson's grand range and 'timbre' of voice; his power of modulation; his great *sostenuto* power; the *portamento* so justly dear to Italian vocalists, might be the truer word; the ample resonant utterance: all was simply no deliberate art of recital but the direct outward representative, the effluence at once of his own deepest sentiment as to what Poetry should be, and of the intention, the aspiration, of his own poems.[4]

He was also, as many witnesses testify, a brilliant conversationalist, often racier and more vigorous than the hushed references to 'the Bard' might lead us to suppose. He once asked 'a rather gushing lady' what birds she imagined were referred to in the famous stanza in *Maud*

> Birds in the high Hall-garden,
> When twilight was falling,
> Maud, Maud, Maud, Maud,
> They were crying and calling.

' "Nightingales," was the rather sentimental answer. "Who ever heard a nightingale say 'Maud'?" was the somewhat stern reply. "They were rooks of course." '[5]

Tennyson had read widely and possessed a large and varied store of information on scientific topics as well as classical and modern literature. 'I hate learning', he once said to Benjamin Jowett[6]— which we may take as meaning that he had a passion for knowledge but a contempt for pedantry and the pursuit of information for its own sake. Knowledge was important to Tennyson because it might turn out to provide the key to an understanding of the meaning of life, and the quest for religious certainty can be said to have dominated his thinking from youth onwards. Although deeply versed in classical literature, he was very much a man of his own age and shared the excitements and doubts that were part of the Victorian intellectual and spiritual experience. *In Memoriam*, one of the most popular poems of its age, is a monument to the doubts; the excitement can be seen, informally and in miniature, in a conversation which took place in 1848 and which was recorded by Mrs Rundle Charles:

> Then he turned to Geology, Weald of Kent, Delta of a great river flowing from as far as Newfoundland. 'Conceive,' he said, 'what an era of the world that must have been, great lizards, marshes, gigantic ferns!' Fancied, standing by a railway at night, the engine must be like some great Ichthyosaurus.[7]

If Virgil and Shakespeare were important to Tennyson's mental development, so were the coming of the railways and Lyell's publications on geology in the 1830s.

Not least, he had a great capacity for friendship; and since he came into contact at one time or another with most of the major figures of the period, from Queen Victoria and Mr Gladstone downwards, an account of Tennyson's life and career is also an account of a large segment of the Victorian age. Especially after he settled on the Isle of Wight in the early 1850s, he entertained in succession an impressive crowd of notabilities: he had retreated from public prying (not entirely successfully), but he was no recluse. His neighbour Wilfrid Ward has given a muster-roll of 'the remarkable people who congregated from time to time round the poet's home in the island. They include Carlyle, Ruskin, Tyndall, Darwin, Lord Dufferin, Palgrave, D. G. Rossetti, Holman Hunt, Lecky, Aubrey de Vere, Sir Henry Taylor, Herschel, Longfellow, Auberon, Herbert, Pollock, Allingham, and many another.'[8] To this list must be added the distinguished residents of the island, such as W. G. Ward, Julia Margaret Cameron, and the Queen herself. As the 1883 cruise on the *Pembroke Castle* amusingly illustrates (see p. 161 below), it was still a time when a poet could consort socially with the crowned heads of Europe.

Tennyson's was a life which possessed something of the quality of legend, but most of the ingredients of the legend seem to have had a firm basis in fact. The final scene, the exemplary death-bed that was an indispensable conclusion to every Victorian *Life*, has an extra-ordinary appropriateness. An eye-witness's account appears near the end of this volume, but Queen Victoria's journal entry for 6 October 1892 manages to catch something of the tableau-like quality and symbolic power: 'He died with his hand on his Shakespeare, and the moon shining full into the window, and over him. A worthy end to such a remarkable man.'[9] Given this legendary quality, no wonder the epithet 'Tennysonian' gained currency in a way that 'Browning-esque' and 'Arnoldian' did not. Elizabeth Barrett's use of it as early as 1845[10] considerably antedates the first example (1853) given by the *Oxford English Dictionary*; 'Browningesque', it seems, appeared only after the poet's death; and 'Arnoldian' does not earn a place in the *OED* at all. The word 'Tennysonian' surely acknowledges the distinctive force of an exceptional personality—a poetic personality, of course, as well as a domestic and social one.

Tennyson was venerated in his later years, and not only for strictly poetic reasons. Jowett's remark that 'merely being in the neighbour-hood of Alfred keeps me up to a higher standard of what ought to be in writing and thinking' conveys something of the inspirational and admonitory power of Tennyson's presence, and many of the accounts written in the years following his death, as well as some written during his lifetime, have a strong flavour of hagiography. The reverent chorus has, however, a few members who sing agreeably out of tune. The impressions of that delightful and irreverent bluestocking Jane Harrison, for instance, come as a refreshing contrast:

He met us at the station, grunting fiercely that he 'was not going to dress for dinner because I had come'. It was rather frightening, but absurd. The vain old thing (he was the most openly vain man I ever met) knew quite well that he looked his best in his ample poet's cloak.... He was very kind to me according to his rather fierce lights; he took me a long, memorable Sunday morning walk, recited *Maud* to me, and countless other things. It was an anxious joy; he often forgot his own poems, and was obviously annoyed if I could not supply the words. He would stop suddenly and ask angrily 'Do you think Browning could have written that line? Do you think Swinburne could?' I could truthfully answer, 'Impossible.' If he posed a good deal, he was scarcely to blame; the house was so charged with an atmosphere of hero-worship that free breathing was difficult....[11]

Among Tennyson's intimates, William Allingham is outstanding for the impression he gives of setting down in his journal (generously represented in this selection) his recollections of the poet's talk with an invigorating immediacy and lack of solemnity. Tennyson hated 'Boswellising', but Allingham's sympathetic and assiduous playing of the Boswellian role is something for which we may be grateful.

The witnesses assembled in this collection were of different generations and enjoyed different kinds of relationship with their subject. Their composite account provides a portrait of the poet and his circle, and to some extent of the Victorian age, throughout most of which his creative life extended. The mainly chronological arrangement means that the material can be read consecutively as a fairly unbroken narrative of Tennyson's life. As with most biographical documentation, material is least abundant for the early years, though FitzGerald and others provide some memorable glimpses of the young Tennyson. The great watershed is 1850: the middle of the century, almost the middle of Tennyson's own life, the year of his long-delayed marriage, of *In Memoriam* and of the Laureateship; thereafter there is an abundance of material of many kinds, in letters, journals, memoirs, articles in periodicals, and the like.

Three works have been of special value to me in annotating the selections. The two volumes of Hallam Tennyson's life of his father, *Alfred Lord Tennyson: A Memoir* (London: Macmillan, 1897), contain a mass of material adequate use of which would have made this selection much longer than it is. It is cited as *Memoir* throughout, and I assume that anyone seriously interested in Tennyson will want sooner or later to turn to it. The Tennyson family tradition of biography has been continued in our own time by the poet's grandson, the late Sir Charles Tennyson, whose books[12] are an important source of information. Christopher Ricks's edition of *The*

Poems of Tennyson in the Annotated English Poets series (London: Longmans, 1969) is indispensable and could hardly be improved on; I have referred to it in my notes as 'Ricks', the number following in each instance being the number assigned by Professor Ricks to the poem in question. Finally, like so many, I owe an enormous debt of profit and pleasure to that remarkable work of reference, the *Dictionary of National Biography*; there can be few standard works of reference at once so useful and so readable. My notes attempt to provide additional information, mainly biographical and bibliographical, that may be helpful to the student and interesting to the reader.

Although Tennyson would probably have taken a dim view of this volume, its editor hopes that readers and students of his poetry will find that the testimony of those who knew him in his habit as he lived significantly enriches their sense of his powerful and many-sided personality. Despite Tennyson's fears, it is a life that can stand the test of multiple close-range scrutiny: it may be that no man is a hero to his valet, but he was unmistakably one to most of those who encountered him. The Queen herself was the most eminent Victorian to be struck by 'the greatness and largeness of his mind', and her phrase is echoed in the pages that follow by many of her subjects.

NOTES

1. *Memoir*, ii, pp. 200–1.
2. *The Autobiography of Margot Asquith* (London: Penguin Books, 1936) p. 166.
3. *Memoir*, i, p. 194.
4. Ibid., ii, p. 493.
5. H. M. Butler, 'Recollections of Tennyson', in *Tennyson and his Friends*, ed. Hallam Tennyson (London: Macmillan, 1911) p. 215. For another version of this anecdote, see p. 67 below.
6. *Memoir*, ii, p. 463.
7. Ibid., i, p. 277.
8. Wilfrid Ward, 'Tennyson and W. F. Ward and Other Farringford Friends', in *Tennyson and his Friends*, p. 229.
9. *Dear and Honoured Lady: the Correspondence between Queen Victoria and Alfred Tennyson*, ed. Hope Dyson and Charles Tennyson (London: Macmillan, 1969) p. 140.
10. In a letter to Miss Mitford dated 4 June 1845—*Elizabeth Barrett to Miss Mitford*, ed. Betty Miller (London: John Murray, 1954) p. 245.
11. Jane Ellen Harrison, *Reminiscences of a Student's Life* (London: Hogarth Press, 1925) pp. 46–7.

12. Sir Charles Tennyson, *Alfred Tennyson* (London: Macmillan, 1949; paperback edn 1968); *Six Tennyson Essays* (London: Cassell, 1954); and, jointly with Hope Dyson, *The Tennysons: Background to Genius* (London: Macmillan, 1974). The last of these has a very interesting appendix on Tennyson's conversation.

A Tennyson Chronology

1809   (6 August) Born at Somersby, Lincolnshire, fourth son of Rev. George Tennyson, Rector of Somersby, and Elizabeth Tennyson.

1815   Attends Louth Grammar School.

1820   Continues his education at home under his father's supervision.

1823–4   Writes verse-drama *The Devil and the Lady*. Father suffers breakdown in 1824.

1827   (April) *Poems by Two Brothers* appears (by Alfred and Charles Tennyson).

        (November) Alfred and Charles enter Trinity College, Cambridge.

1829   Meets Arthur Hallam; becomes a member of the 'Apostles', a select undergraduate debating society; wins the Chancellor's Gold Medal for his poem 'Timbuctoo'.

1830   *Poems, Chiefly Lyrical* appears.

1831   George Tennyson dies in March; Tennyson leaves Cambridge without taking a degree.

1832   Travels to Germany with Hallam; *Poems* published at the end of the year.

1833   (September) Hallam dies in Vienna.

1834   Falls in love with Rosa Baring.

1837   The Tennysons leave Lincolnshire and settle at High Beech, Epping, in Essex.

1838   Becomes engaged to Emily Sellwood.

1840   Engagement broken off; Tennysons move to Tunbridge Wells, Kent; Tennyson begins to suffer from a protracted nervous illness.

1842   Publishes *Poems* in two volumes.

1843   Collapse of the business venture in which Tennyson has invested his inheritance; he takes a 'water-cure' at a hospital near Cheltenham.

1845   Is granted a Civil List pension of £200 a year.

1846   Visits Switzerland.

1847   Publishes *The Princess*.

1848   Visits Ireland and Cornwall.

1850   (May) *In Memoriam* appears.

	(June) marries Emily Sellwood.
	(November) succeeds Wordsworth as Poet Laureate.
1851	Visits Italy.
1852	Birth of Hallam Tennyson.
1853	Moves from Twickenham to Farringford on the Isle of Wight.
1854	Lionel Tennyson born.
1855	*Maud, and Other Poems* published.
1859	*Idylls of the King* appears.
1861	Visits the Pyrenees.
1862	First audience with Queen Victoria.
1864	Publishes *Enoch Arden*.
1868	Begins to build another home at Aldworth, near Haslemere, on the Surrey–Sussex border.
1869	Becomes a founder-member of the Metaphysical Society; publishes *The Holy Grail and Other Poems*.
1872	Publishes 'Gareth and Lynette'.
1875	Publishes his verse-drama *Queen Mary*.
1876	*Queen Mary* produced; *Harold* published.
1880	Publishes *Ballads and Other Poems*.
1881	Henry Irving produces and appears with Ellen Terry in *The Cup*.
1883	Accepts a barony (the offer of a baronetcy had been refused in 1865, 1873 and 1874).
1884	Publishes *Becket*.
1885	Publishes *Tiresias and Other Poems*.
1886	Death of Lionel Tennyson; publishes *Locksley Hall Sixty Years After*.
1889	Publishes *Demeter and Other Poems*.
1892	(6 October) Death of Tennyson.
	The Death of Œnone, Akbar's Dream, and Other Poems published posthumously.

Early Days*

HALLAM TENNYSON

My aunt Cecilia[1] (Mrs Lushington) narrates how in the winter evenings by the firelight little Alfred would take her on his knee with Arthur and Matilda leaning against him on either side, the baby Horatio[2] between his legs; and how he would fascinate this group of young hero-worshippers, who listened open-eared and open-mouthed to legends of knights and heroes among untravelled forests rescuing distressed damsels, or on gigantic mountains fighting with dragons, or to his tales about Indians, or demons, or witches. The brothers and sisters would sometimes act one of the old English plays; and the elder members of the family thought that my father, from his dramatic rendering of his parts and his musical voice, would turn out an actor.

When he was seven years old he was asked, 'Will you go to sea or to school?' He said, 'To school', thinking that school was a kind of paradise; so he was taken to the house of his grandmother at Louth . . . and he was sent to the Grammar School there, then under the Rev. J. Waite, a tempestuous, flogging master of the old stamp. He remembered to his dying day sitting on the stone steps of the school on a cold winter's morning, and crying bitterly after a big lad had brutally cuffed him on the head because he was a new boy . . . .

A few years ago the present master of Louth School gave a holiday in my father's honour. The compliment gratified him; yet he said, 'How I did hate that school! The only good I ever got from it was the memory of the words, "*sonus desilientis aquae*",[3] and of an old wall covered with wild weeds opposite the school windows.' . . .

. . . he wrote the following note for me in 1890:

According to the best of my recollection, when I was about eight years old, I covered two sides of a slate with Thomsonian blank verse in praise of flowers for my brother Charles, who was a year older than I was, Thomson[4] then being the only poet I knew. Before I could read, I was in the habit on a stormy day of spreading my arms to the wind, and crying out 'I hear a voice that's speaking in the wind', and the words 'far, far away' had always a strange charm for me. About ten or eleven Pope's *Homer's Iliad*[5]

Memoir, pp. 5–7, 10–12, 16–17, 20.

became a favourite of mine and I wrote hundreds and hundreds of lines in the regular Popeian metre, nay even could improvise them, so could my two elder brothers, for my father was a poet and could write regular metre very skilfully. . . . At about twelve and onward I wrote an epic of six thousand lines à la Walter Scott[6]—full of battles, dealing too with sea and mountain scenery,—with Scott's regularity of octosyllables and his occasional varieties. Though the performance was very likely worth nothing I never felt myself more truly inspired. I wrote as much as seventy lines at one time, and used to go shouting them about the fields in the dark. . . .

. . . my uncle Arthur adds a few words:

Alfred and I often took long rambles together, and on one particular afternoon, when we were in the home fields talking of our respective futures, he said most emphatically, 'Well, Arthur, I mean to be famous.' (From his earliest years he felt that he was a poet, and earnestly trained himself to be worthy of his vocation.) . . .

There is a story current in the family that Frederick,[7] when an Eton schoolboy, was shy of going to a neighbouring dinner-party to which he had been invited. 'Fred,' said his younger brother, 'think of Herschel's[8] great star-patches, and you will soon get over all that.'

In the summertime Dr and Mrs Tennyson took their holiday by the seaside, mostly at Mablethorpe.[9] From his boyhood my father had a passion for the sea, and especially for the North Sea in wild weather.

NOTES

Hallam Tennyson (1852–1928) was the poet's eldest son and biographer.

1. Tennyson's youngest sister, born in 1817; she married Edmund Lushington in 1842.

2. Arthur Tennyson, born 1814; Matilda, born 1816; Horatio, the youngest child, born 1819.

3. 'The sound of falling water' (Latin). Ovid uses the phrase 'desilientis aquae'.

4. James Thomson's very popular poem The Seasons was published in 1726–30.

5. Pope's translation in heroic couplets appeared in 1715–20 and was widely read.

6. Scott's best-known poems appeared between 1805 and 1815.

7. Frederick Tennyson, born 1807; he contributed four poems to the

inaccurately titled *Poems by Two Brothers* in 1827 (largely by Alfred and
Charles), and subsequently published several volumes of verse.
  8. Sir William Herschel (1738–1822) discovered Uranus and many stars
and nebulae.
  9. On the Lincolnshire coast, about fifteen miles from Somersby.

Lincolnshire Memories*

ROBERT ROBERTS

In an interview about ten years ago with the old Parish Clerk of Bag
Enderby, who was then aged eighty-six, I asked him if he could
remember anything about Tennyson. 'Tennyson,' said he. 'D'ya
meän tha owd doctor?'[1] Said I, 'Not the doctor particularly, but any
of the Tennyson family.' He replied , 'Tha doctor was a fine owd
gentleman. I remember on 'im dying. It's a strange long time agoä,
an' he's in a fine big tomb ageän the church.'
    I asked, 'Do you remember any of the family, any of the
sons—Charles or Alfred?' He began to think, stared vacantly, and, as
the past dimly rose before him, slowly said. 'Y-e-e-s, I do remember
Master Alfred, sewer-ly; he was alus walkin' about tha lanes and
closins wi' a book in 'is 'and; but then he grew up he wornt at 'oäm
much; assiver he went up to Lunnun or some big place, and when he
yeust ta cum 'oäme fur a bit one o' tha sarvants teld me he yeust ta
goä upstairs in a top room, an' 'ing a mat ower 'is doär. I doant kna'
what fur, but they sed he didn't want ta 'ear noa noise.'
    I tried many of the villagers, but the principal things which they
remembered were that the poet's father was a 'fine man, wi' a big
beard'; by which was meant a big, powerful man, and that Alfred was
always 'dawdlin' about wi' a book'. According to rustic notions, such a
young fellow ought to have been rabbiting or rat-catching, or
indulging in some other 'sport'.
    My old friend, the late W. B. Philpot, vicar of South Berstead, who
was once curate to Charles Tennyson Turner,[2] at Grasby, told me
the following characteristic anecdote, which was related by his
rector. It seems it was the custom of the two brothers, when quite
boys, to practise making verses as they walked in the fields; and as
they wished to be in company, but did not want to distract each

* W. Robertson Nicoll and Thomas J. Wise (eds), *Literary Anecdotes of the
Nineteenth Century*, II (London: Hodder and Stoughton, 1906) pp. 422–3,
426.

other's attention, they agreed to walk one on each side of a hedge. One day as they were thus engaged, Alfred called to his brother over the hedge, 'Charles! I have made such a splendid line! Listen!—"A thousand brazen chariots rolled over a bridge of brass." '

NOTES

1. Dr George Clayton Tennyson (1778–1831), Tennyson's father.
2. Charles Tennyson (1808–79), elder brother of Alfred, later adopted the name Turner. He was joint author with Alfred of *Poems by Two Brothers* (1827) and published several volumes of verse on his own account.

At Cambridge*

HALLAM TENNYSON

Fanny Kemble,[1] who used to visit her brother John, said of him when at College, 'Alfred Tennyson was our hero, the great hero of our day.' Another friend describes him as 'Six feet high, broad-chested, strong-limbed, his face Shakespearian, with deep eyelids, his forehead ample, crowned with dark wavy hair, his head finely poised, his hand the admiration of sculptors, long fingers with square tips, soft as a child's but of great size and strength. What struck one most about him was the union of strength with refinement.' On seeing him first come into the Hall at Trinity, Thompson[2] said at once, 'That man must be a poet.' Arthur Hallam 'looked up to him as to a great poet and an elder brother'.

Hallam said to Trench[3] in 1832, 'Alfred's mind is what it always was, or rather, brighter, and more vigorous. I regret, with you, that you have never had the opportunity of knowing more of him. His nervous temperament and habits of solitude give an appearance of affectation to his manner, which is no interpreter of the man, and wears off on further knowledge. Perhaps you would never become very intimate, for certainly your bents of mind are not the same, and at some points they intersect; yet I think you would hardly fail to see much for love, as well as for admiration.' Blakesley[4] described Alfred as 'Truly one of the mighty of the earth.' ...

As a young man my father's friends have often described him to me as having Johnsonian common-sense and a rare power of expression, very genial, full of enjoyment, full of sensitiveness and

* *Memoir*, pp. 35, 40, 48–9.

full of humour, though with the passionate heart of a poet, and sometimes feeling the melancholy of life. He passed through 'moods of misery unutterable', but he eventually shook them off. He remembered how when in London almost for the first time, one of these moods came over him, as he realised that 'in a few years all its inhabitants would be lying horizontal, stark and stiff in their coffins.' . . .

In certain college rooms he was often asked to declaim the many ballads which he knew by heart, 'Clerke Saunders', 'Helen of Kirkconnel', 'May Margaret', and others: and also his own poems 'The Hesperides', 'The Lover's Tale' (written 1827), 'The Coach of Death'; and he would improvise verses by the score full of lyrical passion. I quote . . . from Edward FitzGerald:[5] '"Oriana" Tennyson used to repeat in a way not to be forgotten at Cambridge tables.'

For his exercise he either rowed, or fenced, or took long walks, and would go any distance to see 'a bubbling brook'. 'Somehow', he would say, 'water is the element I love best of all the four.'

NOTES

1. Fanny Kemble (1809–93), a well-known actress who published poems and an autobiography. For her visit to Tennyson at Aldworth in 1871, see *Memoir*, II, p. 108.

2. William Hepworth Thompson (1810–86), Fellow of Trinity College from 1834; subsequently Regius Professor of Greek at Cambridge and Master of Trinity.

3. Richard Chenevix Trench (1807–86), educated at Trinity College, Cambridge, became Archbishop of Dublin and a noted scholar.

4. Joseph Williams Blakesley (1808–85), another Trinity friend of Tennyson, became Dean of Lincoln. The early poem beginning 'Clear-headed friend' (Ricks, 74) is addressed to him.

5. See p. 7.

The Bachelor Years*

EDWARD FITZGERALD

To John Allen from Manchester, 23 May 1835

Alfred Tennyson stayed with me at Ambleside: Spedding[1] was forced to go home, till the last two days of my stay there. I will say no

* From *FitzGerald: Selected Works*, ed. Joanna Richardson (London: Hart-Davis, 1962) pp. 466, 473, 485, 492, 537, 549, 557.

more of Tennyson than that the more I have seen of him, the more cause I have to think him great. His little humours and grumpinesses were so droll, that I was always laughing: and was often put in mind (strange to say) of my little unknown friend, Undine[2]—I must however say, further, that I felt what Charles Lamb describes, a sense of depression at times from the overshadowing of a so much more lofty intellect than my own: this (though it may seem vain to say so) I never experienced before, though I have often been with much greater intellects: but I could not be mistaken in the universality of his mind; and perhaps I have received some benefit in the now more distinct consciousness of my dwarfishness.

To Bernard Barton from London, April 1838

We have had Alfred Tennyson here; very droll, and very wayward: and much sitting up of nights till two and three in the morning with pipes in our mouths: at which good hour we would get Alfred to give us some of his magic music, which he does between growling and smoking; and so to bed.

To Bernard Barton, 17 February 1840

When I got to my lodgings [in London], I found A. Tennyson installed in them: he has been here ever since in a very uneasy state: being really ill, in a nervous way: what with an hereditary tenderness of nerve, and having spoiled what strength he had by incessant smoking etc.—I have also made him very out of sorts by desiring a truce from complaints and complainings—Poor fellow: he is quite magnanimous, and noble natured, with no meanness or vanity or affectation of any kind whatever—but very perverse, according to the nature of his illness—So much for poets, who, one must allow, are many of them a somewhat tetchy race. . . .

To Bernard Barton from London, April 1841

A. Tennyson and I pass some hours together every day and night: with pipes and brandy and water—I hope he will publish ere long. He is a great fellow. But he is ruining himself by mismanagement and neglect of all kinds. He must smoke twelve hours out of the twenty-four . . . .

To Bernard Barton from London, 4 May 1846

Tomorrow Tennyson and I are going to get a pint or two of fresh air at Richmond: and we are to wind up our day at Carlyle's by way of a refreshing evening's entertainment. I met C. last night at Tennyson's; and they two discussed the merits of this world and the next, till I wished myself out of *this*, at any rate.

To E. B. Cowell from London, November 1848

Tennyson is emerged half-cured, or half-destroyed, from a water establishment:[3] has gone to a new doctor who gives him iron pills; and altogether this really great man thinks more about his bowels and nerves than about the Laureate wreath he was born to inherit. Not but he meditates new poems; and now *The Princess* is done,[4] he turns to King Arthur—a worthy subject indeed—and has consulted some histories of him, and spent some time in visiting his tradition-ary haunts in Cornwall.[5] But I believe the trumpet can wake Tennyson no longer to do great deeds; I may mistake and prove myself an owl; which I hope may be the case. But how are we to expect heroic poems from a valetudinary? I have told him he should fly from England and go among savages.

To Frederick Tennyson from Woodbridge, 7 March 1850

I don't find myself growing old about poetry; on the contrary. I wish I could take twenty years off Alfred's shoulders, and set him up in his youthful glory .... He is the same magnanimous, kindly, de-lightful fellow as ever; uttering by far the finest prose sayings of anyone.

NOTES

Edward FitzGerald (1809–83) was a contemporary of Tennyson at Trinity College, Cambridge. He is best remembered as the translator of Omar Khayyam, but he also wrote some very attractive letters; the above selection gives glimpses of the occasional meetings of the two friends during the period 1835–50. They saw little of each other in later years, but for a touching account of their last meeting in 1876 see p. 126.

1. James Spedding (1808–81) had been at Trinity with Tennyson and FitzGerald; he later published an important edition of Bacon.

2. A sylph in the fairy romance of that name by the Baron de la Motte Fouque (published 1811).

3. In the autumn of 1848 Tennyson, anxious concerning his health, took a water cure at Malvern.

4. *The Princess* was finished in 1847 and published on Christmas Day of that year.

5. Tennyson toured Cornwall in May–July 1848: *Memoir*, I, pp. 274–6, quotes extracts from his journal for that period (e.g. on 7 June he 'sought for King Arthur's stone').

'Early Recollections of Tennyson'*

JANE BROOKFIELD

As one of the few surviving friends of his earlier days, I can still remember him in the splendour of his youth and in the dawn of his great reputation. During the many years that have gone by since that time, I can gratefully recall his unvarying friendship towards me and mine. Many months, and sometimes even years, might pass without our meeting, but whenever we were within easy reach again, there was never any change in Alfred Tennyson's kindly welcome to my husband and myself. He took up the thread of former days, and even sometimes of former conversations, exactly as if we had continued to see each other without any break at all; and in the peace and restfulness of his most happy home, those who were dearest to him were equally faithful in their goodness and consideration towards all for whom he cared. He was consistently loyal towards those whom he had once accepted as his friends.

It must have been as long ago as the year 1839, when I was a very young girl, that my future husband, the Rev. W. H. Brookfield, brought his early college friend, Alfred Tennyson, to be introduced to my father, who was himself a poet and of literary and classical reputation.

The name of Alfred Tennyson had long been familiar in our family, as the dearest friend of my first cousin, Arthur Hallam, on whose early death, in 1833, *In Memoriam* was written. Alfred Tennyson was, therefore, gladly welcomed by my father and by the remainder of our family—my mother had died long before.

As I remember him at that time, he was wonderfully handsome, and of tall and stately presence.

Although always courteous, he was on this first visit to us reserved and silent for some time, until he gradually thawed under the sympathetic influence of his friend Brookfield, to whom he was greatly attached, and the conversation became generally interesting and agreeable. But when a slight pause occurred Tennyson slowly rose from his chair, and with grave deliberation laid his hand on my father's remarkably fine and intellectual head, saying, 'You must do

* *Temple Bar*, CI (1894) 203–7.

a great many foolish things, sir, with this great bump of benevolence of yours.' My father answered genially, 'I daresay I do'—and we were all much amused, though a little awed, at the same time. With all Lord Tennyson's depth and originality of thought, the homage and admiration which became so widely accorded to him, never led to his despising 'the day of small things'.

Good-nature is usually treated as a very common-place virtue, the one redeeming quality perhaps allowed to an otherwise stupid man. But when it is combined with the highest genius and the most critical ability, it is a delightful surprise, and this was most conspicuous in Alfred Tennyson: he was so thoroughly kind, compassionate, and sympathetic with all genuine trouble or perplexity.

I remember the exceeding good-nature and interest he took in a very clever and imaginative boy of about twelve years old, who was spending a few days of his holidays with our kind friend Mrs Cameron at Freshwater. Tennyson had heard he was not very happy at school. He invited him to his house, and dispelled all shyness and reserve by conversing with him, on equal terms, as it were, so as to set the dear boy at his ease, by discussing the books that he took interest in reading out of school, and leading him on by degrees to give an epitome, in his own words, of Miss Braddon's latest three-volume novel.[1] Tennyson followed the whole narrative, as told him by his young schoolboy friend, with kindly attention, and this friendly sympathy in his young visitor's pursuits and interests out of school, did more to cheer him, than any questionings about his grievances would have done.

The great charm of Tennyson's sense of humour has made itself felt even in his poetry, but it was always like a reserve fund near at hand in daily life—and the exceeding dignity and seriousness of his usual demeanour made these frequent flashes of amusement, the more welcome.

In his younger days he would allow his friends to laugh at, as well as with him, and receive it with only playful indignation; sometimes, perhaps, he would wilfully provoke their criticisms. On one occasion, after they had left Cambridge, my husband remembered dining with Tennyson, George Venables,[2] and others, at the Reform Club. After dinner, in contempt of all formality, Tennyson persisted in resting his feet on the table. His friends remonstrated in vain, until one of them said, 'Take care, Alfred, they will think you are Longfellow.' Down went the feet.

In later years, it was without the least touch of adapting himself to a lower level, that he would interest himself in ordinary everyday questions. At one time, he told me he very much wished to find out whether ladies liked their male acquaintances to assume a gentler tone of voice, when speaking to them, from that in which they talked to each other. Alfred said he disliked this affection of consideration towards what is called 'the weaker sex', and that he preferred to think that the tone of voice, as well as the subject of conversation, should need no remodelling to make it fit for ladies to hear. Although with his intimate friends his conversation was full of depth and earnestness, on all serious subjects, he would from time to time, greatly amuse them with humorous flights of fancy, amounting sometimes to hyperbolical exaggeration, which those who knew him well, could never misunderstand, but which might easily perplex a new acquaintance.

A very delightful and highly cultivated friend of ours, who belonged to a strictly conventional section of society, had gladly accepted an invitation to meet Tennyson at our house. She had read his poetry with great admiration, and was prepared to make his acquaintance with reverent enthusiasm. He was, however, as retiring as usual, when with absolute strangers, and the graceful deference of our dear friend's demeanour towards him, did not at first tend to dispel his shyness; later in the evening, however, when Alfred had realised that this lady was an intimate friend of ours, and that we particularly wished that he should make himself agreeable to her, he went up to her with good-natured friendliness, saying, 'I could not find anything to say to you before dinner, but now that I have a bottle of port in me, I can talk as much as you like.' My friend was at first rather alarmed at this playful announcement, receiving it as a literal assertion. But she was soon reassured by the serious interest of his conversation, which realised all her expectation. This is but a trifling incident to recall, but it is one of those early reminiscences of his bachelor days, which seems to me to acquire interest from its very simplicity.

In the very early years of our married life, we were for a time in lodgings in Ebury Street; Alfred Tennyson also had rooms on the opposite side of the same street, and we daily met. It was some time before his marriage, and he consulted us as to a dinner he wished to give to a few very intimate friends, ourselves amongst the number—my cousin, Harry Hallam,[3] was also there. The invitations had all been accepted, and the day for the dinner had arrived, when, in the early part of the afternoon, my husband found Alfred Tennyson at his lodging, superintending the dismantling of his bedroom, with workmen taking down his bedstead, as it had occurred to him, that there was no drawing-room for the ladies he had invited, and that we should all have to meet together in his one sitting-room, and remain there through the whole evening. My husband succeeded in persuading him to give up this chivalrous intention, and assured him we should enjoy the novelty of remaining in the dining-room. We had a most agreeable evening, and Alfred's hospitable anxiety on our behalf was entirely relieved, after all this perturbation, by the landlady's placing her own private sitting-room at our service for this special occasion.

I believe we were all of us surprised to find how perfectly everything had been arranged for this party of seven or eight guests. The dinner was excellent, the waiting admirable, and we found that Alfred had quietly secured the best possible assistance from outside resources, beyond the reach even of the most obliging of London landladies.

In the year 1855, just before the publication of Tennyson's *Maud*, I was with my husband and children on a visit to Lord and Lady Ashburton at the Grange, in Hampshire.[4] There was a large party staying in the house, when, to our great joy, Alfred Tennyson also arrived, and, I think, only the next day, the first copy of his latest poem, *Maud,* was forwarded to him. We were, all of us, of course eager to hear his new poem read aloud by himself, and he most kindly agreed to gratify us. But there were difficulties to be got over. Carlyle and his wife were amongst the guests, and it was well known that he could not endure to listen to anyone reading aloud—not even to Alfred Tennyson.

Carlyle was accustomed to take an early walk daily, and to be accompanied by an appreciative companion. What was to be done? All the visitors in the house were presumably anxious to listen to Tennyson's delightful reading. Lord and Lady Ashburton were kept waiting, chairs had been arranged in a quiet sitting-room; the visitors (ourselves amongst the number) were taking their places. Alfred was ready. So was Carlyle—in the hall, waiting for a companion in his walk—and evidently he would not stir without one. It was quite an anxious moment. We each probably wondered which of us would volunteer to leap into the gulf, as it were, like Quintus Curtius of old. At length, to our great relief, Mr Goldwin Smith[5] generously stepped forward, and joined the philosopher, whilst we remained to listen with enthralled attention to the new words of the poet.

I recollect during this same visit at the Grange, Tennyson's coming in to breakfast rather late one morning, with a perturbed expression of face, and his watch in his hand, saying with great gravity, 'My watch has stopped, what am I to do?' We all felt concerned for a moment, until I think it was Mr Fairbairn, who as a practical man, with equal gravity, rose from his chair, took the watch from Alfred's hand, asked for his key, wound it up, and silently returned it to its owner.

On every important occasion in our lives, some kindly word of interest and regard would come from Alfred Tennyson, and when my husband died, in 1874, he wrote a few lines to me, which I have always preserved, ending with the words 'For I believe that the dead live, whatever pseudo-savants may say.'

NOTES

Jane Brookfield (died 1896) married in 1841 William Henry Brookfield, a clergyman who had been a college friend of Tennyson and Hallam. She is also remembered as a friend of Thackeray. After her husband's death in 1874 Tennyson wrote an affectionate sonnet recalling their early friendship (Ricks, 363).

1. Mary Elizabeth Braddon (1837–1915), popular author of 'sensation novels'.

2. George Venables (1810–88), barrister and journalist; he contributed the second line of Book IV of *The Princess*.

3. Henry Fitzmaurice Hallam (1824–50), younger brother of Arthur Hallam.

4. The Ashburtons' country house, The Grange, near Alresford, Hants, became a meeting-place for literary and political figures. *Maud, and Other Poems* was published in July 1855.

5. Goldwin Smith (1823–1910), journalist and controversialist.

A Meeting of Poets*

AUBREY DE VERE

It was in 1841 or 1842 that I first met the poet on whom and on whose works my imagination had rested so often during the preceding ten years; and I lost nothing when the living man stood before me. The large dark eyes, generally dreamy but with an occasional gleam of imaginative alertness, the dusky, almost Spanish complexion, the high-built head and the massive abundance of curling hair like the finest and blackest silk, are still before me, and no less the stalwart form, strong 'with the certain step of man', though some years earlier it might have moved

> Still hither thither idly sway'd
> Like those long mosses in the stream.

* *Memoir*, I, pp. 207–11.

Whenever we were both in London, I met him as often as I could, sometimes at the rooms of James Spedding,[1] or at some late smoking-party consisting of young men, their intimates at the University, the well-known Cambridge 'Apostles'.[2] That was a society unvexed by formalities; and I do not remember that my new friend and I ever called each other otherwise than by our Christian names. He was thus always called by many of his intimates beside; for their affection for him partook largely of domestic affection in its character. He was pre-eminently a *man*, as well as a genius, but not the least the man of the world. He was essentially refined; but convention fled before his face. . . .

The entire simplicity and unconventionality of Alfred Tennyson was part of the charm which bound his friends to him. No acquaintance, however inferior to him in intellect, could be afraid of him. He felt that he was not in the presence of a critic, but of one who respected human nature wherever he found it free from unworthiness, who would think his own thoughts whether in the society of ordinary or extraordinary men, and who could not but express them plainly if he spoke at all. That perfect transparency of mind, like the clearness of air in the finest climates, when it is nearness not distance that 'lends enchantment to the view', I have seen only in three men beside him, Wordsworth, Sir William Rowan Hamilton[3] and one other. His unguardedness, in combination with his unworldliness, made his friends all the more zealous to help him; and perhaps their emulous aid was more useful to him than self-help could have been. . . .

Alfred Tennyson's largeness of mind and of heart was touchingly illustrated by his reverence for Wordsworth's poetry, notwithstanding that the immense merits which he recognised in it were not, in his opinion, supplemented by a proportionate amount of artistic skill. He was always glad to show reverence to the 'old poet', not then within ten years of the age at which the then younger one died. 'Wordsworth', he said to me one day, 'is staying at Hampstead in the house of his friend Mr Hoare; I must go and see him; and you must come with me; mind you do not tell Rogers,[4] or he will be displeased at my being in London and not going to see him.' We drove up to Hampstead, and knocked at the door; and the next minute it was opened by the Poet of the World, at whose side stood the Poet of the Mountains. Rogers's old face, which had encountered nearly ninety years, seemed to double the number of its wrinkles as he said, not angrily but very drily, 'Ah, you did not come up the hill to see me!' During the visit it was with Tennyson that the Bard of Rydal held discourse, while the recluse of St James's Place, whom 'that angle' especially delighted, conversed with me. As we walked back to London through grassy fields not then built over, Tennyson complained of the old poet's coldness. He had endeavoured to stimulate some latent ardours by telling him of a tropical island where the trees, when they first came into leaf, were a vivid scarlet;—'Every one of them, I told him, one flush all over the island, the colour of blood! It would not do. I could not inflame his imagination in the least!' During the preceding year I had had the great honour of passing several days at Rydal Mount with Wordsworth, walking on his mountains and listening to him at his fireside. I told him that a young poet had lately risen up. Wordsworth answered that he feared from the little he had heard that if Crabbe was the driest of poets, the young aspirant must have the opposite fault. I replied that he should judge for himself, and without leave given, recited to him two poems by Tennyson: viz. 'You ask me, why, tho' ill at ease', and 'Of old sat Freedom on the heights'. Wordsworth listened with a gradually deepening attention. After a pause he answered, 'I must acknowledge that these two poems are very solid and noble in thought. Their diction also seems singularly stately.'

There was another occasion on which the poet whose great work was all but finished, and the youthful compeer whose chief labours were yet to come, met in my presence. It was at a dinner given by Mr Moxon.[5] The ladies had withdrawn, and Wordsworth soon followed them. Several times Tennyson said to me in a low voice, 'I must go: I cannot wait any longer.' At last the cause of his disquiet revealed itself. It was painful to him to leave the house without expressing to the old bard his sense of the obligation which all Englishmen owed to him, and yet he was averse to speak his thanks before a large company. Our host brought Wordsworth back to the dining-room; and Tennyson moved up to him. He spoke in a low voice, and with a perceptible emotion. I must not cite his words lest I should mar them; but they were few, simple and touching. The old man looked very much pleased, more so indeed than I ever saw him look on any other occasion; shook hands with him heartily, and thanked him affectionately. Wordsworth thus records the incident in a letter . . . : 'I saw Tennyson when I was in London several times. He is decidedly the first of our living poets, and I hope will live to give the world still better things. You will be pleased to hear that he expressed in the strongest terms his gratitude to my writings. To this I was far from indifferent.'

Our many conversations, in those pleasant years, turned chiefly on poetry, a subject on which Tennyson could say nothing that was not original. It was easy to see that to discern the Beautiful in all around us, and to reveal that beauty to others, was his special poetic vocation. In these conversations he never uttered a word that was disparaging, or tainted with the spirit of rivalship. One of the poets least like himself, Crabbe, was among those whose merits he affirmed most unequivocally, especially his gift of a *hard* pathos. The only poet I heard him criticise roughly or unfairly was himself. 'Compare,' he once said to me, 'compare the heavy handling of my workmanship with the exquisite lightness of touch in Keats!' Another time he read aloud a song by one of the chivalrous poets of Charles I's time, perhaps Lovelace's 'Althea',[6] which Wordsworth also used to *croon* in woods, and said, 'There! I would give all my poetry to have made one song like that!' Not less ardent was his enthusiasm for Burns. . . . 'Read the exquisite songs of Burns', he exclaimed. 'In shape, each of them has the perfection of the berry, in light the radiance of the dewdrop: you forget for its sake those stupid things, his serious pieces!' . . .

NOTES

Aubrey de Vere (1814–1902), Irish poet, prose writer and dramatist. Tennyson visited him in Ireland in 1848: for de Vere's account of the visit, see *Memoir*, I, pp. 287–94.

1. See p. 7
2. Tennyson and Hallam were among the early members of this famous discussion society. Hallam Tennyson's account conveys something of its atmosphere of bold and wide-ranging intellectual enquiry:

> These friends not only debated on politics but read their Hobbes, Locke, Berkeley, Butler, Hume, Bentham, Descartes and Kant, and discussed such questions as the Origin of Evil, the Derivation of Moral Sentiments, Prayer and the Personality of God. . . .
> My father seems to have propounded in some college discussion the theory that the 'development of the human body might possibly be traced from the radiated, vermicular, molluscous and vertebrate organisms'. The question of surprise put to him on this proposition was 'Do you mean that the human brain is at first like a madrepore's, then like a worm's, etc.? but this cannot be for they have no brain.' (*Memoir*, I, pp. 43–44, referring to the period 1828–30)

3. Sir William Rowan Hamilton (1805–65), Irish mathematician; he published verse and was a friend of Wordsworth.
4. See p. 122.
5. See p. 16.
6. 'To Althea, from Prison' by Richard Lovelace (1618–58).

'A Bit of Chaos'*

THOMAS CARLYLE

... Moxon[1] informs us that ... Tennyson is now in Town, and means to come and see me. Of this latter result I shall be very glad: Alfred is one of the few British or foreign figures (a not increasing number, I think!) who are and remain beautiful to me;—a true human soul, or some authentic approximation thereto, to whom your own soul can say, Brother!—However, I doubt h[e] will not come; he often skips me, in these brief visits to Town; skips [every]-body indeed; being a man solitary and sad, as certain men are, dwelling in an element of gloom,—carrying a bit of Chaos about him, in short, which he is manufacturing into Cosmos!

Alfred is the son of a Lincolnshire gentleman farmer, I think; indeed you see in his verses that he is a native of 'moated grange',[2] and green fat pastures, not of mountains and their torrents and storms. He had his breeding at Cambridge, as if for the Law, or Church; being master of a small annuity on his father's decease, he preferred clubbing with his mother and some sisters, to live unpromoted and write poems. In this way he lives still, now here now there; the family always within reach of London, never in it; he himself making rare and brief visits, lodging in some old comrade's rooms. I think he must be under forty, not much under it. One of the finest looking men in the world. A great shock of rough dusty-dark hair; bright-laughing hazel eyes; massive aquiline face, most massive yet most delicate, of sallow brown complexion, almost Indian-looking; clothes cynically loose, free-and-easy;—smokes infinite tobacco. His voice is musical metallic,—fit for loud laughter and piercing wail, and all that may lie between; speech and speculation free and plenteous: I do not meet, in these late decades, such company over a pipe!—We shall see what he will grow to. He is often unwell; very chaotic,—his way is thro' Chaos and the Bottomless and Pathless; not handy for making out many miles upon.

* The Correspondence of Emerson and Carlyle, ed. Joseph Slater (New York: Columbia University Press, 1964) p. 363.

NOTES

Thomas Carlyle (1795–1881): his friendship with Tennyson dated from the latter's bachelor days ('During the "forties" he was in the habit of walking with Carlyle at night'—*Memoir*, I, p. 267). Carlyle, who was noted for his vigorous speech, described Tennyson in 1851 as 'sitting on a dung-heap among innumerable dead dogs' ('Carlyle meant that he was apt to brood over old-world subjects for his poems'—*Memoir*, I, p. 340). For notes on their conversation, see *Memoir*, II, pp. 234–7.

Carlyle corresponded extensively with the American writer R. W. Emerson; the letter quoted from is dated August 1844.

1. Edward Moxon (1801–58) published some of Tennyson's poems.

2. The phrase 'moated grange' occurs in Tennyson's poem 'Mariana' (Ricks, 73) as well as in the epigraph to the poem taken from *Measure for Measure*.

Meetings with Tennyson (1849–89)*

F. T. PALGRAVE

From the Journals

31 March 1849. In the evening to Mr Brookfield's.[1] Found there Lingen, A. Tennyson; afterwards Thackeray and H. Hallam came. Walked towards Hampstead with A. Tennyson. Conversed on Universities, *The Princess*, his plans, etc.; he very open and friendly: a noble, solid mind, bearing the look of one who had suffered greatly: —strength and sensitiveness blended.

2 April 1849. In the afternoon to A. Tennyson's in the Hampstead Road. Long conversation with him; he read me songs to be inserted in *The Princess*, and poems on A. Hallam, some exquisite.

To his father, from Ardtornish, Morvern, Argyllshire, Scotland, 3 August 1853.
I travelled to Oban last night with Tennyson, and came over here to

* *Francis Turner Palgrave: His Journals and Memories of his Life*, ed. Gwenllian F. Palgrave (London: Longmans Green, 1899) pp. 41, 46–7, 98–9, 135, 152–3, 178–9, 202, 217.

Sellar today in an open boat through splendid scenery. We came slowly through Edinburgh, where we stayed three or four days .... Tennyson was in a happy humour, he discussed many matters in his large and noble-natured way: and I was very glad to have had the privilege of accompanying him.

To F. G. Waugh, August 1867

I had a very enviable fortnight whilst in the south with A. Tennyson. We went over Dartmoor and the peninsula of Salcombe together in the finest weather, and enjoyed ourselves like schoolboys in defiance of Time, children, and the other cares of life. If not *noctes coenaeque deum*,[2] the half-hours of talk, or reading Horace together, with a pipe, and in some choice spot of hillside or torrent or woodland, or by the sea, were hardly less divine.

From the Journals

On 14 October 1871 to Aldworth. Found there, besides A. Tennyson and his always charming wife, his very pleasant brother Charles. A. T. himself remarkably full of life and spirit. The country is beautiful, both in the near landscape and the noble view—the 'immense plain', which Tennyson confessed 'sometimes weighed upon his spirits'. He read Wordsworth on Sunday evening, and we had a general service of reverence to that great poet, agreeing that what he had left us was the greatest gift any one poet, since Milton, had conferred on England.

21 June 1876.   This morning Tennyson read to me the last act of *Harold*: it seemed to me full of life, character, and passion.

20 March 1877.   Dined with the Tennysons in Upper Wimpole Street: met Mr and Mrs Gladstone, Joachim,[3] Browning, and Lord Monteagle.

25 August 1883.   Went to Aldworth. Found Mrs Tennyson as bright in mind and charming as ever during the thirty years and more since I first saw her at Twickenham. On Sunday morning I had a longish walk with A. T.; he is as interesting, as rich in mind, almost as ready for humour and liveliness as when he showed his poems to me in MS in his dingy lodging by Mornington Crescent in 1849. He read to me in the evening an old poem[4]—forty years old, he said he believed—

which he had written out from his old sketches, with a prologue to FitzGerald, his college friend, written just before FitzGerald's death. The central poem is in his finest early style; the two other poems seemed to me to be also perfect masterpieces.

10 January 1885. To Aldworth, where I found Jowett. One evening A. T. read us several recent poems in his ballad style of extraordinary power and beauty.

November 1886, Aldworth. Found A. T., though saddened by the loss of Lionel,[5] unbroken in strength and mind. He stoops a little, but strode along steadily down hill and up rough road, through rain and mud, talking much, depressed by the state of England and his own loss.... He read aloud to me a second part of 'Locksley Hall', a long poem of great force; also the third act of *The Promise of May*: this is certainly very tragic and fine.

1 November 1888. A message from Hallam [Tennyson] telling me his father was better and would like to see me brings me to Aldworth. A. T. received me with all his wonted kindness, and presently his voice grew firm and strong, his conversation was full of life as ever. He emphatically repeated to me his constant estimate of Wordsworth as the greatest of our poets in this century. He gave me to read a very lovely and skilful poem on Gifford as Ulysses.

July 1889. To Aldworth, where I found A. T. in full vigour of mind and able to walk a mile. The Duke of Argyll[6] is also here, and there has been much interesting talk; as good conversation, perhaps, as I ever heard for variety, real interest of subjects, and well put remarks.[7]

NOTES

Francis Turner Palgrave (1824–97), civil servant and man of letters, Professor of Poetry at Oxford (1886–95), is best remembered as the editor of the *Golden Treasury* (1861 and later editions), his selections for which were submitted to Tennyson's judgement. He was the son of Sir Francis Palgrave (1788–1861), historian. He met Tennyson in 1849 and they became lifelong friends. Among the many holidays they spent together was a two-week visit to Portugal in 1859, Palgrave's account of which was published in the magazine *Under the Crown* in 1868. When Tennyson died, Palgrave wrote that 'an unvarying friendship from him since 1849, and the many visits and journeys with him, have rendered his death a sort of chasm through my life' (*Journals*, p. 228). He contributed a substantial essay, 'Personal Recollections', to the *Memoir*, ii, pp. 484–512.

  1. See p. 12.
  2. 'Nights and feasts of the gods'.

3. Joseph Joachim (1831–1907), Hungarian violinist and composer.

4. The reference is to 'Tiresias' (Ricks, 219), written in 1833 but not published until 1885 ('forty years old' is thus an understatement). FitzGerald died on 14 June 1883; on the dedicatory poem, see p. 127 below.

5. Lionel Tennyson died in April 1886 on the voyage home from India.

6. The 8th Duke of Argyll (1823–1900), Liberal Cabinet minister and friend of Tennyson. He made a brief contribution to the *Memoir*, ii, pp. 513–16.

7. In a letter to T. H. Warren in May 1897, Palgrave wrote that Tennyson 'was, taken all in all, the best talker I have ever known' (*Journals*, p. 254).

The New Laureate*

W. M. ROSSETTI

30 November 1850.   Woolner . . . was yesterday with Patmore,[1] accompanying Tennyson in the search for a house in the neighbourhood of London, but without result. Tennyson is in a state of disgust at the idea of being presented at court on his appointment to the Laureateship—Patmore says that Tennyson has in his memory, and on occasion recites, an immense quantity of poetry which he never intends to commit to paper.

NOTES

William Michael Rossetti (1829–1910), art critic and man of letters.

1. On Woolner and Patmore, see pp. 84 and 30 respectively.

'Personal Recollections of Tennyson'†

W. F. RAWNSLEY

I can never cease thanking both my parents for treating me . . . as a person, and one who, unaided, could take an interest in what went

The P. R. B. Journal: William Michael Rossetti's Diary of the Pre-Raphaelite Brotherhood, 1849–1853, ed. William E. Fredeman (Oxford: Clarendon Press, 1975) p. 83.

† *Nineteenth Century*, xcvii (Jan 1925) 1–9.

on around him. Thus it came to pass quite naturally that when Alfred Tennyson in December 1850 stayed in our house, the vicarage, at Shiplake, half a year after his marriage, I trotted down the kitchen garden walk one morning between the finish of our nursery breakfast and the beginning of that downstairs, and asked questions of him, and, most gratifying to the childish mind, was talked to as if I was a companion and not a little ignorant child. He picked the leaves of the sage, rubbed his teeth with them, and said: 'That is the best thing in the world to take away the stain of tobacco', for he was a great smoker, and I was turned out of my little bedroom when he visited us so that he might have a place to write and smoke in at pleasure, for my mother would not allow him to smoke in her best bedroom. Many years later he told me how he began to smoke. 'Jackson, the saddler at Louth, once gave me one of his strong cigars when I was a boy of twelve, and I smoked it all and flung the stump into a horse-pond, and was none the worse for it, so I was bound to be a smoker.' ...

In February [1851] Alfred was again at Shiplake, and as I entered the room where he and my father were sitting he greeted me with—

> And oh! far worse than all beside,
> He whipped his Mary till she cried.

'What is that?' I said. 'You'll know tomorrow.' This puzzled me, for I had forgotten that tomorrow was my birthday. But my father and the poet had been into Reading and bought me for a birthday present that delightful book *The English Struwwelpeter*,[1] for, in spite of its abominable name, what a never-failing fount of pleasure it has been, and, indeed, still is, to me, and no doubt to hundreds of others! At that time I think it gave Tennyson as much pleasure as it did me. ....

My father had the invaluable habit of reading to us children in the evenings both prose and poetry; and thus we heard most of Dickens, and also the beautiful songs of *The Princess* before they were published, and the 'Ode on the Death of the Great Duke', which Tennyson himself read to us at Shiplake. Matthew Arnold's 'Merman'[2] Tennyson also read to us aloud at Shiplake, and I heard him say as he finished it 'I should like to have written that.'
    The *sound* of a line of poetry (for poetry, to be fully understood, should be read aloud) was very much to him; and he certainly was unmatched in his use of vowels and in the melody of his verse. In speaking of Browning, he once said to me: 'I don't think that poetry should be *all thought*: there should be some melody'; and he carried his objection to a jingle so far that when, after publishing his first

four *Idylls of the King*, he learnt that 'Enid' was properly pronounced
'Ennid,' he changed his line beginning 'Had wedded Enid' to 'Had
married Enid'; the jingle of 'wedded Ennid' was to his ear quite
impossible. He instanced to me as fine-sounding lines and some of
his best (and he made them all the finer by his magnificent way of
rolling them out) the lines about the burial of Elaine:

> The maiden buried, not as one unknown
> Nor meanly, but *with gorgeous obsequies*
> *And mass and rolling music like a queen.*

Many years later, walking with my wife over the heather on
Blackdown, just outside Aldworth, he sat down on the edge of a deep
cart track and recited in his magnificent voice

> Go fetch to me a pint o'wine,
> And fill it in a silver tassie,
> That I may drink before I go
> A service to my bonnie lassie.
>
> The trumpets sound, the banners fly,
> The glittering spears are ranked ready,
> The shouts o' war are heard afar,
> The battle closes thick and bloody.[3]

He repeated the last two lines, rolling them out with delighted
admiration, and said, 'I would have given anything to have written
that.' A line that he thought one of his best was 'The mellow ouzel
fluted in the elm.'[4] The richness of the bird's note is expressed by the
'u' sound in two consecutive words, and the 'el' in two other words
gives a liquid tone which makes the line perfect. 'And yet,' he said,
'nine-tenths of the English readers would have been just as well
pleased if I had written, 'The merry blackbird sang among the trees.'
Besides the well-known 'moan of doves in immemorial elms, And
murmuring of innumerable bees',[5] another of his best lines he
thought to be that which describes the sound of the bells in the poem
'Far, Far Away': 'The mellow lin-lan-lone of evening bells.'
    He told my sister that the most beautiful and touching lines he
knew were in the anonymous poem 'Forsaken':

> O waly waly up the bank,
> And waly waly down the brae,
> And waly waly yon burn-side,
> Where I and my love wont to gae

ending with

And O! if my young babe were born
And set upon the nurse's knee,
And I myself were dead and gone,
And the green grass growing over me!

But to return to Elaine. Elaine's brother could not conceal his admiration for what he called 'the great Lancelot', but Lancelot answers him

Me you call great: mine is the firmer seat,
The truer·lance: but there is many a youth
Now present who will come to all I am
And overcome it; and in me there dwells
No greatness, save it be some far-off touch
Of greatness to know well I am not great:
There is the man

—pointing to the king. About this passage Tennyson once said to me, 'When I wrote that I was thinking of myself and Wordsworth.' Did ever one poet pay a finer compliment to another? I might add that Wordsworth said of Tennyson, 'I have been trying all my life to write a poem like his "Dora", but in vain.' It is pleasant to hear words of genuine praise from one real poet of another, and Tennyson spoke from his heart when he said, 'Read the exquisite songs of Burns, each perfect as a berry and radiant as a dewdrop. There never was an immortal poet if he be not one'; while of Keats he said to me, 'If Keats had lived he would have been the first of us all.' . . .
We were speaking, as we paced the lawn at Aldworth, of the magnificent sound of some of Homer's lines, but he said that the grandeur of the lines in Homer was due to the Greek words being spoken by the Northern tongue. 'The Greeks,' he said, 'never polufloisboied; they polufleesbeed.'[6] His own translation of Homer, of which he did so little, is so far superior to any other that I asked him when we were on this subject of Homer if he had never thought of doing much more. He said, 'To translate Homer would be the work of a lifetime; and when done the benefit of it rests with the translator.' The lines I was thinking of as even better than the original were those from the *Iliad*, VIII. 552:

As when in heaven the stars about the moon
Look beautiful, when all the winds are laid,
And every height comes out, and jutting peak
And valley, and the immeasurable heavens,
Break open to their highest. . . .

All his classic poems show Tennyson at his best. 'Ulysses' has in it an element of autobiography referring to his turning to work as a remedy for the desolation into which his grief at the death of Arthur Hallam had plunged him; and how fine are 'Oenone' and 'Demeter', and best of all 'Tithonus', with the pathos of the boon granted by love at love's request turning out a curse, and finally 'Lucretius', speaking of which, and especially of the passage about the abode of the gods,

> Where never creeps a cloud or moves a wind
> Nor ever falls the least white star of snow

I said, 'Of course that is Homer', and the poet said, 'Yes, but I improved on Homer, because I knew that snow crystallises in stars.'

I was still a small boy when Tennyson sent to my grandfather his 'Charge of the Light Brigade'. I have it just as he sent it, a cutting from p. 780 of the *Examiner* of 1854. After the first twenty lines as they now stand was a break, and then came four which are now omitted:

> Into the valley of death
> Rode the six hundred,*
> For up came an order which
> Someone had blundered.

The rest is as we have it now, except that ' ."Charge for the guns!" he said' was at first ' "Take the guns", Nolan said', and 'Flashed *as they turned* in air' was well substituted finally for 'Flashed *all at once* in air'.

But even in this early original after the line 'Plunged in the battery smoke' four lines of the *Examiner* cutting had been blacked out, and eight new ones written in by Emily Tennyson, six of which are still retained, ending with

> Then they rode back, but not,
> Not the six hundred.

The metre is very happy, but not a common one, and I once asked Tennyson if he had taken it from Drayton's 'Agincourt'. He said, 'No, when I wrote it I had not seen Drayton's poem, but *The Times* account had "Someone had blundered", and the line kept running in my head, and I kept saying it over and over till it shaped itself into the burden of the poem', where it was repeated at least twice. Knowing that, it is hard to understand how he allowed himself to be persuaded to omit the expression from the poem altogether when it first came out in book form in the *Maud* volume; but Ruskin,

---

* 'Hundred' in Lincolnshire is pronounced 'hunderd'.

remonstrating and telling him that it was the key to the whole thing, got him to put it back.

Another instance of his getting wrong advice, though he did not this time take it, he told me about when we were talking of his Lincolnshire dialect poems. He said that, as it was twenty-seven years since he had left Lincolnshire, he felt that he had probably got some mistakes in his first 'Northern Farmer', so he sent the MS to a friend who lived near Brigg, and he altered it all into the dialect spoken in that northern part of the county. He felt sure that was not the dialect of East or Mid-Lincolnshire, and sent it to my father, who put it all back as he had written it. After that the dialect poems were always sent to one of our family before they were given to the public, but the first 'Northern Farmer' has still in it several traces of the wrong dialect in the use of 'o', as in 'hoight' and 'squoire' and 'doy', in place of 'a', which the poet himself explains in his note to the 'Northern Cobbler' to be the proper vowel sound. He loved Lincolnshire, and the sight of a Lincolnshire face was always a delight to him. Knowing this, I once asked: 'Why did you call it the "Northern" instead of the "Lincolnshire Farmer"?' and he said, 'You see, I was modest: I had been so long out of the county that I did not feel sure my memory would serve me'; but really he was right all through. How careful he was to be perfectly accurate may be shown by the following: Once at Farringford he asked me how they pronounced 'turnips' about Spilsby; he had been told 'turmuts'. I said, 'No, "tonnops" '; and some months later, going to see him again at Farringford, when I had forgotten all about the 'tonnops', his first words to me were, 'You were right about that word.' He also said, 'I think you are right, too, about "greät", not "graät", for I see it is sometimes spelt "greet".' This is an instance of his perfect accuracy, for to many the distinction between 'greät' and 'graat' is hardly perceptible. His poems were always printed and kept by him for some time before he published them, and many a new unpublished poem has he read to me, as to others, under the strictest promise of secrecy, in his study, upstairs, or in the garden, both at Farringford and Aldworth. Those were indeed delightful readings. 'Owd Roä', one of his last dialect poems, he read to my wife and myself, and subsequently he made me read it aloud to him, and encouraged me to make suggestions on certain words, all of which when it came out I saw he had adopted. The line he made most of, speaking it with a kind of awe in his voice, is in the Globe Edition printed in italics: 'But'e coom'd thruf the fire wimy bairn i' 'is mouth to the winder there.'

He liked particularly to find that the hearer appreciated the humour of a line, and he looked up for it. His eye fairly twinkled as he read the lines

When 'e cooms to be deäd
I thinks as I'd like fur to hev soom soört of a sarvice reäd. . . .

I once read 'The Spinster's Sweet-arts' at a penny reading at
Freshwater in the proper Lincolnshire dialect, and next morning the
poet greeted me with 'You gave me a bad night.' 'How?' I said. 'Two
of the maids sleep over my room, and they were laughing half the
night over "The Spinster's Sweet-arts".' I saw by his humorous smile
that I was easily forgiven. The story itself is full of humour, and was,
he told me, entirely spun out of his own brain, 'though the critics say
I have no imagination'.

NOTES

Willingham Franklin Rawnsley was an elder brother of H. D. Rawnsley: on
the latter, and the Rawnsley family in general, see pp. 75–6. A second
instalment of his recollections appeared in *Nineteenth Century* for February
1925.
    1. Book of cautionary verses for children by the German author Heinrich
Hoffman, translated into English as *Shock-headed Peter* in 1847.
    2. 'The Forsaken Merman', published in 1849. Much earlier Tennyson
had himself written two short poems, 'The Merman' and 'The Mermaid'
(Ricks, 76–7).
    3. From the song 'My bonny Mary' by Robert Burns.
    4. 'The Gardener's Daughter', l. 93.
    5. *The Princess*, VII, 221.
    6. The reference is to two different ways of pronouncing the Greek word
for the sound of the sea.

Tennyson at
Twickenham (1851–3)*

WILLIAM ALLINGHAM

I ventured to send my first volume of verse (1850) to Tennyson from
Ballyshannon. I don't think he wrote to me, but I heard indirectly
that he thought well of it; and during a visit to London in the
summer of 1851 Coventry Patmore,[1] to my boundless joy, let me

* *William Allingham: A Diary*, ed. H. Allingham and D. Radford (London:
Macmillan, 1907) pp. 60–5.

know that I might call on the great poet, then not long married,[2] and living at Twickenham.

Saturday 28 June, was the appointed day, and in the warm afternoon I walked from Twickenham railway station to Montpelier Row, quite away from the village. It proved to be a single row of about a dozen moderate-sized houses, that seemed dropped by accident among quiet fields and large trees, 'Chapel House' where T. lived (so called I know not why) being the last at the south end of the terrace, where I think the byroad ended.

I was admitted, shown upstairs into a room with books lying about, and soon came in a tall, broad-shouldered swarthy man, slightly stooping, with loose dark hair and beard. He wore spectacles, and was obviously very near-sighted. Hollow cheeks and the dark pallor of his skin gave him an unhealthy appearance. He was a strange and almost spectral figure. The Great Man peered close at me, and then shook hands cordially, yet with a profound quietude of manner. He was then about forty-one, but looked much older, from his bulk, his short-sight, stooping shoulders, and loose careless dress. He looked tired, and said he had been asleep and was suffering from hay-fever. Mrs Tennyson came in, very sweet and courteous, with low soft voice, and by and by when I rose to take leave she said, 'Won't you stay for dinner?' which I was too happy to do. Mr Tennyson went out, and returning took me upstairs to his study—a small room looking out to the back over gardens and trees. He took up my volume of poems, saying, 'You can see it is a good deal dirtier than most of the books.' Then turing the pages, he made critical remarks, mostly laudatory. Of 'Cross Examination' he said, 'I looked sharp at it to see if any of the rhymes were forced.' He objected to 'rose' and 'clothes' in 'The Touchstone' (since corrected). Then he asked, 'Do you dislike to hear your own things read?' and receiving a respectfully encouraging reply, read two of the 'Aeolian Harps', first 'Is it all in vain?', then 'What saith the River?' The rich, slow solemn chant of his voice glorified the little poems. In reading the last line of the second—'For ever, ever, ever fled away!' he paused after the two 'evers' and gave the third as by an afterthought, thus adding greatly to the impressiveness. He especially admired

> Night with her cold fingers
> Sprinkles moonbeams on the dim sea-waste.

I said, 'That was Donegal Bay.' T. replied, 'I knew you took it direct from nature.' The pieces never seemed to me so good before or since.

At dinner there was talk of Wordsworth, etc. T. spoke of George

Meredith's poems,[3] lately sent to him, author only twenty-three; 'I thanked him for it and praised it—"Love in the Valley" best.' I said I also knew the book, and had bought it. T. gets enough poetry without buying: 'They send me nothing but poetry!'—'As if you lived on jam,' I said.

T.—'And *such* jam! Yes, I did lately receive a prose book, *Critical Strictures on Great Authors*, "a first hastily scribbled effusion", the writer said. There was this in it, "We exhort Tennyson to abandon the weeping willow with its fragile and earthward-tending twigs, and adopt the poplar, with its one Heaven-pointing finger."' 'A pop'lar poet', says I.

After Mrs Tennyson had gone upstairs, Patmore was announced. T. said, 'You didn't know Allingham was here', and it rejoiced me to hear the familiar mention of my name. Over our port we talked of grave matters. T. said his belief rested on two things, a 'Chief Intelligence and Immortality.'—'I could not eat my dinner without a belief in immortality. If I didn't believe in that, I'd go down immediately and jump off Richmond Bridge.' Then to me, rather shortly, 'Why do you laugh?' I murmured that there was something ludicrous in the image of his jumping off Richmond Bridge. 'Well,' he rejoined, 'in such a case I'd as soon make a comic end as a tragic.' I went out to the garden, where were Mrs Tennyson with Mrs Patmore and her sister. Returning to the house there was tea, to which Tennyson came in, muttering as he entered the room 'we exhort Tennyson'.—I smiled. He said, 'What are you laughing at? You don't know what I'm saying.' I said 'O yes, I do.'

After tea he went upstairs and smoked, Patmore and I sitting with him: English and Irish characteristics; the English an ill-mannered people. Edgar Poe:[4] T. did not know 'The Raven', and I recited some lines of it, to which T. listened attentively. New Forest: Tom Taylor's[5] story of artist painting in the Forest suddenly seeing a little brown man, who had crept up unseen and clutched his bottle: 'Gin?' says he; 'Water', says the painter, and the little brown man immediately disappeared. When we took leave T. came out to the gate and again shook hands with me. I said, 'Ask me to find a lodge for you on the West coast of Ireland'; he, 'I should like it very much.' We walked to Richmond railway station, I feeling that a longing of my life had been fulfilled, and as if I had been familiar for years with this great and simple man.

In 1853, being in London, from Ireland, for a short holiday, I wrote to Twickenham and had a kind reply under the Poet's hand asking me to come, and adding, 'As my wife is not very well you must "tread softly and speak low".' So on Thursday the first of November I went from Waterloo Station to Richmond by rail, walked over Richmond

Bridge—a fine day, autumnal woodlands mirrored in the river, struck a field-path on the left, and passing after a bit under some tall trees emerged through a little gate upon the grass-plot fronting Montpelier Terrace. As I came forward to Chapel House two other men approached the door, one of them something like T., and went in, not without a suspicious glance or two at me.

I was soon in the Poet's much-longed-for presence, who shook hands in the most delightful, simple, friendly way, and asked me to stay and dine; then said he had to go away for a little and handed me a book for my amusement. When he returned he was carrying in his arms his baby son, called 'Hallam'; the child had a ball to amuse him, which he liked to drop on the floor exclaiming, 'Tha!' or 'Da!' as it fell. Then T. took me up to wash my hands in the dressing-room, its window looking across several gardens, and a sunset sky shining through the trees. Returning to the drawing-room I found Mrs Tennyson—sweet, pale, and kind; Mr Frederick Tennyson the eldest of the brothers, and Mr Edward FitzGerald (*Omar Khayyám*), the two gentlemen whom I had encountered at the front door. Mr FitzGerald ('Fitz'), an old and intimate friend, told droll stories with a quaint gravity, much amusing Mrs Tennyson in particular. One was about old Miss Edgeworth,[6] whom he knew, and her turban. She used to take it off for coolness and resume it when visitors were announced. One day by some mischance a strange gentleman came into the room and found her writing with her almost bald pate plainly visible. Miss E. started up with the greatest agility, seized her turban which lay close by and darted through an opposite door, whence she quickly reappeared with the decoration upon her head, but unluckily turned wrong side foremost. He also told us of Mr Edgeworth's tombs of his three wives in the park at Edgeworthstown.

After dinner, poetry was the subject. Mr FitzGerald stood up for Pope's 'Homer', and tried in vain to get T.'s approval.

'You think it very wonderful surely?'

T.—'I don't think I do.'

'O yes, you do, Alfred!'

T.—'No, I do not.'

Frederick T. set Schiller above Goethe, to which I strongly objected. A. T. said, 'If one of you is for Goethe and the other for Schiller, you'll never agree on poetry.' Moore was mentioned; his skilful versification in fitting words to music. T. objected to the line 'She is far from the land where her young hero sleeps.' I did not find much the matter with it, but T. would not allow 'young hero' to pass, the metre requiring a dactyl there: 'I wonder you don't see', he said. 'Subaltern', I suggested. 'Yes, that would do, as far as sound goes.' We turned to Campbell's 'Soldier's Dream', and T. objected to

'Our bugles sang truce', both for the two esses and the accentuation. Of the two lines

> And thousands had sunk on the ground overpowered,
> The weary to sleep and the wounded to die

he said, 'Those are perfect.' Then we spoke of Shelley's accents, and I quoted 'Of the snake's adamantine voluminousness', but without effect. I called Browning a *vivid* man, to which T. assented, adding, 'How he did flourish about when he was here!'

Then came on Dickens's cockney *History of England*,[7] Professor Aytoun [8] (not praised), Thackeray's *Book of Snobs*,[9] and Mr Martin Tupper.[10]

I spilt some port on the cloth, and T., with his usual imperturbability spread salt on it, remarking as he did so, 'I believe it never comes out!' Then we went upstairs to tea. I praised the view from the windows at the back. He said nothing would grow in his own garden but stones: 'I believe *they* grow. I pick up all I can see, and the next time I come there are just as many.' Then T., Frederick T., Edward F. and I to the study, where smoking and stories, some of an ammoniacal saltness. When I took leave, Mr Frederick T. shook hands kindly, spite of our differences of opinion, and T. came with me to the front garden gate.

NOTES

William Allingham (1824–89), Irish poet. In 1874 he married Helen Paterson, artist and illustrator.

1. Coventry Patmore (1823–96), poet and prose writer, friend of Tennyson.

2. Tennyson had married Emily Sellwood on 13 June 1850.

3. *Poems* (1851).

4. Edgar Allan Poe (1809–49), American poet, short-story writer and critic. 'The Raven' was written to illustrate his theory of poetic composition. Tennyson regarded him as 'the most original American genius' (*Memoir*, II, pp. 292–3).

5. Tom Taylor (1817–80), dramatist and later editor of *Punch*.

6. Maria Edgeworth (1767–1849), Irish novelist.

7. *Child's History of England*, published 1852–4.

8. William Edmondstone Aytoun (1813–65), Scottish poet, was Professor of Belles-Lettres at Edinburgh University from 1845.

9. This collection of essays contributed by Thackeray to *Punch* appeared in volume form in 1848.

10. Martin Tupper (1810–89) was the author of the enormously popular *Proverbial Philosophy* (1838–42) and other works.

Farringford*

LADY RITCHIE

One autumn, when everything seemed happy at home, Mrs Cameron took me with her to Freshwater for a few delightful weeks, and then, for the first time I lived with them all, and with kind Mrs Cameron, in the ivy-grown house near the gates of Farringford. For the first time I stayed in the island, and with the people who were dwelling there, and walked with Tennyson along High Down, treading the turf, listening to his talk, while the gulls came sideways, flashing their white breasts against the edge of the cliffs, and the poet's cloak flapped time to the gusts of the west wind.

The house at Farringford itself seemed like a charmed place, with green walls without, and speaking walls within. There hung Dante with his solemn nose and wreath; Italy gleamed over the doorways; friends' faces lined the passages; books filled the shelves, and a glow of crimson was everywhere; the great oriel drawing-room window was full of green and golden leaves, of the sound of birds and the distant sea.

The very names of the people who have stood upon the lawn at Farringford would be an interesting study for some future biographer: Longfellow, Maurice, Kingsley, the Duke of Argyll, Locker, Dean Stanley, the Prince Consort. Good Garibaldi once planted a tree there, off which some too ardent republican broke a branch before twenty-four hours had passed. Here came Clough in the last year of his life. Here Mrs Cameron fixed her lens, marking the well-known faces as they passed: Darwin and Henry Taylor, Watts and Aubrey de Vere, Lecky and Jowett, and a score of others.

NOTE

Lady Ritchie (1837–1919), born Anne Isabella Thackeray, was a daughter of W. M. Thackeray and was herself the author of novels and memoirs. She married Richmond Ritchie, a senior civil servant who was knighted in 1907. Farringford is a Georgian country house (now a hotel) at Freshwater on the Isle of Wight; the Tennysons moved there from Twickenham in November 1853, at first leasing it and later purchasing it with the profits from *Maud*.

* *Records of Tennyson, Ruskin and Browning* (London: Macmillan, 1892) pp. 43–4.

A Child's Memories of Tennyson*

AGNES WELD

In his daily walks on the Downs Tennyson was in the habit of chatting with the coastguards whom he met marching along the path that skirted the edge of the cliffs, and many a tale they told him of the fierce contests they used to have with the smugglers; but it was difficult to get the latter to tell of their own daring deeds, though my uncle had quite the knack of drawing out the villagers to talk of the auld lang syne. He would smile at their yarns of how one morning the tidings flew through Freshwater that Bonaparte's fleet was in sight, and forthwith most of the able-bodied men, women, and children hied them up to the top of the Beacon Down and ranged themselves in a long line which they still further lengthened by sheep-pens set up on end, hoping that Napoleon would take the whole lot for soldiers, and be thus scared from his purpose of invasion. With the fishermen and their love for a seafaring life my uncle, who was a splendid sailor, had the fullest sympathy, and he quite agreed with them that it was infinitely preferable to 'wyverning about atop of dry land', as they expressed the act of travelling by rail.

Frequent were the visits we paid together to the cottage of Tennyson's old shepherd, and still more frequently did we watch him as he called out by name the various members of his master's flock, and bid us observe, as each answered to its name, how it differed in countenance and expression from its fellows. In their intense love of Nature, animate and inanimate, Shepherd Paul and my uncle were at one, and indeed the latter's sympathy with Nature led him to mourn the cutting down of trees as if they were, like the grove in Dante's Inferno, the abode of his personal friends, and specially did he grieve if the axe smote them in summer-time. I well remember his gazing long upon a horse-chestnut that had continued to put forth flowers days after it had been felled to the earth. 'Look at it,' he said, 'stretching out a beseeching arm, and blossoming on, its blooms unfolding in all their beauty, quite unconscious that they can

* Glimpses of Tennyson, and of Some of his Relations and Friends (London: Williams and Norgate, 1903) pp. 41–50.

never turn to fruitage. How like they are to some men, who appear blooming outwardly, and think that they are living whilst they are already dead within.'

He scolded me severely, as a child, when he met me trundling along a wheelbarrow that I had filled full of the daffodils I had been picking in Farringford home-park, telling me how wrong it was to waste in that way the good gifts of God, since while I should derive no more enjoyment from these hundreds of plucked blossoms than from half a dozen; if left on their own roots they would have lasted double the time as a joy for many to look upon. Every spring the glory of these 'Lent Lilies' that flooded the grass of the park with their golden sunshine was a fresh delight to him, as were the masses of cowslips that succeeded them. He had the artist's eye for form, and would lay an ivy spray by his side, and crave a faithful copy of its graceful outlines; and this design of his, together with an Agnus Dei, to which he had taken a great fancy, formed the decorative terracotta mouldings round the windows of a model labourer's cottage on his estate, whose erection he used to superintend daily.

Tennyson was by no means blind to the darker side of Nature. 'She will never teach men morality,' he would say, 'and her ravening tooth is a cruel one. Indeed, it was the observed cruelty of Nature that gave rise to the cult of the Khonds, with their human sacrifices. You could not learn to know the higher attributes of God from Nature even with the aid of science.' His mind, however, dwelt far less on her discords than on her harmonies, which he wrought into the harmonies of his verse.

He held strongly that scientific truth can never be really at variance with divine truth, but he considered that men are too apt to mistake what they personally hold to be true for the absolute truth. On this account, when I asked him whether he considered the motto 'Truth against the World' a wise one to be used by people in general, he answered. 'No, I don't exactly think that would be a wise motto to be proposed for universal adoption, because if each man were to stick himself up with his own ideas of truth against all the rest of mankind, and blurt out these ideas in the faces of everybody else, each would be a great bore.' Yet my uncle thought there were certain great moral truths in which all might agree, and he used to explain to me how he had sought to express these in his *Idylls of the King*, though he said that his meaning in these Idylls had not always been fully understood. For instance, that the 'Three Queens' are not faith, hope, and charity; the 'Lady of the Lake' is not the Church, though she teaches Christianity; and 'Arthur' is not the conscience merely, he is the ideal man: the whole man, not the part.

It is surprising how many people still continue to read Tennyson's poetry with their attention so exclusively directed to the beauty of its form that they entirely ignore the soul within it, for whose sake the casket was so exquisitely wrought, and are thus led to assert that it is as an artist, rather than as a teacher, that Tennyson takes his high rank among the great poets of the nineteenth century; whereas he assured me that any measure of perfection to which he might seem to have attained as an artist in metre was imperfect compared with the standard he had set before himself, since he felt that the gift of poetry was bestowed on him by his Heavenly Father as 'a great trust', that it might be a vehicle in which he was permitted to convey to his fellowmen the message he had received from the Master. He told me that his sense of the divine source of this gift was almost awful to him, since he felt that every word of his should be consecrated to the service of Him who had touched his lips with that fire of Heaven which was to enable him to speak in God's name to his age. So that, great as was the delight he felt in the exercise of his art, the constant realisation of his responsibility so far outweighed to him the joy of production that he was wont to say to me that nothing he had ever written seemed to him to have reached that perfection short of which he must never rest, and that all he could hope was that he had brought men a little nearer to God; for as he sat day by day at the Master's feet with that humility of childhood which he kept to his dying hour, he felt no words of his could ever fully reproduce the messages which had been spoken to his own heart, and yet that he must strive with all his might to clothe them in the best language he could find. And so he sang on all through that long life of his, not that he might receive the homage of his own or future ages as a consummate artist, but as one to whom, all unworthy though he deemed himself, the mission had been entrusted of raising the thoughts of all who should come under his influence to a higher, diviner level—the level to which he himself was ever aspiring. . . .

I think no man that ever lived came nearer than he did to perfect truthfulness. He was often a martyr to his determination never to say anything that was not strictly and absolutely true; for none could be more sensitive than he was about paining people, and yet he would discard all smooth speeches that would have given pleasure, but would not have been quite sincere, and would just say right out the wholesome, though sometimes unpalatable truth instead, feeling utterly miserable for hours, and sometimes for days afterwards, with the fear that in this moral surgery he had not handled the knife as gently as he might have done. Unless by his keeping silence the cause of truth would have suffered, he would never mention any matter that might injure a single human being, and he always put the best possible construction upon people's words and actions. I am sure his attitude towards them made them better men and women than they would otherwise have been, for they were ashamed not to be what he showed that he thought them.

He was always far more severe with himself than with others, and would bitterly reproach himself for being brusque in manner to untactful strangers, and for allowing fits of depression to get possession of him at times. In a letter to my father he earnestly warns him to avoid following his example in this latter respect, though after his marriage my uncle found it much easier to shake off these fits of depression than he had done in the days when my mother knew him as one sorely tried by the long deferment of that marriage with her sister which at last brought the 'peace of God' into his life.

NOTE

Agnes Grace Weld was the daughter of Charles Richard Weld, author of a *History of the Royal Society*, who had married Anne Sellwood, a younger sister of Tennyson's wife; she was thus a niece by marriage to the poet. In *Lord Tennyson: A Biographical Sketch* (1884) Henry T. Jennings prints a long letter from her describing Tennyson's friendship with Mrs Cameron, W. G. Ward, and others; an abridged version of this letter is given in *Memoir*, II, pp. 523–5.

Tennyson and Mrs Cameron*

AGNES WELD

I used to feel a sort of proprietorship in the old study, for if the Tennysons happened to be away from Farringford when we were at Freshwater, my uncle would give me the key of the room; but I loved it best when I used to go up to it between eleven and twelve to fetch my uncle down for our morning walk together, before starting on which I used to coax him to read to me from the volume which he generally was holding in his hands when I entered, which sometimes consisted of the MS of his last written poem, and sometimes was a new book of science, history, or philosophy, all of which subjects interested him keenly.

The reading finished, we went down to my aunt in the drawing-

* *Glimpses of Tennyson*, pp. 63–71.

room for a few minutes, and then my uncle donned his large, soft felt hat, and we passed out of the breakfast-room on to the broad lawn, across which Tennyson strode with rapid steps into the winding shrubbery path that had been bordered all through the spring with primroses of many hues, self-sown for the most part. Opening the little wicket gate to which the path led, we passed into the bowery lane and turned down it to the left towards Freshwater Bay, if our first halting-place was to be the picturesque ivy-clad 'Dimbola', garlanded to its very roof with roses, where dwelt that unique personality Julia Margaret Cameron,[1] who seemed to be all the famous women of the French salons of the eighteenth century rolled into one, with an added charm of her own beside. As Sir John Simeon[2] and his eldest daughter were Tennyson's dearest man and girl friends of the Isle of Wight circle, so was Mrs Cameron, whose nature was fully as noble a one as theirs, his dearest woman friend; almost the only woman outside his relations whom he called by her Christian name, and who called him in turn by his. She was a woman of earnest piety and rare intellectual powers, and especially was she the very incarnation of friendship; no trouble was ever too great for her to take to serve or give pleasure to the many she folded to her motherly heart, and when with Mrs Cameron she made each feel that he or she was the only being in the whole universe for whom this Queen of Friends lived. . . .

She refused to be bound by any of the artificialities of modern society life, and her complete freedom from affectation was a great refreshment to Tennyson, and even made him bear patiently the many scoldings she gave him for refusing to waste (as he considered) the precious hours of lovely summer mornings in sitting to her for his photograph. Unfortunately for my uncle she had discovered what an immense source of pleasure to her friends her photographs of him were; and still more unfortunately, from his point of view, she had made the further discovery that this pleasure was greatly enhanced when the said photographs were signed with the poet's own autograph. The more he signed, the more she wanted him to sign; and I have really pitied my uncle when she has come flying up to Farringford with such a huge sheaf of her photographs of him that she has had to hire a carriage to bring them, and has plumped them down before him, with a selection of new pens, so that he might not have the excuse of not having a pen handy to sign them with.

Some of Mrs Cameron's photographs of Tennyson were as successful as were those of her husband, who used to look very patriarchal in his purple caftan, over which flowed his long snowy locks and beard. He had done much active and important work in India, but now led a reposeful existence, absorbed in the classics, of which he had such a thorough mastery that Tennyson loved to discuss them with him.

The Camerons' sons being about the same age as the young Alfred Tennysons were their constant companions, and such was the intimacy between the two families that an introduction from Mrs Cameron was generally an open sesame to the charmed circle of Farringford. I remember witnessing this with a young girl who was paying a short visit to Dimbola, and happened to be looking out of an upper window with Mrs Cameron at the view of the sea which it commanded, when the latter espied a tall figure, in a flowing mantle-like cloak, approaching with rapid strides, and smiling up to her. Instantly she flew out into the garden with both her arms outstretched to meet and greet her honoured guest, to whom she proudly exhibited the good results she was getting from that last negative of him which occupied a large printing frame on the lawn. Tennyson, who remembered what long sittings it involved, shrugged his shoulders at her suggestions of a new pose, in which she declared she could make a quite Rembrandt-like picture of him that very morning, on which the strongly actinic rays of the spring sunshine would be sure to bring out the very best effects of light and shade. Tennyson was not to be moved by her pleadings, eagerly emphasised by gesticulations with those expressive hands of hers, deeply stained by the chemicals in which she was continually soaking them, for she did every part of the process herself, even to the making of those wet plates of the messiness of which modern photographers with the dry plate have so little idea.

She next urged that if the wayward poet would insist on preferring a walk in the sunshine to making the far better use of it of letting it immortalise her through him to future ages, he would at all events congratulate her on a capital illustration to one of his poems she had found in a young lady visitor to Freshwater. She picked up a second printing-frame from the lawn, and releasing the catch disclosed the face of the girl who had been leaning with her out of the window, which Tennyson pronounced to be that of a winsome maiden, but not exactly his conception of the particular character to which Mrs Cameron has fitted her. 'Well, if you won't sit to me today, you must take that girl for a walk', said Julia Margaret in the imperative mood tone, and the poet, glad to grant her a small favour after refusing her a large one, consented at once, and the maiden was beckoned up to at the window out of which she was still leaning. She blushed with awe and shyness as her hostess dragged her forward, and told her she was to put on her hat quickly for a walk with one whom she had hitherto regarded as a being to be almost worshipped for his genius. Before the walk was half over, her fear of him had vanished, but her reverence was intensified. She was amazed at the vast depth of his learning; amazed, too, at the way he managed to make subjects she had hitherto thought far too abstruse and difficult for her quite easy of comprehension.

He gave her his hand to help her down the steep path into Watcombe Bay, which, as I have said, was his own especial bay of which he was extremely proud, and he showed her all the wealth of minute animal and vegetable life that fills its limpid rock-pools. As they gained the summit of the Beacon Down he brought to her mind's eye a graphic picture of the geological changes that have taken place in the extensive landscape upon which they looked, and then brought her back to the life-history of the tiny mollusc, half-hidden in the short turf upon which they were treading. When after lunch at Farringford she returned to Dimbola, that young girl echoed the remark made to me by the late Dean Wellesley[3] of Windsor, 'I honoured Tennyson so highly for his writings that I feared to know him lest I might be disappointed in him; but now that I have seen and known your uncle, I can truly say that he himself is higher and greater than the greatest of all the poems he has written.'

NOTES

1. Julia Margaret Cameron (1815–79), nee Pattle; in 1838 she married Charles Hay Cameron (1795–1880), who after a notable legal career in India returned to England in 1848 and from 1860 to 1875 lived at Freshwater. There the Camerons became close friends of the Tennysons. In about 1865 Mrs Cameron took up photography; she is now recognised as outstanding among Victorian portrait photographers—see Helmut Gernsheim, *Julia Margaret Cameron: her Life and Photographic Work* (1948). Her wit and her disregard for convention are displayed in an anecdote told by V. O'Connor: when some Americans who were visiting her were refused admission at Tennyson's house,

'Oh, he won't see you?' she said. 'Come with me.' And thereupon hastily throwing on her shawl, she took them straightway to Farringford, entered the open hall door, and marched them into the drawing-room, where Mr Tennyson and his wife were seated. 'Alfred,' she said, 'these strangers come from a far country to see the lion of Freshwater; and'—waving her hand—'behold—a bear!' Tennyson, ever gentle with his friends, caught her direct humour, and broke into a hearty laugh, receiving his visitors in the kindliest manner. ('Mrs Cameron, Her Friends and Her Photographs', *Century Magazine*, n.s., xxxiii (1897) 7–8)

She photographed Tennyson, Browning, Darwin, and many others, and was well-known for brooking no refusal from her sitters; when Longfellow visited Tennyson in 1868 (see p. 86 below), 'Tennyson grimly left him to Mrs Cameron, saying: "Longfellow, you have to do whatever she tells you.

I'll come back soon and see what is left of you" ' (O'Connor, pp. 3–4).

2. Sir John Simeon, third baronet, was the Roman Catholic squire of Swainston Hall, near Newport, a few miles from Farringford. He was for a period Member of Parliament for the Isle of Wight. He met Tennyson in 1854 and they became close friends. According to Sir Charles Tennyson, he 'was a fine type of country gentleman: a good scholar, an excellent landlord and Master of the Isle of Wight foxhounds' (*Alfred Tennyson*, 280). When he died in 1870 shock and grief caused Tennyson to delay the move to Aldworth. 'In the Garden at Swainston' (Ricks, 357) was written on the occasion of his funeral. A few weeks later Tennyson described him, in a letter to his widow, as 'my much-loved and ever honoured friend, the only man on earth, I verily believe, to whom I could, and have more than once opened my whole heart' (*Memoir*, ii, p. 98). It seems to have been Simeon who, on coming across the lyric 'Oh! that 'twere possible', urged him to make it the basis of a longer poem—the result being *Maud*.

3. Gerald Wellesley (1809–82), a contemporary of Tennyson at Trinity, became Dean of Windsor, 1854–82.

Walks with Tennyson*

LOUISA WARD

'During my father's absences in London and elsewhere, I was free to go and stay there as often and for as long as I liked. I used to go for long walks, sometimes alone with Mr Tennyson, sometimes in the company of other guests, of whom Mr Jowett was one of the most frequent. Tennyson in these walks would rise to the highest themes, and thread his way through the deepest speculations till I caught the infection of his mind, and the questions of matter and spirit, and of time and eternity, and such kindred subjects, became to me the burning questions, the supreme interests of life. But however absorbed he might be in earnest talk, his eye and ear were always alive to the natural objects around him. I have heard him stop short in a sentence to listen to a blackbird's song, to watch the sunlight glint on a butterfly's wing, or to examine a field flower at his feet.' I [Agnes Weld] cannot resist here interrupting Mrs Ward's notes to illustrate them by telling how, when walking one day with the present Rector of Corfe Castle, along the top of Watcombe Bay—that picturesque little cove dear to Tennyson from a sense of his lord-of-the-manorship over it as well as from its own beauty—my uncle stopped suddenly in a line of argument to point out the sunlight gilding to a

* A. G. Weld, *Glimpses of Tennyson*, pp. 58–61.

deeper golden shade the fragile rock-cistus bloom at his feet, and, tenderly plucking the delicate flower, he held it lovingly in his hand, and, looking up, said 'There is not a flower on all this Down that owes to the sun what I owe to Christ.'

Sir John Simeon's daughter continues, 'The afternoon walks were followed by the long talks in the firelight by the side of Mrs Tennyson's sofa—talks less eager, less thrilling than those I have recalled; but so helpful, so tender, full of the wisdom of one who has learnt to look upon life, and all it embraces, from one standpoint only, and that the very highest. Then came dinner, seasoned with merry, genial talk, unexpected guests arriving, and always finding the same warm welcome, for none came who were not tried and trusted friends. Afterwards we adjourned to the drawing-room, according to the old college fashion, for the delightful dessert. Mr Tennyson went up after dinner to his little study at the top of the house with any men friends who were staying in the house. They smoked there for an hour or two, and then came down to tea, unless, as sometimes happened, we all joined them upstairs; and then there was more talk, and reading aloud of published, or, still better, unpublished poems. He would sometimes read from other poets, Shakespeare, Milton, Pope, and some lyrics of Campbell being what he often chose, and he taught me to know and appreciate Crabbe, whom he placed very high in the rank of English poets.'

NOTE

Mrs Louisa Ward was the eldest daughter of Sir John Simeon (see p. 39).

'A Visit to Tennyson'*

C. L. DODGSON

To William Wilcox from Christ Church, Oxford, 11 May 1859

There was a man painting the garden railing when I walked up to the house, of whom I asked if Mr Tennyson were at home, fully expecting the answer 'No', so that it was an agreeable surprise when he said, He's there, sir', and pointed him out, and, behold! he was not many yards off, mowing his lawn in a wideawake[1] and spectacles. I had to introduce myself, as he is too short-sighted to recognise

* *Strand Magazine*, xxi (1901) 543–4.

people, and when he had finished the bit of mowing he was at, he took me into the house to see Mrs Tennyson, who, I was very sorry to find, had been very ill, and was then suffering from almost total sleeplessness. She was lying on the sofa, looking rather worn and haggard, so that I stayed a very few minutes. She asked me to come to dinner that evening to meet a Mr Warburton[2] (brother of the 'Crescent and the Cross'), but her husband revoked the invitation before I left, as he said he wished her to be as little excited as possible that evening, and begged I would drop in for tea that evening, and dine with them the next day. He took me over the house to see the pictures, etc. (among which my photographs of the family were hung 'on the line', framed in those enamel—what do you call them, cartons?) The view from the garret windows he considers one of the finest in the island, and showed me a picture which his friend Richard Doyle[3] had painted of it for him; also his little smoking-room at the top of the house, where of course he offered me a pipe; also the nursery, where we found the beautiful little Hallam (his son), who remembered me more readily than his father had done.

I went in the evening, and found Mr Warburton an agreeable man, with rather a shy, nervous manner; he is a clergyman, and inspector of schools in that neighbourhood. We got on the subject of clerical duty in the evening, and Tennyson said he thought clergymen as a body didn't do half the good they might if they were less stuck-up and showed a little more sympathy with their people. 'What they want,' he said, 'is force and geniality—geniality without force will of course do no good, but force without geniality will do very little.' All very sound theology, to my thinking. This was up in the little smoking-room, to which we had adjourned after tea, and where we had about two hours' very interesting talk. The proof-sheets of 'The King's Idylls'[4] were lying about, but he would not let me took at them. I looked with some curiosity to see what sort of books occupied the lowest of the swinging bookshelves, most handy to his writing-table; they were all, without exception, Greek or Latin—Homer, Aeschylus, Horace, Lucretius, Virgil, etc. It was a fine moonlight night, and he walked through the garden with me when I left, and pointed out an effect of the moon shining through thin, white cloud, which I had never noticed before—a sort of golden ring, not close round its edge like a halo, but at some distance off. I believe sailors consider it a sign of bad weather. He said he had often noticed it, and had alluded to it in one of his early poems. You will find it in 'Margaret'.[5]

The next day I went to dinner, and met Sir John Simeon,[6] who has an estate some miles off there, an old Ch. Ch.[7] man, who has turned Roman Catholic since. He is one of the pleasantest men I ever met, and you may imagine that the evening was a delightful one: I enjoyed it thoroughly, especially the concluding two hours in the smoking-room.

I took over my books of photographs, but Mrs Tennyson was too tired to look at them that evening, and I settled to leave them and come for them next morning, when I could see more of the children, who had only appeared for a few minutes during dinner.

Tennyson told us that often on going to bed after being engaged on composition he had dreamed long passages of poetry ('You, I suppose', turning to me, 'dream photographs?') which he liked very much at the time, but forgot entirely when he woke. One was an enormously long one on fairies, where the lines from being very long at first gradually got shorter and shorter, till it ended with fifty or sixty lines of two syllables each![8] The only bit he ever remembered enough to write down was one he dreamed at ten years old, which you may like to possess as a genuine unpublished fragment of the Laureate, though I think you will agree with me that it gives very little indication of his future poetic powers:

> May a cock-sparrow
> Write to a barrow?
> I hope you'll excuse
> My infantine muse.

Up in the smoking-room the conversation turned upon murders, and Tennyson told us several horrible stories from his own experience: he seems rather to revel in such descriptions—one would not guess it from his poetry. Sir John kindly offered me a lift in his carriage back to the hotel, and as we were standing at the door before getting in he said, 'You don't object to a cigar in the carriage, do you?' On which Tennyson growled out, 'He didn't object to *two pipes* in that little den upstairs, and *a feebliori*[9] he's no business to object to one cigar in a carriage.' And so ended one of the most delightful evenings I have spent for many a long day.

NOTES

Charles Lutwidge Dodgson (1832–98), Oxford lecturer in mathematics (1855–81) and, as 'Lewis Carroll', author of *Alice's Adventures in Wonderland* (1865), etc. He was also an enthusiastic photographer. Tennyson and Dodgson met in about 1857. William Wilcox, the addressee of the letter from which the above extract is taken, was Dodgson's cousin.

1. Soft felt hat with wide brim and low crown—Tennyson's favourite headgear.

2. William Warburton (1826–1919), later Canon of Winchester. His brother Bartholomew was the author of the popular book *The Crescent and the Cross: or Romance and Realities of Eastern Travel* (1845).

3. Richard Doyle (1824–83), artist, illustrator and caricaturist; he designed the once-familiar cover of *Punch*.

4. *Idylls of the King* was published in July 1859; the volume contained 'Enid', 'Vivien', 'Elaine' and 'Guinevere'.

5. The reference is to lines 19–21 of the poem (Ricks, 175).

6. See p. 39.

7. Christ Church.

8. 'This reminiscence probably gave his guest the idea for "The Mouse's Tale" in *Alice in Wonderland*' (Sir Charles Tennyson, *Alfred Tennyson*, p. 316).

9. Humorous adaptation of the Latin phrase *a fortiori*.

'Recollections of Tennyson'*

H. M. BUTLER

My real acquaintance with the Tennyson family dates from the end of 1861 and the early days of 1862. . . .

The two first incidents that I remember were the Poet showing us the proof of his 'Dedication of the Idylls', and at our request, reading out to us *Enoch Arden*. The 'Dedication' must have been composed almost immediately after the death of the Prince Consort on 14 December. He seemed himself pleased with it. I thought at the time, and I have felt ever since, that these lines rank high, not only among his other tributes of the same kind, but in the literature of epitaphs generally. We felt it a proud privilege to be allowed to stand at his side as he looked over the proof just arrived by the post, and it led us of course to talk sympathetically of the late Prince and the poor widowed Queen.

Very soon after, the Bradleys[1] and we dined at Farringford. The dinner hour was, I think, as early as six, and then, after he had retreated to his *sanctum* for a smoke, he would come down to the drawing-room, and read aloud to his guests. On this occasion he read to us *Enoch Arden*, then only in manuscript. I had before heard much of his peculiar manner of reading, with its deep and often monotonous tones, varied with a sudden lift of the voice as if into the air, at the end of a sentence or a clause. It was, as always, a reading open to criticism on the score of lack of variety, but my dear bride

* Hallam Tennyson (ed.), *Tennyson and his Friends* (London: Macmillan, 1911) pp. 208–14, 216–21.

and I were in no mood to criticise. The spell was upon us. Every note of his magnificent voice spoke of majesty or tenderness or awe. It was, in plain words, a prodigious treat to have heard him. We walked back through the winter darkness to our hotel, conscious of having enjoyed a unique privilege.

During this vacation I had, as often in after years, not a few walks with him on the downs, leaving the Beacon on the left and going on to the Needles. It was a walk of about two hours. It is here that my memory so sadly fails me as to his talk. In tone it was friendly, manly, and perfectly simple, without a touch of condescension. He seemed quite unconscious that he was a great man, one of the first Englishmen of his time, talking to one young and utterly obscure. Almost any subject interested him, grave or gay. He would often talk of metres, Greek and Latin; of attempts to translate Homer; of the weak points in the English hexameter; or again of more serious topics, on which he had thought much and felt strongly, such as the life after death, the so-called 'eternity of future punishment', the unreality of the world as known to the senses, the grander human race, the 'crowning race', still to be born. . . .

I noticed that he never spoke of Wordsworth without marked reverence. Obviously, with his exquisite ear for choice words and rhythm, he must have been more sensitive than most men to the prosaic, bathetic side of Wordsworth; but I never heard him say a word implying that he felt this, whereas I *have* heard him qualify his admiration for Robert Browning's genius and his affection for his person by some allusion to the roughness of his style. This, he thought, must lead to his being less read than he deserved in years to come, and he evidently regretted it.

It was in the period, roughly speaking, between 1862 and 1880 that I saw most of him, for it was then our habit to make frequent visits to Freshwater or Alum Bay, generally at Christmas, and we were always received with the same cordial kindness. It was then that the long walks and the readings of his poetry after dinner continued as a kind of institution, and never palled. Among the poems that he read out to us were 'Aylmer's Field', the 'Ode on the Death of the Duke of Wellington', parts of *Maud*, 'Guinevere', 'The Holy Grail', 'The Charge of the Light Brigade', 'The Revenge', 'The Defence of Lucknow', 'In the Valley of Cauteretz'. With regard to this beautiful poem I cannot help recalling an amusing and most unexpected laugh. He had read the third and fourth lines in his most sonorous tones.

All along the valley, where thy waters flow,
I walked with one I loved two and thirty years ago

and then suddenly, changing his voice, he said gruffly, 'A brute of a
—— has discovered that it was thirty-one years and not thirty-two.
Two-and-thirty is better than one-and-thirty years ago, isn't it? But
perhaps I ought to alter it.'

It was at this time that we used often to meet Mr Jowett and also
the poet's great friend and admirer, the gifted Mrs Cameron and
her dignified and grey-bearded husband, who looked like a grand
oriental chief. . . .

On 13 December [1886] I was invited to Farringford, with the
prospect of returning on the 16th to Davos Platz, where I had left my
invalid daughter. Of this short visit I find I have made a few notes.
The poet was as cordial as ever. After dinner he took me to his
sanctum, and read me his new Jubilee Ode in Catullian metre, and
then 'Locksley Hall Sixty Years After'. Next morning there came a
letter from Dr W. H. Thompson's[2] executor containing an early
poem of Tennyson's of 1826, and a sonnet, once famous, complain-
ing of defects in the college system of his day [quotes 'Lines on
Cambridge of 1830'—Ricks, 140]. About eleven o'clock the Poet
took me out alone. We went first to Freshwater Gate, where he said
the 'maddened scream of the sea' in *Maud* had been first suggested
to him. He talked of our late friend, Philip Stanhope Worsley,[3] the
translator of the *Odyssey* and half of the *Iliad*, who was living there a
good many years ago, and whom I had met at his table. He admired
him much. He talked also, but I forget to what effect, of 'The Holy
Grail' and the old Arthur myth, but before this we talked of the
Cambridge sonnet just mentioned. 'There was no *love*', he said, 'in
the system.' I understood him to mean that the dons, as a rule, were
out of sympathy with the young men. He spoke also of the bullying
he had undergone at his first school; how, when he was a new boy of
only seven and a half, he was sitting on the school steps crying and
homesick. Up came a big fellow, between seventeen and eighteen,
and asked him roughly who he was and what he was crying for, and
then gave him a kick in the wind! This experience had evidently
rankled in his mind for more than seventy years. Again, in April
1890, he told me the same story.

But to return to our morning walk of 14 December 1886.
Something led me to speak of my favourite lines:

> The old order changeth, yielding place to new,
> And God fulfils Himself in many ways,
> Lest one good custom should corrupt the world.

Spedding,[4] it seems, and others had wanted him to alter the 'one *good*
custom'. 'I was thinking', he said, 'of knighthood.' He went on to
speak of his 'Experiments on Quantity', and in particular of the

Alcaic Ode to Milton, beginning 'O mighty-mouth'd inventor of harmonies'. 'I thought *that*', he said, 'a bit of a *tour de force*', and surely he was right there. He tilted a little at C. S. Calverley[5] for demurring to 'God-gifted organ-voice of England'. 'I didn't mean it to be like your "September, October, November"; I was imitating, not Horace, but the original Greek Alcaic, though Horace's is perhaps the finest metre.' The two Latin metres which I have more than once heard him admire were the hexameter and the Alcaic.

I find that in my Journal I wrote as regards this walk: 'I wish I could remember more. He was wholly *facilis*, and I never felt less afraid of him or more reverent.' Perhaps I should add that during the walk he told me an extraordinary number of ghost stories—a man appearing to several people, and then vanishing before their eyes. . . .

At this point I shall do well to insert extracts from my dear wife's journal, describing a few incidents in what proved our last visit to Farringford . . . at the end of January 1892. . . . She writes as follows.

VISIT TO FARRINGFORD, JANUARY 1892

On 26 January Montagu and I left our two small boys at Eton Villa, Shanklin, to spend the night at Lambert's Hotel, Freshwater. After leaving our traps at the hotel we walked up to Farringford in time for two o'clock lunch. I sat next the poet at table, and had some talk with him. He spoke of the metres of Horace, and said that he always thought his Sapphics uninteresting and monotonous. 'What a relief it is', he said, 'when he *does* allow himself some irregularity, for instance 'Laurea donandus Apollinari'. On the other hand, he admired his Alcaics immensely. The discovery for which he always hoped the most was of some further writings of Sappho herself. He considered the metre beautiful under her treatment.

Then we spoke of Schliemann,[6] of whom I had just been reading in Schuchardt's book, and he said he had no faith in him. 'How could a great city have been built on a little ridge like that (meaning Hissarlik)? Where would have been the room for Priam's fifty sons and fifty daughters?'

He also thought the supposed identifications of topography absurd, and preferred to believe that Homer's descriptions were entirely imaginary. When I said that I thought that a disappointing view, he called me 'a wretched localiser'. 'They try to localise me too', he said. 'There is one man wants to make out that I describe nothing I have not seen.' Also, with some irritation, of other accounts of himself: 'Full of lies, and —— made me tell a big one at the end.'

Next day we walked up at about 12.20 to accompany him in his morning walk. Montagu and he were in front, Hallam Tennyson and I behind. Montagu tells me how he was indignant with Z. for charging him with general plagiarism, in particular about Lactantius and other classics, 'of whom', he said, 'I haven't read a word'. Also, of taking from Sophocles, 'whom I never read since I was a young man'; and of owing his 'moanings of the sea' to Horace's 'gementis litora Bospori'. Some one charged him with having stolen the *In Memoriam* metre from some very old poet of whom he had never heard. He said, in answer to Montagu's question, that the metres of both 'Maurice' and 'The Daisy' were original. He had never written in the metre of Gray's 'Elegy', except epitaphs in Westminster Abbey. He admired the metre much, and thought the poem immortal.*

Hartley Coleridge,[7] he said, spoke of Pindar as the 'Newmarket Poet'. He thought the loss of his Dithyrambs most serious, judging from the remaining fragment. He had from early boyhood been familiar with the fact that Wolsey and Cromwell in *Henry VIII*, were by Fletcher, but he felt absolutely certain that the description of the Field of the Cloth of Gold was by Shakespeare's own hand. He quoted it, as well as several lines from Wolsey. When I said how glad I was he had written about the Duke of Clarence, he said, 'Yes, but I wouldn't write an Installation Ode for the Chancellor.'

So far Montagu reported. After this we others came up, and the old poet and I walked home together.

We spoke a little of our projected tour to Greece. He had never been there, but would have greatly liked to go—in a private yacht—'but they tell me an old man is safest at home, and I dare say it is true; and I couldn't stand the vermin!' I told him I was hoping to study classical architecture a little before going out, and he said that he thought, after all, Gothic architecture was finer than classic. 'It is like blank verse', he said; 'it will suit the humblest cottage and the grandest cathedral. It has more mystery than the classic.' He thought many of our cathedrals spoiled by their vile glass. He had been disappointed, in his late visit to Cambridge, to

---

* I can confirm this last statement from more than one talk with him. He would note the perfection of the metre. The second line affords an instance of the delicacy of his ear. We were speaking of the undoubtedly correct reading, 'The lowing herd *wind* slowly o'er the lea'—not, as is so often printed, *winds*. I forget his exact comment, but the point of it was that the double ess, winds slowly, would have been to his ear most displeasing.

Again, speaking of the line 'And all the air a solemn stillness holds', he observed how seldom Gray seemed satisfied with this inversion of the accusative and the nominative, and how he himself endeavoured, as a rule, to avoid it—H. M. B.

notice that the windows in King's seemed to be losing their brilliancy and to look dark.

After we had been walking a few minutes in silence, he said to me, 'Do you see what the beauty is in the line "That all the Thrones are clouded by your loss"?'—quoting from his still unpublished poem on the young Prince. I said I thought it very beautiful; but he asked if I saw why he had used the word *clouded* instead of *darkened* or another. 'It makes you think of a great mountain', he explained. Then he spoke of the great richness of the English language due to its double origin, the Norman and Saxon words. How hard it would be for a foreigner to feel the difference in the line 'An *infant* crying for the light', had the word *baby* been substituted, which would at once have made it ridiculous. He told me that his lines 'came to' him; he did not make them up, but that, when they had come, he wrote them down, and looked into them to see what they were like. This was very interesting, especially as he had told Montagu, at Easter 1890, that he had composed 'Crossing the Bar' in less than ten minutes.

Then he said again, what I have heard him say before, that though a poet is *born*, he will not be much of a poet if he is not *made* too. Then he asked me if I was fond of Pindar. I am very glad that he admires him greatly. He could not believe Paley's[8] theory that Pindar is earlier than Homer. I vented my dislike of Paley's horribly prosaic translations in his notes on Aeschylus, and he said *he* had always used Blomfield,[9] he found his Glossary such a help.

We were now indoors, and in a few minutes went in to luncheon. I was again seated next him, and we had some more talk. He got upon the subject of college life, and told me anecdotes of himself and his friends, one very amusing one about Tom Taylor.[10] During some vacation Tom Taylor's rooms were lent by the college authorities to a farmer, a member of an agricultural society which they were entertaining. Taylor knew this perfectly well; but in the middle of the night suddenly entered the room, in a long traveller's cloak and with a lantern in his hand, 'Pray, what are you doing in my room, sir, and in my bed?' feigning great surprise and indignation. The poor old farmer tried to explain that he was honoured by being the guest of the college, but Taylor refused to be pacified; when suddenly, in the midst of their altercation, enter Charles Spring-Rice,[11] brother of Stephen, personating the Senior Dean, who forthwith laid forcible hands on Tom Taylor. Thereupon ensued a regular scuffle, in which they both tumbled onto the bed, and Tom Taylor got so much the worst of it that the kindly agriculturist began to intercede, 'Oh, please, Mr Dean, don't be too hard on the young man!'

Tennyson himself had been proctorised[12] once or twice. Once, during the first few days of his college life, he came out to receive a parcel by a midnight mail. 'Pray, sir, what are you doing at this time of night?' said the Proctor. 'And pray, sir, what business of yours is it to ask me?' replied the freshman, who in his innocence knew nothing about the Proctor. He was told to call upon him next day, but then explained his ignorance, and was let off.

On one occasion a throng of university men outside the Senate House had been yelling against Whewell.[13] Tennyson was standing by the door of Macmillan's shop, and raised a counter-cry *for* Whewell. He was, however, seen standing, and was sent for to Whewell. 'I was surprised, sir, to see *you* among that shouting mob the other day.' 'I was shouting *for* you', was the reply. Whewell was greatly pleased, and grunted his approbation.

Another funny story. A wine-party was going on in Arthur Hallam's rooms in the New Court, when enter angrily the Senior Dean, 'Tommy Thorp'. 'What is the meaning. Mr Hallam, of all this noise?' 'I am very sorry, sir', said Hallam, 'we had no idea we were making a noise.' 'Well, gentlemen, if you'll all come down into the Court, you'll *hear* what a noise you're making.' 'Perhaps', admits Tennyson, 'I may have put in the *all*.'

So ends my wife's short journal, and it only remains for me to sum up very briefly the impressions left upon me, after a lapse of fifty, forty, thirty, twenty years, by these visits to Farringford which once made so large a part of my interest and my happiness.

Little as I am able to put these impressions into words, I can say with truth that no personality with which I have ever come in close touch, either seemed to me at the time, or has seemed in later recollection, to cover so large, so rich, and so diverse a field for veneration, wonder, and regard.

Tennyson was, and is, to me the most remarkable man that I have ever met. Often when I was with him, whether in long walks or in his study, and when I came to think of him silently afterwards, I used to recall his own lines on Wellington

> Our greatest yet with least pretence . . . ,
> Rich in saving common-sense,
> *And, as the greatest only are,*
> *In his simplicity sublime.*

Simple, natural, shrewd, humorous; feeling strongly on a vast variety of subjects, and saying freely just what he felt; passing rapidly and easily from the gravest matters of speculation or conduct to some trifling or amusing incident of the moment, or some recollection of the years of his youth; he seemed to me unconscious of being a great man, though he must have known himself to be one of the foremost thinkers, and quite the foremost poet of his day. He was wholly free from affectation. He was never an actor of a part. There was about him always an atmosphere of truth. 'Truth-teller was our Alfred named' was a line that again and again recurred to the memory as one heard him speak out his mind either on men, or on politics, or on the deepest mysteries of philosophy or religion. He was pre-eminently one of the Children of Light. Of light, whether from science, or from literary criticism, or from the progress of the human conscience, he hailed thankfully and expectantly every fresh disclosure. There was a deep reverence in him for the Unseen, the Undiscovered, the as yet Unrevealed. This on the intellectual side; and on the moral side there was a manly, a devout, and a tender veneration for purity and innocence and trustfulness, and, to borrow his own stately words, written early in his life, 'Self-reverence, self-knowledge, self-control'.

NOTES

Henry Montague Butler (1833–1918), after twenty-six years as Headmaster of Harrow School, became Master of Trinity College, Cambridge, in 1886.

1. The Rev. G. G. Bradley, Dean of Westminster, and his wife were friends of the Tennysons and contributed some brief reminiscences to the *Memoir*, I, pp. 204–7, 467–9.

2. See p. 5.

3. P. S. Worsley (1835–66) published translations of Homer in 1861 and 1865.

4. See p. 7.

5. Charles Stuart Calverley (1831–84), remembered for his witty verses and parodies.

6. Heinrich Schliemann (1822–90), German archaeologist, had excavated Troy in 1870–82. Tennyson had dined with Schliemann in London in 1877; when Schliemann remarked that 'Hissarlik, the ancient Troy, is no bigger than the courtyard of Burlington House', Tennyson retorted 'I can never believe that' (*Memoir*, II, p. 217).

7. Hartley Coleridge (1796–1849), minor poet and and eldest son of S. T. Coleridge.

8. Frederick Apthorp Paley (1815–88), classical scholar; his translations of Aeschylus began to appear in 1849.

9. Charles James Blomfield (1786–1857) published editions of several plays by Aeschylus from 1810.

10. See p. 30.

11. The Hon. Charles Spring-Rice was a son of Baron Monteagle.

12. Punished (usually fined) by the proctors, university officials charged with maintaining discipline and enforcing regulations governing the behaviour of undergraduates.

13. William Whewell (1794–1866), later Master of Trinity (1841–66), had been Tennyson's tutor.

It is reported that Whewell, recognising his genius, tolerated in him certain informalities which he would not have overlooked in other men. Thus, 'Mr Tennyson, what's the compound interest of a penny put out at the Christian era up to the present time?' was Whewell's good-natured call to attention in the Lecture Room while my father was reading Virgil under the desk. (*Memoir*, i, pp. 38–9)

Visits to Farringford*

WILLIAM ALLINGHAM

Sunday, 20 December 1863. I lunched at Farringford. We all helped in wheeling Mrs Tennyson to the top of High Down. Then A. T., the tutor and myself walked to Totland's Bay, the talk all upon classic metres, of which he is full at present. I am invited for Christmas.

Sunday, 27 December 1863. After dinner more talk of 'classic metres'; in the drawing-room, T. standing on the hearth-rug repeated with emphasis (perhaps apropos of metres) the following lines, in the following way:

> Higgledy-piggledy, silver and gold,
> There's–(*it's nothing very dreadful!*)
> There's a louse on my back
> Seven years old.
> He inches, he pinches,
> In every part,
> And if I could catch him
> I'd *tearr* out his *hearrt*!

The last line he gave with tragic fury. Prose often runs into rhyme. T. imitated the waiter in some old-fashioned tavern calling down to the kitchen—'Three gravies, two mocks, and a *pea*'! ('soup' understood). On 'pea' he raised the tone and prolonged it very comically.

Monday, 28 December 1863. A. T., Palgrave[1] and I walk to Alum Bay

* *William Allingham: A Diary*, pp. 93–4, 117–19, 126–8, 137, 148–51, 156–9, 163.

and look at the coloured cliffs, smeary in effect, like something spilt.
A. T. reproves P. for talking so fast and saying 'of—of—of—of', etc.
He also corrects me for my pronunciation (or so he asserts) of 'dew'.
'There's no *Jew* on the grass!' says he—'there may be *dew*, but that's
quite another thing.'

Saturday, 24 June 1865.   After Custom-House, steamer to Island.
Farringford, hid my bag—find some people in the hay-field and Mrs
Cameron photographing everybody like mad.
    Went to house: A. T. says, 'Are you come to stay?' I confess the bag
and we go to fetch it. Mrs Cameron focuses me, but it proves a failure
and I decline further operations. She thinks it a great honour to be
done by her. Dress for dinner. Mr King, the publisher, at dinner and
Mrs King. Talk of Ireland,—Petrie and other men, of whom A. T.
hardly knows the existence. The cholera. T.'s den at top of house;
smoking,—Public Schools, Charterhouse, etc., effect of a few bad
boys on the rest—Tupper—Swinburne. The Kings take leave, are at
the Albion Hotel. I sit reading and A. T. comes down to me.

Sunday, 25 June 1865.   Fine—at breakfast A. T. with his letters, one
from D. of Argyll. Swinburne—Venables. Out and meet the
Kings—Mrs Cameron. Return to Farringford. Dinner (which is at
6.30 always). Sitting at claret in the drawing-room we see the evening
sunlight on the landscape. I go to the top of the house alone; have a
strong sense of being in Tennyson's; green summer, ruddy light in
the sky. When I came down to drawing-room found A. T. with a
book in his hand; the Kings expectant. He accosted me, 'Allingham,
would it disgust you if I read *Maud*? Would you expire?'
    I gave a satisfactory reply and he accordingly read *Maud* all
through, with some additions recently made. His interpolated
comments very amusing.
    'This is what was called namby-pamby!'—'That's wonderfully
fine!'—'That was very hard to read; could you have read it? I don't
think so.'
    What strikes me most in *Maud* this time, as always, is the section
beginning, 'O that 'twere possible after long grief and pain.' It
contains the *germ of the whole*, and was written many years ago.
    Upstairs, talk of Poe. I praise Emerson,[2] to which T. rather
demurs but says little. By and by he asks me to lend him Emerson's
books, which I will gladly do. I feel his naturalness much.

Monday, 26 June 1865.   Cloudy. Farringford. A. T. last night
intended to come across with me and let me show him some places.
New, at breakfast time, he can't make up his mind.
    The Queen is liberal-minded, she thinks churchmen are in the

way to ruin the Church by bigotry—likes droll stories—story of great fire and little fire to burn doll—When T. visited her she curtseyed very low in receiving him—was there anything particular in this?

Another Majesty, Dowager Queen Emma of the Sandwich Islands, is expected soon on a visit to Farringford.

Saturday, 29 July 1865. To Farringford. After dinner T. spoke of boys catching butterflies.

'Why cut short their lives?—What are we? We are the merest moths. Look at that hill' (pointing to the one before the large window), 'it's four hundred millions of years old;—think of that! Let the moths have their little lives.'

Speaking of the colonies, he said, 'England ought to keep her colonies and draw them closer. She ought to have their representatives sitting in London, either in or in connection with the Imperial Parliament.'

Tennyson is always well at sea. 'To own a ship, a large steam-yacht,' he said, 'and go round the world—that's my notion of glory.'

Of the Norwegian waterfalls he said, 'I never was satisfied with water before. On the voyage out, standing at the door of the deck cabin, I saw a moving hill of water pass the side of the ship. I got on the top of the cabin, and saw the sea like a mountainous country, all hill and valley, with foam for snow on the summits;—the finest thing I ever saw.'

Tennyson loathed the necessity, which he fancied himself under, of writing for money. 'The fine thing would be to have a good hereditary estate and a love of literature.' Of the expenses of land-owning he said, 'it costs £100 an acre, and brings in nothing yet'.

T. said he had read part of Carlyle's *Frederick*[3] till he came to, *'they did not strive to build the lofty rhyme'*, and then flung the book into a corner.

He read some extracts in the *Spectator* about poetry, and referred to Carlyle's contemptuous way of speaking of poets, saying, 'We are all tadpoles in a pool, one a little larger or smaller than others!' How differently Goethe would have spoken of this minor poet: 'he was useful in his own time and degree'. . . .

'I was at an hotel in Covent Garden, and went out one morning for a walk in the Piazza. A man met me, tolerably well-dressed but battered-looking. I never saw him before that I know of. He pulled off his hat and said, "Beg pardon, Mr Tennyson, might I say a word to you?" I stopped. "I've been drunk for three days and I want to make a solemn promise to you, Mr Tennyson, that I won't do so any more." I said that was a good resolve, and I hoped he would keep it. He said, "I promise you I will, Mr Tennyson", and added, "Might I

shake your hand?" I shook hands with him, and he thanked me and
went on his way.'

Wednesday, 1 November 1865. We drive in a fly to Farringford,
where T., Mrs T., Miss T. meet us in the hall. T. and B.[4] at once on
easy terms, having simple poetic minds and mutual goodwill. Talk of
Ancient Britons, barrows, roads, etc. I to upper room and dress, T.
comes in to me and we go down together. Dinner: stories of ghosts
and dreams. To drawing-room as usual, where T. has his port, B. no
wine. T. says, 'Modern fame is nothing: I'd rather have an acre of
land. I shall go down, down! I am up now.' T. went upstairs by
himself.

Tea: enter Mrs Cameron (in a funny red openwork shawl) with
two of her boys. T. reappears, and Mrs C. shows a small firework
toy called 'Pharaoh's Serpents', a kind of pastile, which, when
lighted, twists about in a worm-like shape. Mrs C. said they were
poisonous and forbade us all to touch. T. in defiance put out his
hand.

'Don't touch 'em!' shrieked Mrs C. 'You shan't, Alfred!' But
Alfred did. 'Wash your hands then! But Alfred wouldn't, and
rubbed his moustache instead, enjoying Mrs C.'s agonies. Then she
said to him, 'Will you come tomorrow and be photographed?' He,
very emphatically, 'No.'

She turned to me—'You left a great poet out of your *Nightingale
Valley*,[5] and have been repenting ever since in sackcloth and
ashes—eh?' She meant Henry Taylor.[6]

I tried to say that the volume was not a collection of specimens of
poets, but she did not listen. Then she said graciously 'Come
tomorrow and you shall be taken.'

T. and I went out to the porch with Mrs C., where her
donkey-chaise was waiting in the moonlight.

Tennyson now took Barnes and me to his top room. Darwinism—
'Man from ape—would that really make any difference?' Huxley,
Tyndall.[7]

'Time is nothing,' said T., 'are we not all part of Deity?'
'Pantheism?' hinted Barnes, who was not at ease in this sort of
speculation. 'Well!' says T., 'I think I believe in pantheism, of a sort.'
Barnes to bed, T. and I up ladder to the roof to look at Orion. Then
to my room, where more talk. He likes Barnes, he says, 'but he is not
accustomed to strong views theologic'.

We talk of Browning, for whom T. has a very strong personal
regard. 'Browning must think himself the greatest man living. I can't
understand how he should care for my poetry. His new poem[8] has
15,000 lines—there's copiousness! I can't venture to put out a thing
without care. Good-night.' Bed about one, sleep middling.

22 July 1866. After dinner we talk of dreams. T. said, 'In my boyhood I had *intuitions* of immortality—inexpressible! I have never been able to express them. I shall try some day.'

I say that I too have felt something of that kind; whereat T. (being in one of his less amiable moods) growls, 'I don't believe you have. You say it out of rivalry.'

Friday, 24 January 1867. Lymington. Fine and vernal. Ferry to steamer—delightful colours of earth, sky and sea, a bloom upon the landscape. From the Solent see the woody background of Lymington recede, the Island approach with a welcome; a boat with red sails passes in the sunshine. I feel tranquilly happy. Yarmouth, send two bottles of whisky to A. T. by Lambert's driver. Walk to Farringford, field-path, warm. Drawing-room. Mrs T. (looking ill), Miss T., T. He and I walk on the downs; very friendly talk. I said I felt happy to-day, but he—'I'm not at all happy—very unhappy.' He spoke of immortality and virtue,—man's pettiness,—'Sometimes I have a kind of hope.' His anxiety has always been great to get some real insight into the nature and prospects of the human race. He asks every person that seems in the least likely to help him in this, reads every book. When *Vestiges of Creation*[9] appeared he gathered from the talk about it that it came nearer to an explanation than anything before it. T. got the volume, and (he said to me), 'I trembled as I cut the leaves.' But alas, neither was satisfaction there.

Plato: T. says he has not really got anything from him. Aeschylus is great; he quoted from a chorus in the *Agamemnon.*

Women in towns, dangers to health, horrible diseases, quack-doctors, etc. T. would have a strict Contagious Diseases Act in force everywhere.

We go through kitchen garden, lane and gate to the road as usual, where we take leave after some talk upon Christ and the people. T. loves the spirit of Christianity, hates many of the dogmas.

Saturday, 2 February 1867. T. and Lionel just starting for a walk; we took the green road at foot of downs. T. had in his pocket a volume, or pamphlet, of Edwin Waugh's *Lancashire Songs*,[10] and when we paused he read, 'Coam whoam to thy childre and me', with praise. We went to the end of the downs overlooking the Needles. T. spoke of Campbell—his vanity—'has written fine things.'

Edge of cliff, wind blowing in from the sea; a ship ashore at Brook.

Sunday, 3 February 1867. Walk with T. to Brook Bay, ship ashore, the *Fannie Larabee* of Bath, large, three masts, good model. There are people on the shore, but T. doesn't seem to mind. We walked to next point and saw a steamer ashore at Atherfield; then turned up to downs and came back by a path slanting along the cliff side, like a frightful dream rather, my head being lightish. T. tells of people who have fallen over, and at one place is a monumental stone to commemorate such an accident. I said (walking close behind him) 'suppose I were to slip and catch hold of you, and we both rolled down together,' on which T. stopped and said, 'You'd better go on first.'

We talked of Dryden, Campbell, etc. T. told me he was prevented from doing his Arthur Epic, in twelve books, by John Sterling's review of 'Morte d'Arthur' in the *Quarterly*. 'I had it all in my mind, could have done it without any trouble. The king is the complete man, the knights are the passions.' Home a little late for dinner. Afterwards T. rose to leave the room. Matilda (I think) asked, 'Where are you going?'

'To read the Scriptures.'

Later in the drawing-room he read aloud some of Goethe's lyrics.

Monday, 18 February 1867.   Mist. Steamer to Yarmouth. Flags flying. The Queen expected from Osborne, coming to take a look at this part of the island. I to Farringford. I say to T., 'Perhaps the Queen will visit you today.' He thinks it possible.

'Then I had better go?'

'No, stay by all means.'

Talking of the Queen, when T. was at Osborne Her Majesty said to him, 'Cockneys don't annoy *us*,' to which T. rejoined, 'If I could put a sentry at each of my gates I should be safe.'

'She was praising my poetry; I said "Every one writes verses now. I daresay Your Majesty does." She smiled and said, "No! I never could bring two lines together!" '

Wednesday, 3 April 1867.   Farringford. Tennyson and I busied ourselves in the shrubberies, transplanting primroses with spade, knife, and wheelbarrow. After dinner T. concocts an experimental punch which whisky and claret—not successful. Talks of publishers, anon of higher things. He said, 'I feel myself to be a centre—can't believe I shall die. Sometimes I have doubts, of a morning. Time and Space appear thus by reason of our boundedness.'

We spoke of Swedenborg,[11] animals, etc., all with the friendliest sympathy and mutual understanding. T. is the most delightful man in the world to converse with, even when he disagrees.

Friday, 23 August 1867.   Very fine. Steamer 11.40 to Yarmouth.
Tennyson on the quay, also his brother Frederick and two
daughters. A. T. is going to Lyme Regis alone.
    'I have wanted to see the Cobb there ever since I first read
Persuasion.[12] Will you come?'
    Can I possibly? Yes, I will!
    We cross to Lymington. I rush up and make hasty arrangements at
Custom-House and lodgings; then off go A. T. and I, second class, to
Dorchester, A. T. smokes. (T. is a great novel-reader, very fond of
Scott, but perhaps Miss Austen is his prime favourite.)
    In our carriage a Cockney clock-winder, who gets out at every
station to regulate the railway company's clock.
    Once safely *incognito* T. delights in talking to people, but touch his
personality and he shuts up like an oyster. Ringwood, Wimborne,
Poole Harbour, Wareham (mounds), Dorchester. Walk in the warm
afternoon, through stubble fields and reapers at work, to the grand
old Celtic fortress now called 'Maiden Castle', view the great green
mounds, and lie on a slope looking over autumnal landscape. Then
descend and return, finding corn-flowers and 'Succory to match the
sky.' Shall we stay to-night at Dorchester? T. vacillates, at last agrees.
We go to the 'Antelope', rooms not good—out, and into the
Museum, up a backyard,—British antiquities, Roman pottery, etc.
High Street, at its foot a clear little river, *the Frome.* A tipsy cobbler
accosts us. Riverside walk through meadows. County Jail looks like a
pleasant residence. Return by back street to the 'Antelope', which
produces a pint of good port at dinner. The twilight being fine I
propose that we should visit William Barnes, whom T. personally
knows, and whose poems in the Dorset dialect[13] T. knows and likes. I
show the way to Came Vicarage, where I had enjoyed hospitality
from a Saturday to a Monday a year or two before. The cottage
parsonage lies in a hollow among trees about a mile from Dorchester, separated from the public road by a little grass-plot and
shrubbery. We find the gate by starlight and reach the house door
between 9 and 10 o'clock. The worthy old poet–vicar is truly
delighted ,to see us, especially such a guest as T. (whose poetry, he
used to say, has a 'heart-tone' in it).
    Barnes himself lets us in or comes out at once into the passage—
'Here's an honour!' Little Miss Barnes and Mrs Shaw, a married
daughter, appear. B. says, 'put out something! put out something!'
with hospitable fervour, tho' we lack no bodily refreshment. Barnes
himself, by the way, though not a teetotaller, is an abstemious man,
very plain and inexpensive in his diet. We are pressed to stay but
can't. Talk of Maiden Castle, Irish dūns and raths. T. tells his story of
his car-driver, 'The King of Connaught'. Then we go, Barnes with us

to near Dorchester, talking of British antiquities, Wareham, sun-worship, etc.

Saturday, 24 August 1867.   Dorchester—To Maiden Newton—Bridport. We start off to walk to Lyme Regis, leaving bag to come by carrier. Uphill, view of sea, down to Chidiock, pretty village, old church, flowery houses. We push on (as like two tramps as need be) along the dusty road to Martin's Lake, sea on one hand, shore hills on the other. Down a long hill to Charmouth, where we have beer and cheese in a little inn, then T. smokes in the porch and chats to the waitress. She says she is from the Isle of Wight. 'So am I,' says T.,—'what part?' 'From Cowes,' says the girl. 'I come from Freshwater,' says T., which surprises me,—but he revels in the feeling of anonymosity [*sic*]. We see Lyme below us and take a field-path.

Down into Lyme Regis, narrow old streets, modest little Marine Parade. 'The Cups' receives us in the fair plump good-humoured person of a house-keeper–barmaid. T. gets a good bedroom and I a tolerable one; we go into garden sloping down-hill and out by some back steps to a Mrs Porter's, where the F. Palgraves are lodging—not in.

Back to 'The Cups' and order dinner; then by myself up steep street to top of the town, pleasant, view of shore and headlands, little white town far off. Dinner. Then T. and I out and sit on bench facing the sea, talking with friendly openness. Marriage,—'how can I hope to marry? Some sweet good woman would take me, *if I could find her.*' T. says, 'O yes,' adding, 'I used to rage against the social conditions that made marriage so difficult.'

Sunday, 25 August 1867.   Lyme Regis. Very fine. T. up first and at my door. He has been on the Cobb, and eats a hearty breakfast. We go down to the Cobb, enjoying the sea, the breeze, the coast-view of Portland, etc., and while we sit on the wall I read to him, out of *Persuasion*, the passage where Louisa Musgrave hurts her ankle. Palgrave comes, and we three (after Manor House and some talk of Chatham) take a field-path that brings us to Devonshire Hedge and past that boundary into Devon. Lovely fields, an undercliff with tumbled heaps of verdure, honeysuckle, hawthorns and higher trees. Rocks peeping through the sward, in which I peculiarly delight, reminding me of the West of Ireland. I quote, 'Bowery hollows crowned with summer sea'. T. (as usual), 'You don't say it properly'—and repeats it in his own sonorous manner, lingering with solemn sweetness on every vowel sound,—a peculiar *incomplete* cadence at the end. He modulates his cadences with notable subtlety. A delightful place. We climb to the top, find flat fields, and down again. Stile and path—agrimony—we sit on a bank, talk of Morris, Ned Jones,[14] Swinburne, etc. Whitechapel Rock. Then return by winding paths to the town. Miss Austen, Scott, novel-writing. P. counsels me to write a novel. Inn, dinner, fat waitress, port. In the coffee-room a gentleman, who joins in conversation—High Church, etc., State of England,—and speaks well but guardedly. T. talks freely—human instincts, Comte, etc.

We go to Palgrave's, who says, 'Thought you were not coming.' They smoke. When T. and I are walking back to the Inn he takes my arm, and by and by asks me *not* to go back to Lymington. I (alas!) have to reply that I must. 'Well then,' says T., 'arrange your business there and come back.' I doubted if I could. 'Is it money?' says he,—'I'll pay your expenses.' Most delicious! that the man whose company I love best should care about mine. Most mortifying! for I am tied by the leg.

Tuesday, 8 October 1867.   Steamer to Yarmouth. To Mrs Cameron's, Henry Taylor and his daughter Emily. Luncheon. To Farringford, and walk with A. T. to near Alum Bay. He thinks 'England is going down'—Christianity becoming extinct? 'There's something miraculous in man.' 'There's more in Christianity than people now think.'

NOTES

On Allingham, see p. 30.
1. See p. 19.
2. See p. 17.
3. *History of Frederick the Great*, published 1858–65.
4. William Barnes (1801–86), philologist and Dorset dialect poet; he was Rector of Came, near Dorchester, from 1862.
5. An anthology of 'the choicest lyrics and short poems' edited by Allingham (1860).
6. Sir Henry Taylor (1800–86), author of numerous verse-dramas.
7. On Huxley, see p. 109. John Tyndall (1820–93) wrote and lectured widely on scientific topics.
8. Presumably refers to *The Ring and the Book*, published 1868–9.
9. Robert Chambers's pioneering work on evolution appeared in 1844.
10. Waugh (1817–90) was a Lancashire dialect poet; the reference is to his *Lancashire Songs* (1863).
11. Emanuel Swedenborg (1688–1772), Swedish philosopher and mystic.
12. A dramatic episode in Jane Austen's novel takes place on the Cobb, a harbour wall in Lyme Regis, Dorset.
13. The third series had appeared in 1862.
14. Edward Burne-Jones (1833–98), painter and designer.

'Memories of Farringford'*

H. D. RAWNSLEY

I do not remember ever to have found such seclusion as was here possible. It seemed as if every tree that grew had felt a kind of personal responsibility to keep the intruder out. The very walks in the lime-tree alleys were ungravelled and hushed, and when one came upon the lawn it seemed more velvet soft and mossy silent than woodland lawns are wont to be. As for the house itself, it was so swathed in magnolia and heavy ivy garniture that it seemed part of the woodland itself, and it was not till one came from under the cedars and caught sight of the glass conservatory that one was sure that here mortal as well as immortal had his dwelling.

Anyone who approaches Farringford by the ordinary park drive will be struck by the absolute simplicity of it all. No pompous gateway, no pretentious lodge—a simple gate, such as might be found at the entrance of any farm in the Midlands. A simple drive up through the meadow, with the big thatched lowly cottages of the Home Farm nestling away under the trees on our right, and then, beyond the ilex and the pines, a simple, unassuming house front, or perhaps, more accurately, house back, with quiet entrance and unpretentious hall.

How well I remember the poet's greeting! 'Now come to the light. Whose eyes have you? Ah, I see; a son of your mother,—a Franklin. Well, I've read your sonnets,[1] and I know you like what I like', and saying this he led me up to his den, as he called it, and in a very few moments, was reading a bit of work he was busy upon—the making of an epitaph for the De Redcliffe statue in the Abbey.[2]

'I hate doing this kind of thing,' he said; 'but they bother one out of one's life if one refuses. It is the best way to peace. I never wrote but one that was at all to my mind, and that was to your great-uncle, Sir John Franklin',[3] and he recited as he spoke.

> Not here! the white North has thy bones; and thou,
> Heroic sailor soul.

He read me three alternatives for the epitaph he was engaged

* *Memories of the Tennysons* (Glasgow: James MacLehose, 1900) pp. 93–116, 120–21, 138–48.

upon, and it was very interesting to hear him speak of the *pros* and *cons* of the word arrangements.

The first began

> De Redcliffe, now thy long day's work hath ceased,
> Stand here among our noblest and our best.

The second was like it, but with a difference of arrangement:

> Stand here, among our noblest and our best,
> De Redcliffe, now thy long day's work hath ceased.

And he was in doubt as to whether he should, in the second couplet, write

> Silent, in this great minster of the West,
> *Who wast* the voice of England in the East.

or,

> Silent, in this great minster of the West,
> *But once* the voice of England in the East.

He was not satisfied—the rhymes of the quatrain were too nearly akin; but he wished to emphasise the difference between West and East, and he risked the assonance. We had a long talk over the esses, and I was struck with his own self-criticism upon the use of the sibilant. That he felt it too preponderating in the quatrain is, I think, clear from the fact that, in the final form in which it may be read upon the base of the statue in the Abbey, he has substituted the use of 'our' and 'wert' for the words 'this' and 'wast'.

> Thou third great Canning, stand among our best
> And noblest, now thy long day's work hath ceased,
> Here silent, in our minster of the West,
> Who wert the voice of England in the East.

But it was not till a day or two after that one realised how, to his finely trained ear, the sibilant was positive pain.

He had, in the late afternoon, read to me his touching poem dedicated to General Hamley, 'The Charge of the Heavy Brigade', and then we wandered out and up to the Down, and the stars were over us before we reached the ridge. The thrushes, singing their hearts out between the sunset and the star time, made music for us all the way, but I could only think of the rhythm and music of the poem he had rehearsed to me.

Next day, as we wandered out again in the morningtide, I recited to him a sonnet which tried to put the effect of that recitation of 'The Charge of the Heavy Brigade' upon record. It began.

When thrushes sang, between the day and night,
And you clomb up the Down toward the stars. . . .

He listened, and then said: 'No, no; "When thrushes sang", that will never do. Thrushes *called* or *blackbirds* sang, if you like, but can't you hear the hissing of it? Was it not Madame de Stael who said we English folk all hissed like geese and serpents? No, no, let it be, "When blackbirds called, between the day and night".'

To return to one's first impression of the poet. I had expected much. I knew the stately presence of his brother Charles and the fine head of his younger brother Arthur, but the Laureate was grander in build, it seemed to me, and more impressive than either.

Nor was it possible not to feel that one was talking to something more than common mortality. The sound of the seer was in his voice. The air of a prophet was round about him. This may seem exaggeration, but there was something about his look that was more than distinction. It seemed as if one was suddenly brought into the presence of one who lived in another world, and could make one feel the atmosphere of other worldliness in which he lived and moved and had his being. I had seen many great men. I had not *felt* one before. The tone of his voice was to my ears fuller than the tone of his brother Charles's, was richer than the full-chested voice of Arthur, but it was not only in tone that his voice struck one. It was in the exquisite nicety of speech which, with all its simpleness, seemed to have just the added subtleties that you would expect from a man who had spent all his life in word selection and in the phrasing of language with exquisite delicacy.

There was about his face that same foreign look which the old peasants at Somersby had remembered, and of all the softest hands I ever shook his seemed the softest. And last, one noticed just that picturesqueness of attire one had associated with him. The loose collar, the loosely tied cravat, the loosely fitting alpaca coat—all this seeming not careless, but rather with care and thoughtfulness for use and effect.

That evening we dined, and, as was the Farringford wont, passed out of the dining-room to dessert in an adjoining room, where, at a horseshoe mahogany table, we sat, with the fire pleasantly burning on the inner side of the curve; it gave rosy light to the glitter of the glass and fruit, and seemed to add a sense of genial warmth to the pleasantry and wit of the talk that went forward.

I had noted how, through dinner, the poet had been almost silent, but a change came over him, and humour and good sayings and capital stories of old Lincolnshire days, and quaint Lincolnshire sayings, kept the whole table alive. I did not know till that evening what a splendid mimic Tennyson was. He altered his voice from the deep-toned bass of the master of the farm to the shrill treble and cracked voice of the farmer's dame, and capped story after story with infinite zest. The dialect of his Somersby days was evidently as fresh in his ears as though he had never left the county, and the delight in hearing the old Doric of the land of the northern farmer seemed to warm him up to early reminiscences of the quaint ways and quaint sayings of the country folk amongst whom he had spent his boyhood.

'After the walnuts and the wine' below stairs, came wine of other sort in the great study up aloft. There, bedroom candlestick in hand, and sitting on a plain sort of high-backed kitchen chair—if my memory serves—we heard the poet read not what we chose, though he gave us choice in most courteous manner, but what he would. He read a passage from *Maud*, 'The Northern Farmer' (old style), 'The Spinster's Sweet-arts', and 'The Ode to the Duke of Wellington', and to this day I hear the almost moan as of a far away cathedral organ in his voice, with which he began: 'Bury the Great Duke with an empire's lamentation', how he lengthened out the vowel *a* in the words 'great' and 'lamentation' till the words seemed as if they had been spelt 'greaat' and 'lamentaation', and how he rolled out and lengthened the open oes in the words 'To the nooise of the moourning of a mighty naation'; nor shall I cease to remember the way in which, as he approached the end of the line 'Warriors carry the warrior's pall', one felt as if the whole procession was in a kind of slow trot, or rather one seemed to see that curious up and down motion a great line of men makes on the march.

Nor can I forget how, at the intervals or ends of a phrase such as 'And sorrow darkens hamlet and hall', the whole voice which had been mourning forth the impassioned lament suddenly seemed to fail for very grief, to collapse, to drop and die away in silence, but so abruptly that the effect upon one was—'He has come to a full stop; he will not read another line.'

The next day I went for a morning walk with him upon the Down. As we went through the little wicket gate that let us out from the seclusion of the garden grove into the lane, I noticed that a rogue had written in chalk upon it beneath the word 'Private' these other words, 'Old Tennyson is a fool.' I half hoped the old poet would not see it, but his eye caught sight of it, and he said, in a sort of cheery way, 'The boy's about right; we are all of us fools, if we only knew it. We are but at the beginning of wisdom.'

We spoke of other poets—of Wordsworth, whom he called, 'very great when he is great, but there are long barrennesses in him ; of Browning, of whom he said, 'He can conceive of grand dramatic situations, but where's the music?'; of Burns, of whom he said glowingly, 'Yes, if ever man was inspired, Burns was', and at once he broke into one of Burns's songs, and enjoyed himself vastly.

In answer to the question as to which of all the lines he had written he was proudest of, he said, 'I think I am most glad to have written the line "The mellow ouzel fluted in the elm." ' 'I believe', he added, 'I was the first to describe the ouzel's note as a flute note.'

'But', said I, 'what about "The moan of doves in immemorial elms,/And murmuring of innumerable bees,"?' 'Well,' he answered, 'I am glad to have written those also.'

So on we fared, talking, amongst other things, of Charles Turner's sonnets,[4] and hearing him say, 'Yes they are wonderful. I sometimes think that, of their kind, there is nothing equal to them in English poetry.' All the while, as we went along, his eyes were on the ground, and he was constantly turning over the leaf of this or that weed and flower with his stick, as if he expected to find some secret about its life's history hidden away beneath.

Now and again he would push a bit of hedgerow branch with his walking-staff up again the sky that he might see its outline. It seemed a habit, he said nothing, just gazed intently and passed on. Once in sight of the sea, he sang out a passage of Homer, and spoke enthusiastically of the educative power, for the sense of sound, that a good course of Homer gave one; and then we turned for home.

As we came back towards the Home Farm, and were in one of the lanes or roads near by, I saw a charabanc of tourists approaching. Lord Tennyson turned his face to the bank and began prodding violently with his stick.

'Are they looking?'

'Yes', said I.

'Let them look then', said the poet, and they did look, but they saw nothing but the broad back of his cape and the flap of his ample wideawake.

'It's horrible the way they stare', he continued when he was released. 'And their impudence is beyond words. An American lady walked right up to me on the lawn in front of the house one day and asked if I had seen Mr Tennyson, and I said "Yes." Where was he? I told her I had seen him, half an hour before, down there, and she scuttled off like a thing possessed. It was true enough,' added the Bard, 'for I had been down there half an hour ago. It's horrible; what have I done that I should be thus tormented?'

As we came towards the house, he spoke of his peerage. 'I did not want it, what can I do? How can I take off a cocked hat and bow three times in the House of Lords?' he said, 'and that is all it amounts to. I don't like this cocked-hat business at all, but Gladstone showed me that it was an honour not to me so much as to letters, and I learned that the Queen wished it, and that was enough. It would have been disloyal and graceless to refuse it, so I must take off my cocked hat three times, I suppose, and make my bow, but I don't like it.'

He spoke of Gladstone—'I love him,' he said, 'but I hate his politics', and then he spoke of the Queen. I have never heard such full-hearted praise of her as 'the wisest Sovereign upon a throne' as I then heard. Such loyalty to her person and affectionate regard for her womanliness, so sincere, so simple, touched me deeply. I did not understand it all, till I read the correspondence between Her Majesty and the Laureate, which was published in the Tennyson Memoir.

He spoke sadly of politics; the time had come when it seemed to him that all were for the party and none were for the state. He spoke bitterly of France and the poison which he thought was working to infect Europe from Paris. He seemed to see that the day of Armageddon was not so far off as men thought; that there was brewing a terrible storm in which all the forces of evil would be let loose upon the world, and in which the social fabric would be shaken to its foundations. I remember the emphasis with which he said, 'The storm will break; I shall not live to see it, but you will', and he added, 'Except the days be shortened, who shall be saved?'

I tried to find out what he really meant by this gloomy foreboding, but he was silent. He added, 'I have no doubt the old order will yield place to new, and we shall yet find higher gods than Mammon and materialism. But the storm will come, the battle of Modred in the West will yet be fought.'

Each morning of the week I was at Freshwater he would say, 'Well, have you done anything?' as if he felt that as he worked every day at his art, all other verse-writers ought to be doing likewise, and then would add, 'Let me hear.' And as we walked along he would say, 'That will do', or 'I don't like that.' The sonnets written then have since appeared—some of them in memory of the poet, in a little volume called *Valete*, but I never look at the ones written at Freshwater, 'Farringford', 'After the Epilogue to The Charge of the Heavy Brigade', 'On Hearing Lord Tennyson read his Ode on the Death of the Duke of Wellington', without a thought of the kindly criticism, the fatherly tenderness, if I may use the word, with which he would listen, and approve or blame these simple attempts in verse. The thought still stays with me of the humble-heartedness in the innermost, that I seemed to see in that skilled artificer of song. If ever man was, 'as the greatest ones only are, in their simplicity sublime', it was Alfred, Lord Tennyson. He talked as if he felt, after fifty years of work at it, that he was only at the beginning of his task.

He spoke of the next world as assuredly accomplishing the beginnings of this. And whether he had any presage of death I know not, but as he said, 'Farewell', he said, 'Come again, my time cannot be long.'

The next time I saw him was in May of 1889. He had been very ill in 1888—indeed hard at death's door. Rheumatic gout, with some complication, had made recovery slow, but with May his strength came back to him, and he ventured with his son ever tenderly at his side, to accept the offer of Lord Brassey's[5] yacht, and to have a cruise down channel and round the coast. I went with my brother and his pupils, the grandchildren of the poet, to meet him in Southampton Roads.

It was a magnificent May day. The Solent lay smooth as a mirror, the yacht, owing to the light air, was late in coming to her haven, and we sat down by the sunny shore loud with the song of the nightingales in the thickets hard by, and awaited the coming of the Bard.

> We watched the ship from speck to phantom grow,
> From phantom to its three fair towers of sail.

As it neared, the level sunset light flashed on its bows and turned the vessel into gold. We rowed towards it, and we saw Tennyson at the bows in his great cape, waving his hat in kindliest manner. He welcomed us aboard. Then, after a little talk about the beauty of the Solent, and the shining woodland to the west, he said, 'Come down to the cabin, I want to read a bit of "Linkishire" to ears that understand.'

Down we went, and he read with evident enjoyment the manuscript poem of 'Owd Roä'.[6] Now and again he paused and said, 'Is that a Linkishire word still?', and I remember doubting if the word 'wud', for mad, was still in vogue, but he had chapter and verse for it, and had made a pretty full inquiry. He asked if the word 'solidly' in the line. 'An' she didn't not solidly mean I wur gawin that waäy to the bad' was rightly used in such connection; the delightful way in which he rolled out the next line, with all the Lincolnshire singsong in his tone, 'Fur the gell wąs as howry a trollope as iver traäpes'd i' the squad', still remains with me. But the two or three lines which he seemed, at that reading, to most chuckle over were the following:

> And I says, 'If I bëant noäwaäys—not nowadaäys—good fur nowt,
> Yit I bëant sich a Nowt of all Nowts, as 'ull hallus do as 'e's bid.'

And the verse which describes the old dog which was lying, after its gallant rescue of the child, senseless in the barn reek:

Fur 'e smell'd like a herse a-singein', an' seeamed as blind as a
poop,
An' haäfe on 'im bare as a bublin', I couldn't wakken 'im oop.

I remember discussing the spelling of the word 'wakken', and much
wished it should be spelled 'waaken', but I was thinking of the way
my father's coachman pronounced it, and he was thinking of the way
his father's coachman used to say it, and it remains 'wakken' to this
day. The other line which he read through twice with real gusto was
the couplet describing the crash of the barn-roof.

An I'cärd the bricks an' the baulks rummle down when the roof
gev waay,
Fur the fire was a-raägin' an' raävin' an' roarin' like judgment
daäy.

He laughed heartily as he finished the reading of it, and fell to
discussion as to the proper spelling of the word 'wersens' in the next
couplet. I urged that it should be spelt 'hoursens'; but he stuck to his
own 'wersens', saying he supposed that in fifty years there must have
come differences in the dialect, and he wished to put it on record as
he remembered it. He told many 'Linkishire' stories, he talking in
broadest dialect and with delightful humour.

We left when twilight was falling on flood and forest, and the last I
saw of him was the fine cloaked figure taking a turn on deck at his
favourite time—the coming of the stars.

It was my lot only to see him once again. This was in the spring of
1890. He had had a bad attack of influenza, but was recovered
sufficiently to take short walks, though, as a precaution against any
sudden attack of faintness, he never went unaccompanied either by
his devoted son or his nurse. What he looked like in that Spring can
best be seen by a visit to Trinity, Cambridge. In the hall hangs the
fine portrait his dear old friend Watts drew of him in May of that
year.

In one of his short walks to his garden seat in the arbour of the
garden between the house and the home farm, he spoke of the
blindness with which people go through this beautiful world of ours,
neither seeing nor hearing the voices of God that are round about
them. 'It's a sham this nineteenth century education', he said. 'It
turns men and women out like machines, and never once makes
them open eyes and ears to the beauty of the common world about
them.' He instanced the way in which an educated woman had
questioned him as to what bird it was that said 'Maud! Maud! Maud!'
in the High Hall Garden when twilight was falling, and asked if it was
a blackbird. 'Yes,' he replied, 'a very black bird and a big one too;

can't you hear them now, what are those rooks saying overhead?'
He said that he had been asked times out of mind what he meant
by those lines in *Maud*,

> For her feet have touched the meadows,
> And left the daisies rosy.

'Anyone with eyes could surely have known how a lady's dress,
brushing across the daisies, tilts their heads and lets us see the rosy
under-petals, but there are a greater number of no-eyes than eyes in
the world, the more the pity of it.'
We then passed on to speak of the line in *In Memoriam* 'Flits by the
sea-blue bird of March.' 'I don't know,' he answered, 'but I suppose
it's the kingfisher; don't they come up from the sea about that time? I
think I remember that used to be so in the Steeping River.'
'But', I rejoined, 'you, with your accuracy of eye, would not speak
of any kingfisher as flitting. A kingfisher shoots by, flashes by, but
never flits.'
He smiled and said, 'Yes, you are right, but then what bird could it
have been?'
'Well,' I replied, 'you alone can know that, but there is a bird that
does seem in March to shine blue and blue-green with especial
brilliancy, by reason, as I think, of the red contrast that has come into
the thorn-bush buds. I have often been astonished at the March
brightness of the blue tit, and that bird flits.'
'Well,' said the old poet, 'make it a tit; I daresay it was a tit, but I
have quite forgotten, and I know I have told other folk it was a
kingfisher.'
The next day we were again sitting on a garden seat in the sun, and
fell to talking about the fame of a poet, and the mission of a poet.
'A poet must teach, but not preach,' he said, 'and woe to the man
who leaves behind him a note of evil suggestion. I have in my time
heard many pretty things—some I believed, most of them I
disbelieved, but to my way of thinking the tenderest and best praise
that has come to cheer me in my old age is a message from a young
girl who sent it timidly by the lips of a friend. "Tell him," she said,
"that I read his poems and always rise determined to be better, and
feeling wiser than I was." I should wish to go down to posterity, as
Wordsworth will go down to it, as a poet who uttered nothing base.'
Struck by the thought of that young girl's message, I put it into
simple sonnet form and read it the next day, and he said, 'Yes, that's
true, and that young girl's words deserved a sonnet.'
We continued our talk, on the garden seat, and he said, 'The worst
of folk is that they are so unable to understand the poet's mind. I
describe something which is the result of the impression of a

hundred sights and scenes woven into one, and first one localises it here and then another localises it there, and they pin me down to this spot and this meaning, till they make me almost sorry I had written at all. I don't know of how many moated granges it has been asserted that I had it, and it alone, in mind when I wrote "Mariana". But', he added, 'there's a worse lack of insight than this—people who criticise me seem to be lacking in a sense of humour, and you know', he added, 'a man without humour is a fool. Some of the best things I have written are those Lincolnshire sketches, "The Northern Farmer", but it needs humour to understand them.'

Next day we walked to the Briary. It was, he said, the furthest walk he had taken for some time; as we went he spoke of the certainty of life beyond, and quoted a verse from the 'Crossing the Bar'.

His son has told us that his father had the thought of that poem given to him one day when he crossed the Solent from Lymm to Yar, but the working out of it must have taken place in the walk between the Briary and Farringford, for he said, after finishing the quotation, 'I wrote that between here and home in a single walk', and he turned to the nurse who was with us and said, 'Did I not, nurse?'

She replied, 'I know it was written down when you got home from your walk.'

It did not seem strange that it should have been so swiftly composed. It reads so simply and inevitably that one can well believe it was written right off; so I said, 'Yes, but then you had been thinking over it for years.'

And he answered, 'Well, I suppose the most of us think a good deal, do we not, of the time when we shall put out to sea.'

One thing I noted in that walk was the poet's evident sensibility, almost hypersensibility to criticism. He spoke of certain things that had been said of him by men long since dead, and the bitterness of the criticism remained with him. He said of one man whom, I knew, he loved and honoured dearly, 'I wish he had never spoken of my "Battle of Brunanburh" as reminding him of the "House that Jack built"!' It was clear that the wit, whether it was deep or shallow, that had, in any way, seemed to him to have criticised ungently, vexed his poet's mind beyond what one would have thought at his age was likely. He ended the talk by saying,

> In my youth the growls!
> In mine age the owls!
> After death the ghouls!

That evening Lord Tennyson was in his best humour. The talk was brilliant and the good stories never ending. I told him the story of how my father's churchwarden greeted me on my return from ordination, and gave a bit of his mind as to how to proceed to episcopal honours. He was delighted, and said, 'Give me that and I will make something of it.'

It is perhaps worth while to repeat it, for it will show how inimitably the tale is worked up as it were into poetic form from the rough. I jotted it down for him that evening. It must have been written soon after, for I find a note in his son Hallam's diary, published in the *Life* of his father, under date 23 June: 'Aldworth. Walked on the Common. My father is working at his Lincolnshire poem "The Churchwarden",[7] and laughed heartily at the humorous passages as he made them.'

The story, then, in the rough, before it went to the singer's anvil is as follows. I returned to my father's parish, Halton Holegate, near Spilsby, in Lincolnshire, from my ordination, and found my father's churchwarden, G. R., upon the platform. He saw I had a white tie on, and he said cheerily, 'Well, Mr Rownsley, I can sea by that white thing round youre throat that they've gone and maade a parson on you!'

'Well, well, 'he added,' God Omighty knows theer mun bea parsons as well as farmers, and you'd be a fool i' the crewyard along o' the beästs, I reckon, and I should mebbe beä as big a fool in the pulpit o' Sunday. Now, doänt be stunt, I'm youre feyther's church-warden, and I'm goaip' to giv' you a bit o' my moind.'

I assured him that so far from my being stunt, I should take it as a compliment; and he continued, 'Theers no daub about you, I know (he meant, I think, no sham). Thou'lt be maain and plaain and straäight, I know, but, hooiver, tek my advice, doant thou saay nowt to noabody for a year more, but crip and crawl and git along under the hedge bottoms for a bit, and they'll maake a bishop on ye yit'.

The same evening I told him the story of the farmer in the fenside whose cows took bad ways, and who blamed a great 'Baptist dipping' which had taken place in the pond where the cows came to drink. The farmer had waxed quite furious as he told my father of his loss, and said, 'The poor thing was bound to die, dal it, I blaam them howry owd Baptisses for it all, coomin' and pizening my pond by leavin' their nasty owd sins behint 'em. It's nowt nobbut their dippin' as did it, we may be very sartain sewer.'

I can hear the laughter, deep-chested, hearty, full-breathed laughter of the poet as he heard that 'Linkishire' story, and readers of the 'Churchwarden and Curate' will remember how he treated it, how it rings up twice, and how the last two lines of the poem run

Fur they've bin a-preächin' meä down, they heve, an' I haätes 'em now,
Fur they leäved their nasty sins i' my pond, an' it poison'd the cow.

I left Farringford with the feeling that here was a man close on his eightieth birthday with his eye undimmed and his natural powers unabated, and I felt that, humanly speaking, we might still expect much music from him, to the helping of the nation. On the 13th of the month following, he would keep his fortieth wedding day with her whose fancy was

> as summer new
> As the green of the bracken amid the gloom of the heather

that was still dark on the top of that Aldworth Down, where he walked and wrote his last poem in the dialect he had learned as a boy, and loved to hear talked to the last days of his life. . . .

Next to Mr Gladstone, I should certainly put Tennyson as a talker. He did not always talk in company, but with one or two friends he was unsurpassed. Can I ever forget the brightness of the talk at dinner one evening when Jowett and the President of Magdalen[8] were present in the little dining-room at Farringford? Tennyson, too, had huge stores of information. He had seen and heard much, and always read a great deal, and he, too, had a most prodigious memory. And he had, what Gladstone had not, a wonderful sense of humour. He was brimful of stories; and, walk with him as often as you might, he always had something new to tell you, while his humorous stories extended over half a century . . . .

He was always very sensitive to the remarks of the critics, whether they attacked his powers of observation or denied him any originality. One especially annoyed him by suggesting sources from which he had copied or borrowed similes and expressions, often mentioning writers whom Tennyson declared that he had never read or heard of, and quite ignoring the fact that the same thought can strike various people at different times, and that it is not necessary to hunt for the source of all that a poet gives us, if only we will allow that poet some power of imagination of his own.

'They allow me nothing,' he once said to me. 'For instance, "The deep moans round with many voices." "The deep", Byron; "moans", Horace; "many voices", Homer; and so on.'

I once ventured to ask where he got the metre of 'The Charge of the Light Brigade', a metre of which I only knew one other instance, in Drayton's 'Battle of Agincourt'. He said he did not take it from that, but The Times, in giving the account, said, 'Someone had blundered.'[9] He said he kept saying that to himself, and the words kept on sounding in his head, and made the metre of the poem; and, indeed, as it was first printed, the line occurs twice: 'For up came an order which someone had blundered' being afterwards omitted.

He would in the course of an hour's walk on the downs at Farringford talk on an endless variety of topics, telling me the most humorous stories of my grandfather and the old Somersby days, and other good things that his friend Ward had told him, asking for Lincolnshire stories and telling them himself with faultless dialect. His command of the dialect after so many years' absence from Lincolnshire was very wonderful. In three or four of his poems he incorporated stories which originated in or near my father's parish of Halton, but the 'Spinster's Sweet-arts', which is as racy as anything ever written, was entirely spun out of his own brain . . . .

We spoke of the sonnet. He praised some of Shakespeare's, Milton's, and Wordsworth's very highly, and added, 'I have written a few; I think "Montenegro" is a good one.' From this we passed to translations, of which he used to say that the benefit lay with the translator. Of Worsley's translation of the *Odyssey* he said that by the Spenserian stanza a poet was so fettered and constrained that it made it exceedingly difficult. His own few bits of Homeric translation are so good that it was not unfrequently suggested to him to translate the whole *Iliad* or *Odyssey*, but he did not think it a poet's task, although perhaps none but a poet could do it. The pronunciation of Homer we had several talks about. He always maintained that the Greeks themselves never heard the full significance of Homer, the sound of which was only heard at its best when rendered by a northern tongue; and after rolling out a few lines in his own unapproachable manner, he would add, 'The Greeks never *poluphloisboied*, they *poluphleesbeed*.' Sappho he was extremely fond of, and quoted the beautiful line about the apple on the topmost bough, 'ἀκροτατῶ ἔπι δενδρῷ'. Virgil he loved, especially Book VI and the last part of Georgic II, and Catullus, the sweet singer. What can be more beautiful than his own lines to Virgil, written in a charming metre of his own:

> Wielder of the stateliest measure
> ever moulded by the lips of man.

Of English hexameters for serious work he had no opinion. Walking along the terrace of Aldworth with its splendid view, and talking of English hexameters, he rolled out three or four lines, beginning, 'Aldworth that stands on the height o'erlooking the woods and the champain', continuing, 'I could go on for ever like that, but what is its worth?'

Perhaps not much; but it was worth a good deal to hear him declaim them. He addresses Milton in those remarkable experiments in metre, as 'O mighty mouthed inventor of harmonies' and

'God-gifted organ voice of England'. And certainly I never heard any sounds of the human voice so magnificent as the reading by the poet of *Maud* and 'Boädicea'. The long lines were rolled out in rhythmic beats, and the tones involuntarily brought up to one's mind the line 'And let the bass of Heaven's deep organ blow'.

Once at Farringford, when the Dean of Westminister was staying with him, and I had come over from the New Forest for the day; after the poet had already had a good long walk, of which the Dean said to me, 'He walks me quite off my legs', Edison's present of a phonograph was got out, and the poet at the Dean's suggestion spoke some of his own well-known lines into the machine, after which we sat side by side on the little sofa with the conductors in our ears, and heard the grand voice come back from the cylinder: an experience never to be forgotten.

His powers of walking up to almost the last were quite wonderful, and his raven locks gave no signs of his age. Once, soon after the publication of 'Locksley Hall Sixty Years After', I found him rather angry at the critics' having taken the old man who speaks in the poem as intended for a picture of himself. 'I "this old white-headed dreamer", as if I should call myself that! I that have not a white hair in my head!'

I have said that he spared no pains to avoid even the slightest error, and the immense care that he took in polishing and repolishing every verse until he was satisfied with it is common knowledge. Once at Aldworth I saw him walking about the room with an etui-case of Lady Tennyson's in his hand, in which was set a fine piece of the stone called avanturine, so called from its likeness to the Venetian glass, which is brown and full of golden specks, and which, having been first discovered *a ventura* by the chance of some brass filings having fallen into molten glass, was called avanturine. He showed it to us and said, 'Look at it, see the stars in it, worlds within worlds.' He was quite bent on making a simile from it for use in the poem he was writing; and later in the evening, he came downstairs and read aloud the two lines which he then had got in three different ways; one verse was 'Shone gem or jewel in their dewy hair', or

Then glanced
Or dew or jewel from their golden hair

or

Or gem or jewel sparkled in their hair
Like stars within the stone Avanturine.

But when the poem came out ('Gareth and Lynette') it was found to read:

> and the hair
> All over glanced with dewdrop or with gem
> Like sparkles in the stone Avanturine.

Both words, lines, and portions of lines were often changed in the course of construction. For instance, my wife and I were at Farringford just after the death of the Duke of Clarence in January, 1892; and the poet was kind enough to read us the seven lines he had then composed in memory of that sad event.[10] He did not seem satisfied with them, excellent as they were; he always found a difficulty in doing what he called poems to order, but when they were published he had added four at the beginning and six more at the end. In the same way *Maud* was built, as it were from the centre outwards.

His carefulness in choosing his words made him sensitive to the wrong use of words, or the use of wrong words even in conversation; and once when I was walking with him, he pulled me up sharply for using the word 'awful'. 'You have used that word twice this morning; I can't bear it.' I said, 'I know I have, and I hate the slang use of it; but each time I used it today was in its legitimate sense was it not?' He gave a doubtful assent, but I was very sorry I had used it. Once later he corrected me. It was at Aldworth. He was looking for a letter which Browning had written him on his last volume, speaking in high praise of it, and the genuine kindness of the letter had moved Tennyson greatly. We turned over two or three drawers of letters as we sat side by side on the sofa in his room upstairs. He spoke of the time when Mr Gladstone had offered him the peerage and how he took it as a tribute to letters, caring himself nothing for all the peerages in the world; which was no more than true; there never was the slightest suspicion in his manner that being made a peer had altered him in the very least degree. He was if possible simpler in his views and ways afterwards than before, and straightforward simplicity was his strong characteristic. He commended it once to me as the thing he liked so much in my grandfather;[11] and in a man of his own great position and powers it seemed always most noticeable.

But to return. We were looking for Browning's letter, and I used the word 'knowledge', pronouncing it as a rhyme to 'college'. He looked at me and said, 'Knōwledge, I say.' I said, 'Do you say acknōwledge too?' He thought a moment and then said, 'Yes, I do', and there can be no doubt that he was quite right. Though we did not find the letter, he told me the substance of it, and called it a very kind and friendly letter. But our search led to a most interesting talk;

and how interesting his talk could be, only those who had the privilege of knowing him well can realise.

Once when I drove from Winchester to Haslemere with my wife, we walked up to Aldworth in the morning and found the poet ready for a walk on Blackdown, and for a couple of hours he walked and talked on every variety of topic with a life and brightness and humour which we can never forget. He complimented my wife on her costume, because she had not fallen a victim to the horrible custom then in vogue of wearing what was called a 'dress improver', or, as he called it in his straightforward manner, a 'bustle'.

This led him to speak of dress, and he told us that he had lately had a visit from a friend of his who had been in office, I think, in some Pacific isles, where the rarest apology for dress was all that was needed or worn. But the head man of the place had imbibed some European notions and insisted on his wife going to call on the White Chief in a European dress. He said that she came to him positively blushing at what seemed to her the immodesty of her costume, and she apologised to him for appearing before him in clothes. She would have come *in puris naturalibus* without *gene*. 'It is clothes', said Tennyson, 'that make the immodesty, not the want of them. There is nothing immodest in your natural skin.'

The last time I saw him, in the summer of 1892, the last year of his life, he was sitting on one of the green secluded lawns at Aldworth. Mrs Allingham[12] was sitting with us, to whom he paid a very prettily turned compliment on her beautiful water-colour pictures, for though he was called brusque, sometimes he could say very pretty things, and he valued them too. For instance, he told me once how when he went to see the Queen, and she had received him and put him at his ease at once, making him sit down beside her, with the words, 'You and I, Mr Tennyson, are old people, and like to sit down'; he went on to speak with some despair of the irreligion and socialism which seemed to pervade everything, and how the Queen in the prettiest way had said to him in answer,

> Oh yet we trust that somehow good
> Will be the final goal of ill

and he added, 'I thought that very pretty to quote my own words in answer to me.'

NOTES

The Rev. Hardwicke Drummond Rawnsley (1851–1920) became Canon of Carlisle. He was a son of the Rev. Drummond Rawnsley, who had officiated at Tennyson's wedding; his mother was a cousin of Lady Tennyson. He first met Tennyson in 1884. As well as *Memories of the Tennysons* he published *Homes and Haunts of Famous Authors* (1906) and an article 'Memories of the Tennysons at Somersby' in the *Cornhill* in 1912.

1. Rawnsley had published three volumes of verse, the most recent being *Sonnets at the English Lakes* (1881).

2. 'Epitaph on Lord Stratford de Redcliffe' (Ricks, 403).

3. 'Sir John Franklin' (Ricks, 364), written in 1875.

4. Charles Tennyson Turner: see p. 4.

5. Thomas, 1st Earl Brassey (1836–1918), politician and yacht-owner.

6. Published in *Demeter and Other Poems* in December 1889 (Ricks, 421).

7. Published posthumously in 1892 (Ricks, 444).

8. T. H. Warren: see p. 158.

9. As Ricks points out (p. 1034), the phrase used in *The Times* was actually 'some hideous blunder'. For a fuller comment on the same subject, see p. 24.

10. 'The Death of the Duke of Clarence and Avondale' (Ricks, 453).

11. The author's grandfather, Rev. T. H. Rawnsley, had been Rector of Halton, a parish near Somersby, during Tennyson's youth, and the two families had been on terms of close friendship.

12. On Helen Allingham, see p. 30.

Tennyson in Cornwall (1860)*

CAROLINE FOX

22 September 1860. Alfred Tennyson and his friend, Francis Palgrave, [are] at Falmouth, and made inquiries about the Grove Hill Leonardo, so of coure we asked them to come and see it; and thus we had a visit of two glorious hours both here and in the other garden. As Tennyson has a perfect horror of being lionised, we left him very much to himself for a while, till he took the initiative and came forth. Apropos of the Leonardo, he said the head of Christ in the *Raising of Lazarus* was to his mind the worthiest representation of the subject which he had ever seen. His bright, thoughtful friend, Francis Palgrave, was the more fond of pictures of the two: they both

* *The Journals of Caroline Fox*, ed. Wendy Monk (London: Elek, 1972) pp. 229–31.

delighted in the little Cuyp and the great Correggio; thought the Guido a pleasant thing to have, though feeble enough; believed in the Leonardo, and Palgrave gloated over the big vase. On the leads we were all very happy and talked apace. 'The great T.' groaned a little over the lionising to which he is subject, and wondered how it came out at Falmouth that he was here—this was apropos of my speaking of Henry Hallam's story of a miner hiding behind a wall to look at him, which he did not remember; but when he heard the name of Hallam, how his great grey eyes opened, and gave one a moment's glimpse into the depths in which *In Memoriam* learnt its infinite wail. He talked a good deal of his former visit to Cornwall, and his accident at Bude, all owing to a stupid servant-maid. In the garden he was greatly interested, for he too is trying to acclimatise plants, but finds us far ahead, because he is at the western extremity of the Isle of Wight, where the keen winds cut up their trees and scare away the nightingales in consequence. But he is proud and happy in a great magnolia in his garden. He talked of the Cornish, and rather liked the conceit of their countryism; was amused to hear of the refractory Truro clergyman being buried by the Cornish miners, whom he forbade to sing at their own funeral; but he thought it rather an unfortunate instance of the civilising power of Wesley. By degrees we got to Guinevere, and he spoke kindly of S. Hodges's picture of her at the Polytechnic, though he doubted if it told the story very distinctly. This led to real talk of Arthur and the *Idylls*, and his firm belief in him as an historical personage, though old Speed's narrative has much that can be only traditional. He found great difficulty in reconstructing the character, in connecting modern with ancient feeling in representing the Ideal King. I asked whether Vivien might not be the old Brittany fairy who wiled Merlin into her net, and not an actual woman. 'But no,' he said; 'it is full of distinct personality, though I never expect women to like it.' The river Camel he well believes in, particularly as he slipped his foot and fell in the other day, but found no Excalibur. Camel means simply winding, crooked, like the Cam at Cambridge. The Welsh claim Arthur as their own, but Tennyson gives all his votes to us. Some have urged him to continue the *Idylls*, but he does not feel it expedient to take people's advice as an absolute law, but to wait for the vision. He reads the reviews of his poems, and is amused to find how often he is misunderstood. Poets often misinterpret poets, and he has never seen an artist truly illustrate a poet. Talked of Garibaldi,[1] whose life was one out of Plutarch, he said, so grand and simple; and of Ruskin as one who has said many foolish things; and of John Sterling,[2] whom he met twice, and whose conversational powers he well remembers.

Tennyson is a grand specimen of a man, with a magnificent head set on his shoulders like the capital of a mighty pillar. His hair is long and wavy, and covers a massive head. He wears a beard and moustache, which one begrudges as hiding so much of that firm, powerful, but finely chiselled mouth. His eyes are large and grey, and open wide when a subject interests him; they are well shaded by the noble brow, with its strong lines of thought and suffering. I can quite understand Samuel Laurence[3] calling it the best balance of head he had ever seen. He is very brown after all the pedestrianising along our south coast.

Mr Palgrave is charmingly enthusiastic about his friend; if he had never written a line of poetry, he should have felt him none the less a poet . . . .

NOTES

Caroline Fox (1819–71) was a member of a prominent Cornish Quaker family. A selection from her journals was first published in 1882. Tennyson toured Cornwall and the Scilly Isles in August–September 1860; for his own notes on the tour, see *Memoir*, I, pp. 460–66.

1. Giuseppe Garibaldi (1807–82), Italian patriot; in connection with his later visit to Farringford (1864), Hallam Tennyson wrote, 'My father was always an enthusiast for Italian freedom' (*Memoir*, II, p. 1).

2. John Sterling (1806–44) had been a friend of Tennyson and had reviewed the 1842 poems. A biography of him by Carlyle had appeared in 1851.

3. See p. 158.

Interviews with Tennyson*

QUEEN VICTORIA

Osborne, 14 April 1862.   I went down to see Tennyson who is very peculiar looking, tall, dark, with a fine head, long black flowing hair and a beard—oddly dressed, but there is no affectation about him. I told him how much I admired his glorious lines to my precious Albert[1] and how much comfort I found in his *In Memoriam*. He was full of unbounded appreciation of beloved Albert. When he spoke

* *Dear and Honoured Lady: the Correspondence between Queen Victoria and Alfred Tennyson*, ed. Hope Dyson and Charles Tennyson (London: Macmillan, 1969) pp. 69, 79, 102.

of my own loss, of that to the Nation, his eyes quite filled with tears.

9 May 1863.   Afterwards saw Mr and Mrs Tennyson and their two sons. Had some interesting conversation with him and was struck with the greatness and largeness of his mind, under a certainly rough exterior.

Speaking of the immortality of the soul and of all the scientific discoveries in no way interfering with that, he said, 'If there is no immortality of the soul, one does not see why there should be any God', and that 'You cannot love a Father who strangled you', etc.

7 August 1883.   After luncheon saw the great poet *Tennyson* in dearest Albert's room for nearly an hour;—and most interesting it was. He is grown very old—his eyesight much impaired and he is very shaky on his legs. But he was very kind. Asked him to sit down. He talked of the many friends he had lost and what it would be if he did not feel and know that there was another world, where there would be no partings; and then he spoke with horror of the unbelievers and philosophers who would make you believe there was *no* other world, no immortality—who tried to explain *all* away in a miserable manner. We agreed that were such a thing possible, God, who is Love, would be far more cruel than any human being . . . .

NOTES

Queen Victoria (1819–1901) came to the throne in 1837; Tennyson became her Poet Laureate in succession to Wordsworth in 1850. The first of the three extracts from her journal refers to his first audience with her. A selection from their correspondence is given in *Memoir*, ii, pp. 433–55. When Tennyson died, Victoria described the event in her diary (6 October 1892) as 'a great national loss. He was a great poet, and his ideas were ever grand, noble, elevating. He was very loyal and always very kind and sympathising to me, quite remarkably so. . . .' (*Dear and Honoured Lady*, p. 140).

1. The blank verse 'Dedication' for a new edition of *Idylls of the King* (Ricks, 463), written in December 1861 or January 1862. Albert had died on 14 December 1861. For Tennyson's letter to Princess Alice on the subject, see *Memoir*, i, p. 479.

'An Evening at Thomas Woolner's'*

J. A. SYMONDS

My father came to us this afternoon. He is going to dine with Woolner[1] to meet Tennyson, Gladstone,[2] and Holman Hunt.[3] I am to go in the evening at 9.30.

When I arrived at Woolner's, the maid said she supposed I was 'for the gentlemen'. On my replying 'Yes', she showed me into the dining-room, where they were finishing dessert. Woolner sat, of course, at the bottom of the table, Tennyson on his left, my father on his right hand. Next Tennyson sat Gladstone, and Hunt next my father. I was seated in an armchair between Woolner and my father.

The conversation continued. They were talking about the Jamaica business, Gladstone bearing hard on Eyre,[4] Tennyson excusing any cruelty in the case of putting down a savage mob. Gladstone had been reading official papers on the business all the morning, and just after I had entered said with an expression of intense gravity: 'And that evidence wrung from a poor black boy with a revolver at his head!' He said this in an orator's tone, pity mingled with indignation, the pressure of the lips, the inclination of the head, the lifting of the eyes to heaven, all marking the man's moral earnestness. He has a face like a lion's; his head is small above it, though the forehead is broad and massive—something like Trajan's in its proportion to the features. Character, far more than intellect, strikes me in his physiognomy, and there is a remarkable duplicity of expression—iron, vice-like resolution combined with a subtle, mobile ingenuousness.

Tennyson did not argue. He kept asserting various prejudices and convictions. 'We are too tender to savages; we are more tender to a black than to ourselves.' 'Niggers are tigers, niggers are tigers', in *obbligato, sotto voce*, to Gladstone's declamation. 'But the Englishman is a cruel man—he is a strong man', put in Gladstone. My father illustrated this by stories of the Indian Mutiny. 'That's not like Oriental cruelty', said Tennyson; 'but I could not kill a cat, not the tom-cat who scratches and miaows and keeps me awake'—thrown in

* 'Recollections of Lord Tennyson: An Evening at Thomas Woolner's', *Century Illustrated Monthly Magazine*, n.s., XLVI (1893) 32–4.

with an indefinable impatience and rasping hatred. Gladstone looked glum and irate at this speech, thinking probably of Eyre. Then they turned to the insufficiency of evidence as yet in Eyre's case and to other instances of his hasty butchery—the woman he hanged, though she was recommended to mercy by court-martial, because women had shown savageness in mutilating a corpse. 'Because *women*, not the *woman*—and that, too, after being recommended to mercy *by courtmartial*, and he holding the Queen's commission!' said Gladstone with the same hostile emphasis. The question of his personal courage came up. That, said Gladstone, did not prove his capability of remaining cool under, and dealing with, such special circumstances.

Anecdotes about sudden panics were related. Tennyson said to my father: 'As far as I know my own temperament, I could stand any sudden thing; but give me an hour to reflect, and I should go here and go there, and all would be confused. If the fiery gulf of Curtius opened in the City, I would leap at once into it on horseback. But if I had to reflect on it, no—especially the thought of death—nothing can be weighed against that. It is the moral question, not the fear, which would perplex me. I have not got the English courage. I could not wait six hours in a square, expecting a battery's fire.' Then stories of martial severity were told. My father repeated the anecdote of Bosquet[5] in the Malakoff. Gladstone said Cialdini[6] had shot a soldier for being without his regimental jacket. Tennyson put in, *sotto voce*, 'If they shot paupers, perhaps they wouldn't tear up their clothes,' and laughed very grimly.

Frank Palgrave here came in, a little man in morning dress, with short beard and moustache, well-cut features, a slight cast in his eye, an impatient, unsatisfied look, and some self-assertion in his manner. He directed the conversation to the subject of newspapers. Tennyson all the while kept drinking port, and glowering round the room through his spectacles. His moustache hides the play of his mouth, but, as far as I could see, that feature is as grim as the rest. He has cheek-bones carved out of iron. His head is domed, quite different from Gladstone's—like an Elizabethan head, strong in the coronal, narrow in the frontal regions, but very finely moulded. It is like what Conington's head seems trying to be.

Something brought up the franchise. Tennyson said, 'That's what we're coming to when we get your Reform Bill, Mr Gladstone; not that I know anything about it.' 'No more does any man in England', said Gladstone, taking him up quickly, with a twinkling laugh; then adding, 'But I'm sorry to see you getting nervous.' 'Oh, I think a state in which every man would have a vote is the ideal. I always thought it might be realised in England, if anywhere, with our constitutional history. But how to do it?' Soon after came coffee. Tennyson grew impatient, moved his great gaunt body about, and finally was left to smoke a pipe. It is hard to fix the difference between the two men both with their strong provincial accent—Gladstone with his rich, flexible voice, Tennyson with his deep drawl rising into an impatient falsetto when put out; Gladstone arguing, Tennyson putting in a prejudice; Gladstone asserting rashly, Tennyson denying with a bald negative; Gladstone full of facts, Tennyson relying on impressions; both of them humorous, but the one polished and delicate in repartee, the other broad and coarse and grotesque. Gladstone's hands are white and not remarkable, Tennyson's are huge, unwieldy, fit for moulding clay or dough. Gladstone is in some sort a man of the world; Tennyson a child, and treated by Gladstone like a child.

Woolner played the host well, with great simplicity. His manner was agreeably subdued. He burst into no unseasonable fits of laughing, no self-assertive anecdotes. Palgrave rasped a little. Hunt was silent. My father made a good third to the two great people. I was like a man hearing a concerto; Gladstone first violin, my father second violin, Tennyson violoncello, Woolner bass viol, Palgrave viola, and perhaps Hunt a second but very subordinate viola.

When we left the dining-room we found Mrs Woolner and her sister, Miss Waugh (engaged to Holman Hunt), in the drawing-room. Miss Waugh, though called 'the goddess', is nowise unapproachable. She talked of Japanese fans like a common mortal. Mrs Woolner is a pretty little maidenly creature, who seems to have walked out of a missal margin.

Woolner gave Gladstone a manuscript book to read containing translations from the Iliad by Tennyson. Gladstone read it by himself till Tennyson appeared. Then Woolner went to him and said, 'You will read your translation, won't you?' And Palgrave, 'Come you! A shout in the trench!' 'No, I shan't,' said Tennyson in a pettish voice, standing in the room, and jerking his arms and body from the hips. 'No, I shan't read it. It's only a little thing. Must be judged by comparison with the Greek. Can be appreciated only by knowing the difficulties overcome.' Then, seeing the manuscript in Gladstone's hand, 'This isn't fair; no, this isn't fair.' He took it away, and nothing could pacify him. 'I meant to read it to Mr Gladstone and Dr Symonds.' My father urged him to no purpose, told him he would be reading to an intelligent audience; but he cried, 'Yes, you and Gladstone; but the rest don't understand it.' 'Here's my son, an Oxford first-class man.' 'Oh, I should be afraid of him.' Then my father talked to him about his poems—'Mariana in the Moated Grange'. This took them to the Lincolnshire flats, as impressive in their extent of plain as mountain heights. My father tried to analyse the physical conditions of ideas of size, but Tennyson preferred fixing his mind on the ideas themselves. 'I do not know whether to think the universe great or little. When I think about it, it seems now one and now the other. What makes its greatness? Not one sun or one set of suns, or is it the whole together?' Then to illustrate his sense of size, he pictured a journey through space like Jean-Paul Richter's, leaving first one galaxy or spot of light behind him, then another, and so on through infinity. Then, about matter. Its incognisability puzzled him. 'I cannot form the least notion of a brick. I don't know what it is. It's no use talking about atoms, extension, colour, weight. I cannot penetrate the brick. But I have far more distinct ideas of God, of love, and such emotions. I can sympathise with God in my poor way. The human soul seems to me always in some way—how, we do not know—identical with God. That's the value of prayer. Prayer is like opening a sluice between the great ocean and our little channels.' Then of eternity and creation: 'Huxley[7] says we may have come from monkeys. That makes no difference to me. If it is God's way of creation, he sees the whole, past, present, and future, as one.' Then of morality: 'I cannot but think moral good is the crown of man. But what is it without immortality? Let us eat and drink, for tomorrow we die. If I knew the world were coming to an end in six hours, would I give my money to a starving beggar? No; if I did not believe myself immortal. I have sometimes thought men of sin might destroy their immortality. The eternity of punishment is quite incredible. Christ's words were parables to suit the sense of the times.' Further of morality: 'There are some young men who try to do away with morality. They say, "We won't be moral." Comte,[8] I believe, and perhaps Mr Grote,[9] too, deny that immortality has anything to do with being moral.' Then from material to moral difficulties: 'Why do mosquitos exist? I believe that after God had made his world the devil began and added something.'

A move was made into the dining-room Tennyson had consented to read his translations to Gladstone and my father. I followed them, and sat unperceived behind them. He began by reading in a deep bass growl the passage of Achilles shouting in the trench. Gladstone continually interrupted him with small points about words. He has a combative House-of-Commons mannerism, which gives him the appearance of thinking too much about himself. It was always to air some theory of his own that he broke Tennyson's recital; and he seemed listening only in order to catch something up. Tennyson invited criticism.

Tennyson was sorely puzzled about the variations in Homeric readings and interpretations. 'They change year after year. What we used to think right in my days I am told is all wrong. What is a poor translator to do?' But he piqued himself very much on his exact renderings. 'These lines are word for word. You could not have a closer translation: one poet could not express another better. There! those are good lines.' Gladstone would object, 'But you will say "Jove" and "Greeks". Can't we have "Zeus" and "Achaeans"?'

'But the sound of Jove! Jove is much softer than Zeus—Zeus—Zeus.'

'Well, Mr Worsley gives us Achaeans.'

'Mr Worsley[10] has chosen a convenient long meter; he can give you Achaeans, and a great deal else.'

Much was said about the proper means of getting a certain pause; how to give equivalent suggestive sounds, and so on.

NOTES

John Addington Symonds (1840–93), versatile man of letters who spent much of his life abroad on account of ill-health, was the son of a noted Bristol physician of strong literary tastes. His account is based on his diary for 8 December 1865 and was reprinted, with minor changes, in *Letters and Papers of John Addington Symonds*, ed. Horatio F. Brown (London: John Murray, 1923) pp. 1–10.

1. Thomas Woolner (1825–92), sculptor and poet, one of the original members of the Pre-Raphaelite Brotherhood. He was one of the group of friends who had toured Cornwall with Tennyson in 1860.

2. William Ewart Gladstone (1809–98), Liberal statesman and man of letters.

3. William Holman Hunt (1827–1910), painter, another original member of the Pre-Raphaelite Brotherhood, and another member of the Cornish tour.

4. Governor Eyre's suppression of a slave rebellion in Jamaica in October–November 1865 had given rise to a heated controversy in the British press.

5. Pierre Bosquet (1810–61), French marshal.

6. Enrico Cialdini, Duke of Gaeta (1811–92), Italian general, diplomat and politician.

7. See p. 109.

8. Auguste Comte (1798–1857), French Positivist philosopher.

9. See p. 163.

10. See p. 50.

'A Visit to Farringford' (1868)*

ANNE LONGFELLOW PIERCE

Thursday, 16 July 1868 (a.m.). A short drive through the narrow winding roads of Freshwater, between stone walls overhung with ivy, or hedges of sweet briar, or a mixture of thorns, eglantine, privet, ivy and all growing things combined, brought us to the simple gate of Farringford—a long winding avenue through fine tall trees led us with many turns to the house of Tennyson—we entered, under the arches of the piazza, covered with ivy and honeysuckles, a simple rambling mansion, plainly furnished but the walls covered with pictures—the whole length of the stair way hung with photographs of places and persons, hung one above the other in rows like steps. A mask of Dante, with red velvet back and sort of cowl, among them in a conspicuous place—at the foot—the large Dante, with the impression of the nail, near it, and a bust of Dante on the table—a narrow passage led us through a breakfast room to the drawing-room full of everyday comfort—table with books, newspapers and writing materials stood in the centre—sofa, couches and a variety of armchairs offered attractive seats—the only window in the room, a large oriel making a deep recess opposite the fire place, looked out upon the lawn through two very large shade trees, of elm, I believe, to the two pines—a border of sweet and bright flowers under the window and continued all around the somewhat irregular house—A small mask of Shakespeare over the book shelves in the wall at the end of the room—with endless and various small things, in photo and painted, around the walls—a low red screen standing beside one of the couches was covered with photos—one the figure of a beautiful dark-haired boy, Hallam, the eldest son, among them. Each side of the book shelves a small recessed arch, in one a low organ, in the other an étagère with books and little things—picture over each, a room of comfort and refinement.

Here we were received with most friendly cordiality by the wife of Tennyson, a very lovely and attractive lady, exceedingly delicate looking in health—dressed in black silk deeply trimmed with

* *Boston University Studies in English*, 1 (1955) 96–8.

crape—with a most simple bit of white lace edged with silk gimp
falling from the front of her head back, and down to her
shoulders—plain black hair tied behind at the neck with broad black
ribbon the ends trimmed with crape—A spinster sister of the poet's,[1]
dyspeptic and angular, was not so attractive.

Summoned to the dining room to lunch, a most attractive room
only one window, a large oriel filling nearly one end—opposite to this
a buffet—opposite the fireplace on the side of the room a large
sideboard in full blast of usefulness—over it hung an oil *Holy
Family*—all the pictures in this room were in oils, except a large print
of the Queen and Prince Albert framed together—of which T. said
'There's a hateful picture hanging there, but as the Queen presented
it to me I felt obliged to hang it up.' On one side of the window was a
beautiful picture of two handsome youths, with frills round their
necks, portraits of Hallam and Lionel the sons—or as the father said,
'those are my boys when they were girls', a very charming picture,
faces handsome and fine in colouring—on the other side of the
window was a lovely portrait of Mrs T by the same artist, the name I
forget. In front of the window grows a very large ilex, or Italian oak,
almost if not quite as fine as the one we saw on the grounds at Wilton,
at Lady Herbert's.

All the appointments of the lunch were exceedingly simple and
refined—mutton of his 'own raising' etc. etc. exquisitely nice in
cooking, and dessert.

Our first introduction to Mr T. was very informal as we were
seated and had begun our lunch before the gentlemen came in—
our names were all pronounced and he graciously shook hands
with each one on our side of the tables as he passed down to take his
seat.

NOTES

When the American poet Henry Wadsworth Longfellow visited England in
1868 one of the members of his family party was his sister, Anne Longfellow
Pierce. Her impressions of their visit to the Tennysons were recorded in
her journal (now in the Longfellow House at Cambridge, Massachu-
setts). Hallam Tennyson dates the visit 15 July (*Memoir*, ii, p. 55); he
notes that Longfellow was accompanied by 'a party of ten', that 'we invited
forty or fifty neighbours to tea', and that the two poets discussed spiritualism.

1. Matilda Tennyson (1816–1913), who spent most of her time at her
brother's home after their mother's death in 1865.

'A Personal Reminiscence'*

JAMES KNOWLES

More than thirty years ago I had the happiness of making his acquaintance. I was about to publish a little book on King Arthur,[1] chiefly compiled from Sir Thomas Malory, and, as a stranger, had written to ask leave to dedicate it to him—a leave which was directly granted.

For some time afterwards I knew him merely by correspondence, but being in the Isle of Wight one autumn I called to thank him personally for what he had written to me, and then first saw him face to face. I found him even kinder than his letters, and from that time our acquaintance grew gradually closer until it became intimate.

Before long he asked me to become his architect for the new house he proposed to build near Haslemere ('Aldworth' as it was finally called), and the consultations and calculations which naturally followed as to his way of living, the plans, and the cost of building, led to much business confidence. This presently extended to the field of his own business transactions with his publishers, and from these in time to confidences about his work and art; until at length he came to tell me of poems not yet in being, but contemplated, and to talk about them and show me their progress.

Then, and for many years after, under his roof or under mine, it was my great privilege to see and know him intimately; and the more he was known the more impressive were his greatness, tenderness, and truth. The simplicity, sensitiveness, freshness, and almost divine insight of a child were joined in him, as in no other man, to the dignity, sagacity, humour, and knowledge of age at its noblest. An immense sanity underlay the whole—the perfection of common-sense—and over all was the perpetual glamour of supreme genius.

Affectation was so alien from him that he spoke and acted exactly as he felt and thought everywhere and about everything. This at times would perplex and bewilder strangers. The shy were frightened at it; the affected took it for affectation (for, as he was fond of saying, 'every man imputes himself'), the rough for roughness, the bears for bearishness; whereas it was but simple straightforward honesty, and as such of the deepest interest to all

* 'Aspects of Tennyson, II: A Personal Reminiscence', *Nineteenth Century*, XXXIII (1893) 164–74, 181–7.

who could watch and learn in it the ways of Nature with her greatest men.

The little affectations and insincerities of life so troubled him, and his natural shyness, increased by his disabling short sight, so fought with his innate courtesy to all, that general society was always an effort and a burden to him. His fame increased the trouble, and he often told me how he wished he could have had all the money which his books had made without the notoriety. Even a single stranger was, as such and at first, always a trial to him, and his instinctive desire was to hide as much of himself as possible from observation until he found his companion sympathetic. Then he expanded as a flower does in the sunshine, and he never hoarded or kept back any of the profuse riches and splendour of his mind. When Frederick Robertson[2] of Brighton—the great preacher, who had written much and admirably about his poems, and for whom he had a high regard—first called upon him, 'I felt', said Tennyson, 'as if he had come to pluck out the heart of my mystery—so I talked to him about nothing but beer.' He could not help it; it was impossible for him to wear his heart upon his sleeve.

The shortness of his sight, which was extreme, tormented him always. When he was looking at any object he seemed to be smelling it. He said that he had 'never seen the two pointers of the Great Bear except as two intersecting circles, like the first proposition in Euclid', and at my first visit to him he warned me, as I left, to come up and speak to him wherever I next met him, 'for if not,' he said, 'I shouldn't know you though I rubbed against you in the street'. His hearing, on the other hand, was exceptionally keen, and he held it as a sort of compensation for his blurred sight; he could hear 'the shrieks of a bat', which he always said was the test of a quick ear. Its real compensation, however, was in the quickness of his mental vision, which made more out of the imperfect indications of his bodily eyes than most men with perfect sight would see. I remember his telling me (in explanation of a passage in *Maud*)—If you tread on daisies they turn up underfoot and get rosy.'[3] He could read a man through and through in a flash even from his face, and it was wonderful to hear him sum up a complex character in some single phrase. He told me that he was once travelling with an unknown person whose countenance he caught but for an instant from behind a newspaper, but whom he set down, from that flying glimpse, as a rogue. To his surprise he turned out to be somebody of the highest local standing and repute, but he nevertheless held by his impression and in the end was justified; for presently the man fled from justice and the country, leaving hundreds ruined who had trusted him.

His judgement of men was the more terrible because so naturally charitable and tender. Seldom, if ever, did he carry beyond words his anger even with those who had gravely injured him. 'I eat my heart with silent rage at——' he said one day of such a one. How different in this from Carlyle, whose open rage with mankind was so glaring! 'Ha! ye don't know,' he cried out to me one day, 'ye don't know what d——d beasts men are.' Tennyson, quite otherwise, had the tenderest thought and hope for all men individually, however much he loathed that 'many-headed beast' the mob. 'I feel ashamed to see misery and guilt', he said as he came out from going over Wandsworth Jail; 'I can't look it in the face.' Yet he had no love for milksops. 'The only fault of So-and-so', he said, 'is that he has no fault at all'.

It was touching to see his playfulness with children, and how he would win them from their nervousness of his big voice and rather awful presence. I have seen him hopping about on the floor like a great bird, enveloped in his big cloak and flapping hat, in a game of pursuing a little band of them until they shrieked with laughter. It reminded me of a scene in his Cambridge days which he had described to me when he, 'Charles Tennyson, Spedding, and Thompson[4] of Trinity, danced a quadrille together in the upper room of a house opposite the "Bull" '. There was a great abundance of playfulness under the grimness of his exterior, and as to humour, that was all pervading and flavoured every day with salt. It was habitual with him, and seemed a sort of counteraction and relief to the intense solemnity of his also habitual gaze at life in its deeper aspects, which else would almost have overwhelmed him with awe. He had a marvellous fund of good stories which he loved to recount after dinner and over his 'bottle of port'. In later life he gave up the port, but not the stories. He used to say there ought to be a collection of the hundred best ones in the world chosen from different countries so as to show the national diversities, and he would give illustrations of such, declaring that for true and piercing wit the French beat all the others. Could they have been reported *verbatim* as he gave them, they would have been models of English prose. More serious narratives he told thrillingly—one especially of how his own father escaped from Russia as a young man after an incautious speech about the recent murder of the Emperor Paul; how he wandered for months in the Crimea, where 'the wild people of the country came about him' and explained to him that twice a year only, at uncertain times, a courier passed through the place blowing a horn before him, and that then was his only chance of safety; how he lay waiting and listening through the nights until the weird sound came, and how he fared through all the hair-breadth 'scapes that followed.

He would pretend to look upon his bottle of port as a sort of counsellor to be heard sometimes before finally making up his mind upon moot-points, and after the varying moods of the day about them. For instance, he told me, 'The night before I was asked to take the Laureateship, which was offered to me through Prince Albert's liking for my *In Memoriam*, I dreamed that he came to me and kissed me on the cheek. I said, in my dream, "Very kind, but very German." In the morning the letter about the Laureateship was brought to me and laid upon my bed. I thought about it through the day, but could not make up my mind whether to take it or refuse it, and at the last I wrote two letters, one accepting and one declining, and threw them on the table, and settled to decide which I would send after my dinner and bottle of port.'

A notable thing was his comparative indifference to music as a separate art: it almost seemed as if the extreme fineness of his hearing was *too* fine for the enjoyment of its usual intervals and effects and craved the subtler and multitudinous distinctions and inflections and variations of sound, which only the instrument of language can produce. Certainly I hardly ever knew him to care greatly for any 'setting' of his own songs, which he justly felt had already their own music that was confused by the 'setting'. It is curious that Browning, whose music is so rare in his verse, was a masterly musician outside of it, while Tennyson, whose every line was music, cared so little for it except in poetry.

His way of working was much less like 'work' than inspiration. 'I can always write', he said, 'when I see my subject, though sometimes I spend three-quarters of a year without putting pen to paper.' When he did 'see' it, his mind dwelt on it at all times and seasons, possessing him until he possessed and perfected it. Sparkles and gleams might flash out at any moments from the anvil where his genius was beating his subject into shape, but the main creative process, where the vision was condensed into art, went on when he had shut himself up in his room with his pipe. He would do this two or three times a day—his 'most valuable hour', as he often told me, being the hour after dinner—and then with his pipe in his mouth and over the fire he would weave into music what things 'came to him'; for he never accounted for his poetry in any other way than that 'it came'. 'Many thousand fine lines go up the chimney', he said to me, and indeed the mechanical toil of writing them down, made heavier by his short sight, was so great that it was easy to believe in the sublime waste—the characteristic profuseness of genius. When he came out from his room at such seasons, he would often have a sort of dazed and far-off dreamy look about him, as if seeing 'beyond this ignorant present', and such as Millais[5] alone has caught in his great portrait, where he looks like the prophet and bard that he was. And then he might perhaps say aloud, and almost as it were to himself, some passage he had just made, but seldom twice in the same words, and, unless written down at once, the first and original form of it was often lost or 'improved'. This was the beginning of that process of refinement by art until absolute perfection was attained which he always carried on—the cutting and polishing of the native diamonds into complete and brilliant beauty. If interrupted during his hours of seclusion—which of course never happened except upon emergency—his look of 'sensitiveness' was surprising. He seemed ready to quiver at the faintest breath, or sound, or movement, and as though suddenly waked up out of a dream.

After his hour of privacy he would often ask his friends to come to his room with him, and then would talk of present, past, and future in a way which was, in the Arab phrase, like 'the opening of many gates'.

Many personal things he told me at such times when alone with him, which are of course sacred from repetition; but of many other things he spoke openly to whomsoever might be there, and especially he loved to speculate freely on theological and metaphysical subjects.

He formulated once and quite deliberately his own religious creed in these words: *'There's a something that watches over us; and our individuality endures: that's my faith, and that's all my faith.'* This he said with such a calm emphasis that I wrote it down (with the date) exactly and at once. But he was by no means always so calm. His belief in personal immortality was passionate—I think almost the strongest passion that he had. I have heard him thunder out against an opponent of it, 'If there be a God that has made the earth and put this hope and passion into us, it must foreshow the truth. If it be not true, then no God, but a mocking fiend, created us, and' (growing crimson with excitement) 'I'd shake my fist in his almighty face, and tell him that I cursed him! I'd sink my head to-night in a chloroformed handkerchief and have done with it all.'

To one who said, 'My dearest object in life, when at my best, is to leave the world, by however little better than I found it—what is yours?' he answered, 'My greatest wish is to have a clearer vision of God.'

He said, 'Men have generally taken God for the devil. The majority of Englishmen think of Him as an immeasurable clergyman in a white tie'.

He inclined somewhat to the theory of a demiurge with whom alone man comes into direct contact, saying that this was perhaps 'the nearest explanation of the facts of the world which we can get';

and this he put into the mouth of the King in 'The Passing of Arthur', where he cries

> O me! for why is all around us here
> As if some lesser God had made the world,
> But had not force to shape it as he would,
> Till the High God behold it from beyond,
> And enter it and make it beautiful?

He was disposed to doubt the real existence of a material world, and frequently adduced the infinite divisibility of matter as a difficulty which made it unthinkable. He leaned to the idealism of Berkeley,[6] and in physical science preferred the term 'centres of force' to 'atoms' as not involving the idea of matter. He said to me one day, 'Sometimes as I sit here alone in this great room I get carried away out of sense and body, and rapt into mere existence, till the accidental touch or movement of one of my own fingers is like a great shock and blow and brings the body back with a terrible start.'

All such subjects moved him profoundly, and to an immense curiosity and interest about them. He told me that 'Tears, Idle Tears' was written as an expression of such longings. 'It is in a way like St Paul's "groanings which cannot be uttered".[7] It was written at Tintern when the woods were all yellowing with autumn seen through the ruined windows. It is what I have always felt even from a boy, and what as a boy I called the "passion of the past". And it is so always with me now; it is the distance that charms me in the landscape, the picture and the past, and not the immediate today in which I move.'

At one time he contemplated writing a metaphysical poem on Spinoza,[8] and talked much about it, but finally gave it up, saying he could not quite warm to it, 'from Spinoza's want of belief in a God'.

It was as the result of many such speculative debates with him that the idea of founding the late Metaphysical Society occurred to me.

He and the Rev. Charles Pritchard (the Savilian Professor of Astronomy) were both staying in our house as guests, and one morning, after breakfast and much psychological guessing and wondering, one of us said: 'What a pity it is that these subjects cannot be investigated thoroughly in a scientific way and without prejudice and vehemence!' 'Modern science', said Tennyson, has surely learned this much—how to separate heat from light.' 'Well,' I said, 'if you and Mr Pritchard[9] will agree to join it, I will try to get together in London a Society to discuss metaphysics and theology in the manner and with the method of the learned societies.' They promised to become the first members, and I then proceeded to enlist others until the roll of membership was completed. . . .

At its first formal meeting a poem especially written by Tennyson, and afterwards published as 'The Higher Pantheism', was read by the Secretary in the absence of the author. In a note he sent me with it, Tennyson said, 'I am not coming up for your meeting—i.e. I believe so today—and your request that you may read the poem at that meeting abashes me. If you are to read it, it ought to be stated surely that I have but ceded to your strongly exprest desire. Hutton can have a copy of it if he choose; but an I had known that such as he wanted it, I would have looked at it again before I let it go.' He did not often come to the meetings, and when he did so spoke but little. But he read with avidity all its transactions and discussed the subjects of them privately with endless interest. His reverence for Dr Martineau[10] was extreme, and he frequently declared that he was 'by far the greatest among us'.

A frequent subject of his talk in the evenings, or in the long afternoon walks which were his habit, was, as might be expected, poetry and the poets. His acquaintance with all previous poetry was unlimited, and his memory of it amazing. He would quote again and again with complete delight the passages which were his favourites, stopping and calling upon his hearer to consider the beauty of this or that line, and repeating it to admire it the more.

His reading was always in a grand, deep, measured voice, and was rather intoning on a few notes than speaking. It was like a sort of musical thunder, far off or near—loud-rolling or 'sweet and low' —according to the subject, and once heard could never be forgotten.

It made no difference whence a fine line or passage came; it struck him equally with pleasure, when he heard or came across it, whether it were another man's or his own. He would pause in precisely the same way to call out 'That's magnificent', 'What a line!', 'Isn't that splendid?' whether reading Shakespeare, Milton, Wordsworth, or himself. He was struck by the beauty of the art without thinking for one moment of the artist. The shallow-pated, hearing him thus apostrophise his own work, which they may have begged him to read to them, might think in their vain hearts 'How vain!' But vanity had no more to do with it than they had; he was thinking solely of the subject and the music, and only cried out to his hearers for the sake of an echo to his own absorbing pleasure.

He often insisted that the grandest music in the English language was in Milton, and especially in the first book of *Paradise Lost*. . . . As a single line he said he knew hardly any to exceed for charm 'Of Abbana and Pharphar, lucid streams', unless it were Wordsworth's great line in 'Tintern Abbey' 'Whose dwelling is the light of setting suns'. 'Poetry', he would say at such times, 'is a great deal truer than fact.'

His own poetry, he declared, was easy enough to read aloud, if people would only read it just as it was written and not try to scan it or to force the accent. Some few passages, he admitted however, were difficult, such as that in *Maud* beginning 'O, that 'twere possible', but this because 'it ought to be read all through without taking breath'; the 'Bugle song' in *The Princess* was another.

The first thing I ever heard him read was his 'Boädicea', for I said 'I never can tell how to scan it.' 'Read it like prose,' he said, 'just as it is written, and it will come all right.' And then, as if to confute himself, he began it, and in his weird and deep intoning, which was as unlike ordinary prose as possible, sang the terrible war song, until the little attic at Farringford melted out of sight and one *saw* the far-off fields of early Britain, thronged with the maddened warriors of the maddened queen, and heard the clashing of the brands upon the shields, and the cries which 'Roar'd as when the rolling breakers boom and blanch on the precipices'. The image of some ancient bard rose up before one as he might have sung the story by the watch-fires of an army the day before a battle. It was perhaps from some such association of ideas that his name among his intimates became 'The Bard'—a way of recognising in one word and in ordinary talk his mingled characters of singer, poet, and prophet.

When building Aldworth he desired to have, whenever the room was finally decorated, the following names of his six favourite poets carved and painted on the six stone shields which I had designed as part of the chimney-piece in his study, and in front of which be always sat and smoked—namely, Shakespeare, Chaucer, Milton, Wordsworth, Dante, and Goethe.

He used to say 'Keats, if he had lived, would have been the greatest of all of us'; he considered Goethe 'the greatest artist of the nineteenth century, and Scott its greatest man of letters'; and he said of Swinburne, 'He's a tube through which all things blow into music.' He said, 'Wordsworth would have been much finer if he had written much less', and he told Browning in my presence that 'if he got rid of two-thirds, the remaining third would be much finer'. After saying that, and when Browning had left us, he enlarged on the imperative necessity of restraint in art. 'It is necessary to respect the limits', he said; 'an artist is one who recognises bounds to his work as a necessity, and does not overflow illimitably to all extent about a matter. I soon found that if I meant to make any mark at all it must be by shortness, for all the men before me had been so diffuse, and all the big things had been done. To get the workmanship as nearly perfect as possible is the best chance for going down the stream of time. A small vessel on fine lines is likely to float further than a great raft.'

Once, as we stood looking at Aldworth just after its completion, he turned to me and said, 'You will live longer than I shall. That house will last five hundred years.' I answered him, 'I think the English language will last longer.'

Another frequent subject of his talk was the criticism on his own work, *when unfavourable*. All the mass of eulogy he took compara- tively little notice of, but he never could forget an unfriendly word, even from the most obscure and insignificant and unknown quarter. He was hurt by it as a sensitive child might be hurt by the cross look of a passing stranger; or rather as a supersensitive skin is hurt by the sting of an invisible midge. He knew it was a weakness in him, and could be laughed out of it for a time, but it soon returned upon him, and could be laughed out of it for a time, but it soon returned upon him, and had given him from his early youth exaggerated vexation. When remonstrated with for the Hogarth's perspective he thus made, he would grimly smile and say, 'Oh yes, I know. I'm black-blooded like all the Tennysons—I remember everything that has been said against me, and forget all the rest.' It was his temperament, and showed itself in other matters besides criticism. For instance, the last time I went with him to the oculist, he was most heartily reassured about his eyes by the great expert after a careful and detailed inspection. But as we left the door he turned to me and said with utter gloom, 'No man shall persuade me that I'm not going blind.' Few things were more delightful than to help chase away such clouds and see and feel the sunshine come out again, responsive to the call of cheerfulness. To one who had so cheered him he said, 'You certainly are a jolly good fellow, you do encourage me so much.' And at another time: 'I'm very glad to have known you. It has been a sort of lift in my life.' The clouds would gather on him most in the solitude of the country, and he often told me it was needful for him to come from time to time to London to rub the rust from off him. It must be added that so soon as ever the rust was rubbed off he hastened to be back among the woods and hills. . . .

From time to time and bit by bit he read over to me almost all his poems, commenting on them as he read, and pausing to dictate a few words here and there for me to take down from his lips. The following are extracts from the notes so dictated by him.

As to the *Poems by Two Brothers*,[11] he said, 'it was really by three brothers, for Frederick as well as Charles and myself wrote some of them—a very few—and would not acknowledge any, or allow his name as one of the brothers. The bookseller gave £15 in money and £5 worth of books, but the copyright was invalid, the authors being under age. This was tested afterwards when the successor to the original publisher wanted to republish, saying he could make £12,000. The three brothers bound themselves to each other never to reveal who wrote this or that. None of the authors had ever been beyond their native county, and hardly beyond their native town. There were twenty-six misprints, but the publisher would not make a longer list of errata' than the seven which appear.

Of *The Idylls of the King* he said, 'When I was twenty-four I meant to write a whole great poem on it, and began it in the "Morte d'Arthur". I said I should do it in twenty years; but the reviews stopped me. . . . By King Arthur I always meant the soul, and by the Round Table the passions and capacities of a man. There is no grander subject in the world than King Arthur.'

When reading *In Memoriam* he said. 'It is rather the cry of the whole human race than mine. In the poem altogether private grief swells out into thought of, and hope for, the whole world. It begins with a funeral and ends with a marriage—begins with death and ends in promise of a new life—a sort of *Divine Comedy*, cheerful at the close. It is a very impersonal poem as well as personal. There is more about myself in "Ulysses", which was written under the sense of loss and that all had gone by, but that still life must be fought out to the end. It was more written with the feeling of his loss upon me than many poems in *In Memoriam*. . . . It's too hopeful, this poem, more than I am myself. . . . The general way of its being written was so queer that if there were a blank space I would put in a poem. . . . I think of adding another to it, a speculative one, bringing out the thoughts of the "Higher Pantheism", and showing that all the arguments are about as good on one side as the other, and thus throw man back more on the primitive impulses and feelings.'

He explained that there were nine natural groups or divisions in the poem, as follows: from stanza I to stanza VIII; from IX to XX; from XX[12] to XXVII; from XXVIII to XLIX; from L to LVIII; from LIX to LXXI; from LXXII to XCVIII; from XCIX to CIII; from CIV to CXXXI. . . .

When reading *Maud*, he said, 'It should be called *Maud, or the Madness*. It is slightly akin to *Hamlet*. No other poem (a monotone with plenty of change and no weariness) has been made into a drama where successive phases of passion in one person take the place of successive persons. . . . The whole of the stanzas where he is mad in Bedlam, from "Dead, long dead", to "Deeper, ever so little deeper", were written in twenty minutes, and some mad doctor wrote to me that nothing since Shakespeare has been so good for madness as this.'

At the end of *Maud* he declared, 'I've always said that *Maud* and "Guinevere" were the finest things I've written.'

NOTES

James Knowles (1831–1908), journalist and architect, was a friend of Tennyson and Gladstone. He edited the *Contemporary Review* from 1870 to 1877 and in the latter year founded and became first editor of the *Nineteenth Century*. In 1869 he founded the Metaphysical Society, of which Tennyson was a member. He was knighted in 1903.

1. *The Story of King Arthur and his Knights* (1862).
2. F. W. Robertson (1816–53), clergyman, was the incumbent of Trinity Chapel, Brighton, from 1847 to 1853. Knowles's anecdote appears in a slightly fuller form in *Memoir*, I, p. 264.
3. *Maud*, I, xii, 1. 24.
4. On Charles Tennyson, Spedding and Thompson, see pp. 4, 7 and 5, respectively.
5. Sir John Everett Millais (1829–96) painted Tennyson in 1881; according to the *Memoir* (II, p. 261), the portrait passed into the possession of Knowles.
6. George Berkeley (1685–1753), Irish philosopher.
7. Romans 8:26.
8. Spinoza (1632–77), Dutch philosopher.
9. Charles Pritchard (1808–93), joint founder (with Knowles) of the Metaphysical Society and Savilian Professor of Astronomy at Oxford from 1870.
10. James Martineau (1805–1900), Unitarian philosopher and theologian.
11. *Poems by Two Brothers* was published at Louth in 1827. On Frederick Tennyson, see pp. 2–3.
12. This seems to be an error for 'xxi' (see the transcription of Knowles's manuscript notes by Professor Gordon Ray in *Tennyson Reads 'Maud'*, Sedgewick Memorial Lecture 1968, University of British Columbia).

'Tennyson: a Reminiscence'*

WILFRID WARD

'Doric beauty' is the phrase by which the late Mr Huxley[1] once expressed the special character of Tennyson's conversation—with its terse simplicity and freedom from artificial ornament: 'and yet', he added, 'on hearing the first few words one might only say,— "Exactly, this is the man who wrote the 'Northern Farmer'." '

My first recollections of Tennyson date back as far as 1869, or

* *Problems and Persons* (London: Longmans Green, 1903) pp. 196–217.

earlier. As a boy, living near him in the Isle of Wight, I was somewhat in awe of the mysterious figure, whom I often saw in company with his friend and neighbour, Mrs Cameron, or at times with my father, tall and thin, enveloped in a huge cloak, walking rapidly, with a slight stoop, on the Beacon Down or in the Freshwater lanes. He seldom spoke to me in those days, although I was intimate with his second son, Lionel. I think it was the report of a careful study I made of the Holy Grail, in Rome, in the year 1879, which changed this. On my return to England our acquaintance was at once on a new footing. I stayed with him at Aldworth in the following year: and thenceforward walks and talks with the poet were frequent.

There were several things which struck me for the first time after I came to know him better. One was, that even at a time when I was walking with him often, and enjoying the real intimacy which was my privilege, his shyness on first coming into the room, before we started for our morning walk, remained. One had noticed it less when it appeared to be only the slowness of a man of a certain age to talk to a boy. But to the very end it was the same, even with those whom he was most frequently seeing. How familiar the picture yet remains! One waited, perhaps, in the anteroom at Farringford for a few minutes before he appeared. And when he did so there was the far-off look in his eyes, something between the look of a near-sighted man and a very far-sighted man;—due, no doubt, partly to defective vision, but conveying also a sense that his imagination was still occupied with itself, and that his mind was not yet 'focused' on the world immediately about him. I have known him stand for several minutes, after a half-absent 'How d'ye do?' in this dreamy state, with his curious look of high-strung sensitiveness, before he began to talk. And if one waited silently for him to speak, one might have to wait in vain. To tell him an amusing story was the best means of breaking the spell. The gleam of humour came to his face at once, he broke into laughter, left the regions of mental abstraction, and probably at once capped the story himself.

If a stranger had come to see him, the shyness and abstraction might last longer. I remember once going to Farringford with a friend—a true worshipper of his genius—and after the first words of greeting he seemed to be entirely in the clouds; until, after long waiting, we hit upon a device to arouse him. A picture by Edward Lear[2] hung in the room, and under it were four lines from the 'Palace of Art':

> One seem'd all dark and red—a tract of sand,
>   And some one pacing there alone,
> Who paced for ever in a glimmering land,
>   Lit with a low large moon.

We were looking at the picture, and I said to my companion, 'Read the lines.' She read them, giving them a kind of metrical jingle. In a moment Tennyson, who had been standing alone at the other side of the room, stepped rapidly across, seized her arm, and said, 'Don't read them like that', and went on with his deep, sonorous voice to read or rather *chant* them himself, with the roll which was so well known to his friends.

When once the spell had been thus broken, the absolute freedom and naturalness of his conversation came on those who had not seen him before as a surprise. And no doubt the impression left on some, of his being difficult and holding himself aloof, came partly from meeting him on occasions when the first shyness failed to pass away.

The earliest walks I remember with Tennyson were large parties. Six or eight would often go with him; and he himself talked with one at a time, changing his companion occasionally. But from about 1882 onwards I frequently went out with him *tête-à-tête*. And it was then that he waxed most earnest on problems connected with metaphysics and religious philosophy. Before we started there would be a good deal to district his attention. First there was the unloosening of the dogs who were to go with us. Don and Duke in earlier days, and later the beautiful stag-hound Lufra or the graceful Karenina, are an inseparable part of the picture of those walks that lives in the memory. And conversation was from time to time suspended while he dealt condign chastisement for their occasional misdemeanours—the chasing of a sheep, or the fighting with another dog.

As we crossed the 'careless-ordered garden' he would call attention to some little alteration or addition, in which he was sure to be keenly interested. 'Did you ever see a cypress growing as a creeper before?' he asks, as he points to a dark tree nailed against a wall. 'We have *crucified* that tree to make it grow thus.' We stop again at the tennis-lawn: 'The rabbits look on the chalk-line as marking out charmed and forbidden ground.' And he traces with his stick the minute disturbances of the turf which his watchful eye has noted near the outer line of the court, nowhere passing within it. A hundred yards outside the park gates we pause at the shop of Rogers, the naturalist, who has been stuffing a heron or a monkey which one of the Freshwater sailors may have given him, and the poet will study it with keen interest. Then the walk is resumed, but before we have gone far along the road to Freshwater Bay some tree or plant will again stop him. Then he suddenly breaks off with 'But what is the good of speaking to you about this? You are as bad as your father, who noticed nothing, and did not even know his own fields from mine. You once took a lily of the valley for a snowdrop.'

And then the conversation passes to literature, or personal

reminiscence, or poetry, or metaphysics. But soon the sound of the
cuckoo, perhaps, brings it back. 'Do you hear that note? It differs
from what we heard a week ago. If you want to remember when to
listen for the cuckoo learn the lines I learnt in Lincolnshire as a boy.'
And he repeats the old verse

> In April he opens his bill,
> In May he sings all day,
> In June he changes his tune,
> In July away he does fly,
> In August go he must.

Conversation never flagged: neither did the rapid pace at which the
poet walked—except when he would stand still for a minute to tell
some story with particular emphasis. I remember his humorous
satisfaction at Aldworth in 1881 because he and I had distanced Mr
(now Sir Richard) Jebb[3] and another friend, who were detected
sitting down to rest some hundred yards or more behind us. 'I am
over seventy and he is not forty, yet I can outwalk him', Tennyson
said. The remarkable suppleness of his joints remained until a year
before his death, and at Christmas 1891, as we came home from our
walk, he climbed a difficult gate without help; and as we approached
Farringford he ran—literally ran—down a hill, as he had often done
in earlier years. He was then eighty-two years old.

Before passing to some of our talks on matters of deep and
permanent interest, I must give as their setting some sayings and
stories on various subjects which I noted down between the years
1884 and 1887; and I will put together as though belonging to one
walk sayings which really belong to several.

His companion had been reading Browning and had found
Sordello somewhat difficult. This confession amused Tennyson.
'When *Sordello* came out,' he remarked, 'Douglas Jerrold[4] said to me,
"What has come to me? Has my mind gone? Here is a poem of which
I can't understand a single line?" Browning', he added, 'has a genius
for a sort of dramatic composition and for analysing the human
mind. And he has a great imagination. But a poet's writing should be
sweet to the mouth and ear, which Browning's is not. There should
be a "glory of words" as well as deep thought. This he has not got. In
his last work he makes "impulse" rhyme with "dim pulse".' He spoke
of Browning's love of London society: 'I once told him he would die
in a white tie, and he rather liked it.'

This led to a discussion of Goethe's saying 'Es bildet ein Talent sich
in der Stille.'[5] Some poets seem, he said, to find solitude necessary. I
remarked that Arthur Clough[6] 'in his Oxford days shrank from
general society. 'I knew him well in later life', Tennyson said. 'He

once travelled with us in France. He was a delightful companion, but was rather wanting in the sense of humour. He had great poetic feeling. He read me his "In Mari Magno", and cried like a child as he read it.' I spoke of Clough's friendship with some of the Oxford Tractarians, and of their separation owing to Clough's movement towards religious negation. This led Tennyson to tell me of a talk he had with George Eliot on the subject of her negative religious views: 'How difficult it is to repeat a thing as it really happened! George Eliot had this conversation with me at Aldworth, and the account of it which got into print was that I disputed with her till I was red in the face, and then roared, "Go away, you and your molecules!" The real fact was that our conversation was "sweet as summer", and at parting I shook her hand, and said very gently, "I hope you are happy with your molecules." ' He spoke with admiration of George Eliot's genius and insight into human character, but maintained that she was not quite so truthful as Shakespeare or Miss Austen: 'The character of Adam Bede is not quite true to human nature. It is idealised. I am reported to have said that Jane Austen was equal to Shakespeare. What I really said was that, in the narrow sphere of life which she delineated, she pictured human character as truthfully as Shakespeare. But Austen is to Shakespeare as asteroid to sun. Miss Austen's novels are perfect works on a small scale—beautiful bits of stippling. His companion remarked that Macaulay's well-known comparison probably meant no more than this.[7] We thus passed to his impressions of Macaulay himself, and these he gave with grim humour: 'I only met him once. I was introduced to him in the 1850s by Guizot.[8] Macaulay bowed and went on talking to Guizot, addressing no word to me. Then he turned to me, and said, "I am very glad to have made your acquaintance", and walked away. He did not show much sign of being glad to make my acquaintance.'

I told him Jowett's account of a talk with Macaulay: that it was as though Macaulay were delivering a lecture to an audience of one person. This led to a comparison of Macaulay's monologue with Carlyle's. Of Carlyle he said, 'He was at once the most reverent and the most irreverent man I have known. I admire his estimate of Boswell, and hate Macaulay's. Mrs Carlyle was a most charming, witty converser, but often sarcastic. She never spoke before her husband, who absorbed the conversation.' I asked, 'Did he not listen to *you* when you talked?' 'In a way,' he replied; 'but he hardly took in what one said. Carlyle was at his best, *rollicking* at the Ashburtons' house—the Grange.[9] He and Lady Ashburton were the life of the party. Those parties were very interesting, and Lady Ashburton was a woman of great brilliancy. She liked Carlyle, but I think at that time, if she had a favourite, it was George Venables.[10] Carlyle had a great feeling that we needed a strong man in England. "Our Cromwell is being born somewhere", he used to say.'

This led us to speak of our modern statesmen. He seemed disposed to agree with Carlyle, and would not accord to any the title of a really great ruler. Speaking of Mr Gladstone, he said, 'You cannot rule, as he thinks he can, with a silk glove. You must have an iron gauntlet; though you need not always make people feel the iron.' He went on to contrast Gladstone and Disraeli, doing full justice to the gifts of the former as an orator, and to the latter's 'diplomatic craft': 'The great fault of Disraeli's character was that he was scornful. Gladstone is genial and kindly.' He was very grand on contemptuousness. It was, he said, a sure sign of intellectual littleness. Simply to despise nearly always meant not to understand. Pride and contempt were specially characteristic of barbarians. Real civilisation taught human beings to understand each other better, and must therefore lessen contempt. It is a little or immature or uneducated mind which readily despises. One who has lived only in a *coterie* despises readily. One who has travelled and knows the world in its length and breadth, respects far more views and standpoints other than his own. . . .

His companion mentioned a friend who had lately become a vegetarian. This brought back to him an experience of his own: 'Once, in imitation of my friend FitzGerald, the translator of *Omar Khayyam*, for ten weeks I ate only vegetables. At first it gave great lucidity of mind. At the end of that time I felt light, and almost foolish. I ate one chop; and a more genial glow came over me than if I had drunk brandy.' This led naturally to the dedication of 'Tiresias', and he recited the lines

> And once, for ten long weeks, I tried
>   Your table of Pythagoras,
> And seemed at first 'a thing enskied'
>   (As Shakespeare has it), airy light,
> To float above the ways of men,
>   Then fell from that half-spiritual height,
> Chilled till I tasted flesh again,
>   One night when earth was winter-black,
> And all the heavens flashed in frost;
>   And on me, half asleep, came back
> That wholesome heat the blood had lost.[11]

'Belle comme la prose', he said, 'is the French expression for that kind of poetry, and a very good one. It applies also to my lines of invitation to F. D. Maurice.[12] Browning's obscurity of style makes this impossible to him. The great aim in such poems is to say what

you have to say with melody, but with perfect simplicity. When I felt that I had done this in the dedication of "Tiresias", the fools in the *Edinburgh Review* condemned it as "prose in rhyme".[13]

Then the subject of a forthcoming poem of his own might be broached, and its plan discussed with that absolute simplicity in which he had, I think, no rival in private conversation, although the presence of numbers occasionally brought with it an element of self-consciousness. And here I may remark that this truly great simplicity led him invariably to accept criticism which he felt to be honest and just. 'Quondoque bonus dormitat Homerus';[14] and Tennyson, too, would at times overlook an obviously unsatisfactory line in his first draft. I recall his reading to me and to another friend (the late Mr Locker Lampson)[15] 'Vastness' before he published it in *Macmillan's Magazine.* The stately couplets—each descriptive of some phase of the universe or of human existence—were given with grand effect until he read this one.

> Love for the maiden crowned with marriage,
> No regret for aught that has been.
> Debtless competence, comely children,
> Happy household, sober and clean.

His hearers smiled very visibly at the last words. Tennyson looked up.

'Why are you laughing? he asked.

'If we laughed perhaps others might laugh', ventured.

'True', he said, and closed his book. Next day he called us, and read as follows:

> Love for the maiden crowned with marriage,
> No regrets for aught that has been.
> Household happiness, gracious children,
> Debtless competence, golden mean.

I think I am right in saying that the great problems of metaphysics and of man's destiny and origin occupied a larger share of his thoughts than heretofore, during the last ten or twelve years of his life. But indications of the trains of thought which he afterwards matured are to be found comparatively early. I asked him which was the earliest poem in which he had begun seriously to consider these problems, and he said, 'The Two Voices'. Two couplets [*sic*] therein express his method in nearly all his great metaphysical poems:

> As far as might be, to carve out
> Free space for every human doubt,
> That the whole mind might orb about.

> To search thro' all I felt or saw
> The springs of life, the depths of awe,
> And reach the law within the law.

It was by allowing the most free and explicit voice to doubt that he gradually worked further and further towards the solution of the mysteries of life and of the world. He was a thoroughgoing idealist; and his conclusions recall in some respects portions of the writings of three great thinkers—Kant, Berkeley, and Father Malebranche....[16]

Bacon has grandly described that attitude of humility and sensitiveness to all facts which is indispensable to the student of nature. Tennyson had this humility pre-eminently in metaphysics. Bacon's bugbears, the *intellectus sibi permissus*, mere speculation, mere prejudice, which lead to the ignoring of facts which do not square with preconceived theories, have their counterpart in the upholders of dogmatic metaphysical systems. Tennyson, on the contrary, showed a passionate yearning simply to learn facts as they are. There was no pride, no dogmatism, but the simplicity of a child—of 'an infant crying for the light'—alongside of the penetrating and sensitive intellectual nature. To the very end he had the teachableness of true greatness, and his views seemed to grow more accurate and mature to his last year.

And here we have, I think, the quality which made his conversation on these subjects so peculiarly impressive. One felt its intense candour and truthfulness. I use the word 'intense' advisedly. With many a man one knows that on such subjects there is no lack of ability or sincerity. But he is ready to theorise and to develop a theory with ingenuity; and what began as a candid attempt to solve the mysteries of the universe soon becomes untrue to fact. Tennyson, on the other hand, tested every step; questioned and questioned again his own conclusions; detected and allowed for the least shadow of prejudice or prepossession; re-examined his own old statements in the light of further experience. He seemed to be ever looking upward at the mysteries of the world behind the phenomena of sense, intently eager to miss no flash of light, however momentary, which might break through the clouds and reveal the heavens beyond. He carried into metaphysics the extraordinary accuracy of perception which he showed with physical nature, and indeed with all the facts of life. That this habit was lifelong in the case of physical nature we are reminded by such a poem as the 'Progress of Spring', first written in youth. Such lines as 'The starling claps her tiny castanets,' and the description (elsewhere) of the sunflower which 'rays round with flames her disc of seed', are specimens given only to indicate the habit to which I refer, instances of which are too abundant to need further specification. The 'thing as it was', instead of being confused by imagination or associations, made an indelible impression on him.

His accuracy as to quite trivial matters was even scrupulous. If a story were told with the slightest inaccuracies of detail he would spoil it by repeated interruptions, rather than let them pass. He was equally severe with himself if memory tripped in the smallest degree. In his 'All along the valley', the opening lines run thus:

> All along the valley, stream that flashest white,
> Deepening thy voice with the deepening of the night,
> All along the valley, where the waters flow,
> I walk'd with one I loved two-and-thirty years ago.

One day he discovered that he was wrong by one year—that only thirty-one years had passed when he wrote the poem. He was much vexed, and talked seriously of changing the line. So, too, in speaking of historical or social facts, dates and numbers were always prominent and always accurate. Talking of Buddhism and its later division into so many sects, he gave at once, with perfect exactness, their number and the dates and circumstances of the chief schisms. And above all, he remembered and delighted in the facts of astronomy. Such a book as Ball's *Astronomy*[17] filled his imagination. He would point to a fixed star and tell one the exact pace at which it was moving, and give the distance from us of each planet, and calculate the time the sun's light takes to reach us, and make his figures still more vivid by comparing them with the speed of things familiar to us on our own earth.

This habitual accuracy of memory and perception, and knowledge of detail, instead of being confused when his imagination became most vivid, came out all the more clearly. Ruskin, in *Modern Painters*, names three kinds of imagination:

> The man who perceives rightly because he does not feel, and to whom the primrose is very accurately the primrose because he does not love it; secondly, the man who perceives wrongly because he feels, and to whom the primrose is anything else than a primrose—a star or a sun or a fairy's shield or a forsaken maiden. And then there is lastly the man who perceives rightly in spite of his feelings, and to whom the primrose is for ever nothing else than itself—a little flower apprehended in the very plain and leafy fact of it, whatever and how many soever the associations and passions may be that exist around it.

Tennyson's imagination was eminently of the third kind. The

vividness it gave was not a halo which may blur or obscure the true features it surrounds, but a strong limelight which shows the minutest details accurately. The new light was never confused or dazzling; and it was always focused precisely.

It was then, I think, partly this close truthfulness in his perception and memory of all he spoke of, which gave one such a strong sense of the reality of his metaphysical thought. He was no theoriser to spin a web of fancy on such questions. One felt that his was peculiarly a mind which could not be constantly brooding on the subject (as it was), and constantly revising and retouching his analysis of its problems, if those problems and his solutions were not very real indeed. Some characteristics which often mar philosophical speculation were entirely absent from him. He was incapable of confounding mistiness with mystery, incapable of occupying his mind with anything which it did not definitely *ap*prehend, although he recognised as much as any one how large is the sphere of mystery which no man can *com*prehend. On the other hand, his clearness never led to the unreal completeness of lovers of system. One felt confidence in his glimpses all the more from the frankness with which he recognised that they were but a partial insight into truths beyond us. What he said won assent not from any logical completeness, but from absolute truth to fact; though it often had the characteristics ascribed by George Eliot to truth under the limitations of our present condition—of being 'complex' and 'fragmentary'. On such subjects this was an additional sign of its exactness.

The problems of the physical universe and of man's physical life alternated as a theme of conversation with metaphysics themselves, and thus claim their share in my notes. Nearly all the sayings I have set down belong to the years 1885–1887. He spoke of the mysteries of metaphysics. 'After religion,' he said, 'metaphysics are the great hope for mankind. They must stem the tide of materialism. They show materialists that you can't escape from mystery by escaping from religion.' A subject which especially exercised him in this connexion was the mystery attaching to space and to extended matter, indications of which are in 'Vastness', the second 'Locksley Hall', the 'Ancient Sage' and 'De Profundis'. We were passing one day through a ploughed field, and, pointing to the clods, he remarked that to a woodlouse they might look as grand as the Swiss Alps to us. 'All greatness is relative', he said. 'What are the Swiss mountains themselves when you know their proportion to the earth; and the earth itself when you know its proportion to the universe?' A little later on I returned to this subject, and instead of 'woodlouse' said a 'flea'. He stopped me at once. 'Not a flea: it could jump to the top in a moment, and that would prevent the idea of such greatness.' On my saying, then, that it was painful to look on one's impression of the beauty of Swiss mountains as only a subjective feeling, without corresponding objective reality, he said he did not mean this. The *size* is relative; but the *beauty* may be real. The clods in the ploughed field may be really beautiful, but one needs to be as small as a tiny insect to appreciate the beauty. Then, too, what mystery there is in a grain of sand! Divide and divide it as you will, you never come to an end of it. All that has magnitude is divisible; two atoms without magnitude cannot make one with magnitude. So you can always divide.' He passed, then, from the consideration of infinite littleness in matter to that of infinite greatness: 'Think of the proportion of one human eye to our earth; of our earth to the sun; of the sun to the solar system; of that to the universe; and then think that one human eye can in some sense be in contact with the stars of the Milky Way.'

Another saying of his connected with this subject is all the more interesting, because he immediately afterwards embodied it in eight lines of great beauty. Walking one day on the down which stretches from Freshwater Bay to the Freshwater Beacon, his conversation was chiefly of two subjects. One was the mad lawlessness of the Celtic character, which he illustrated by items of news from Ireland—fresh instances of maiming cattle, and of murder and outrage, and the other all the mass of confusion and crime which a great town brought together. Paris was worse than London, he said, because of the Celtic element in the French character. About half-way between Freshwater Bay and the Beacon, he suddenly stopped and pointed with his stick to a star, quite visible, though it was almost daylight. 'Do you see that star?' he asked, in his abrupt way. 'It is the evening star. Do you know that if we lived there this earth would look to us exactly like that. Fancy the vice and confusion of London or Paris in that peaceful star.' He looked again at the star with an expression half of horror, half of grim humour. We walked on. I did not know at the time that he was writing the second 'Locksley Hall',[18] and it was with a curious sensation that one read afterwards the exquisite lines which that walk had (apparently) suggested. His few words on the subject proved to have been, what his talk so often was, condensed prose notes of coming poetry:

Hesper, whom the poet called the bringer home of all good things,
All good things may move in Hesper, perfect peoples, perfect
   kings.

Hesper, Venus, were we native to that splendour, or in Mars,
We should see the globe we groan in, fairest of our evening stars.

Could we dream of wars and carnage, craft and madness, lust and
   spite,
Rearing London, raving Paris, in that point of peaceful light?

Might we not in glancing heavenward on a star so silver fair,
Yearn and clasp the hands and murmur, 'Would to God that we
were there!'

He insisted strongly on misuses of the word 'God', and often
condemned the immorality of extreme Calvinism. One could not but
trace to the memories of the Calvinistic surroundings of his boyhood
the deep feeling evident in such poems as 'Despair' and 'Demeter'
against the conception of a vindictive Deity. 'I remember one woman
who used to weep for hours because God was so infinitely good. He
had predestined (she said) most of her friends to damnation, and
herself, who was no better than they, to salvation. She shook her
head at me sadly, and said, "Alfred, Alfred , whenever I look at you I
think of the words of Scripture, 'Depart from me, ye cursed, into
everlasting fire.' " The Calvinist minister, who was spiritual guide to
the neighbourhood, had typhoid fever. To the horror of his
congregation, on recovering he became a Universalist, and ceased to
believe in hell.' He told me of another Calvinist minister who argued
with a clergyman of more liberal views on the ways of Providence.
'Wait a moment,' interrupted the latter, 'we have not defined our
terms. We are using them in different senses. Your God is my devil.'

This vindictive idea of God was perhaps his greatest trial in
popular religion. Another was the anthropomorphism which regarded the Supreme Being as a sort of 'magnified clergyman'. But he
admitted that this was almost inevitable with some of the uneducated. 'These misuses of the word "God" make me prefer another
name' he said. 'I prefer to say the Highest or the Supreme Being. In
the "Ancient Sage" I have called God "the Nameless". I have
sometimes demurred to the phrase "personal" as applied to God, for
that same reason. It has been used as though personality were quite
similar in God and in man. But I only mean that His personality is
higher than ours. Lotze[19] says the lack of personality is in us. God is
unknowable as he is in Himself, but He touches us at one point. That
point is the conscience. If the conscience could be further de-
veloped, we might in some sense see God.' And again: 'The
conception in us of a perfect being realising our highest ideals is
some proof of God's existence, though not a conclusive proof. Why
should we conceive of such a being unless it were put into us to do so?'

'Lushington[20] used to say to me', he continued, 'that if there were
no other world, this world would be all the more valuable. I, on the
contrary, feel that it is only the light shed on our earth from another
world which gives it any value. The thought of working for the
human race is not incentive enough to virtue if man is not immortal.
The whole race will be extinct, probably, in a few thousand years. All
the greatest aspirations are without meaning if man be not immortal.

Religious belief is necessary to give life any meaning or value. A man without religious aspirations is only half a man.

Speaking of free will, he said, 'Man is free, but only free in certain narrow limits. His character and his acquired habits limit his freedom. They are like the cage of a bird. The bird can hop at will from one perch to another, and to the floor of the cage, but not beyond its bars.' And of the Buddhist Nirvana: 'Place a cork at the bottom of a jar of water. Its tendency will be to work its way upwards, whatever obstacles you may place in the way. At last it reaches the top and is at rest. That is my conception of Nirvana.'

Evolution was a very favourite topic with him. He had made a close study of it, and Huxley once said to me that Tennyson's grasp of the principles of physical science was equal to that of the greatest experts. Wallace's book on Darwinism[21] was not published until 1889, but long before that time Tennyson often spoke of his genius, and was disposed to think his conclusions more exact in some respects than Darwin's: 'Wallace pointed out that man has a prospective brain—that he has faculties in excess of his physical needs. This would show that you can't account for his higher faculties by natural selection.' Again: 'The descent of man's body from lower animals,' he once said, 'if it is true, helps to solve the mystery of man's dual nature. We naturally inherit a great deal from our brute ancestors. The spiritual nature is something superadded, but the brute nature is there, and remains side by side with the other.'

NOTES

Wilfrid Ward (1856–1916), Roman Catholic biographer of Cardinal Newman and Cardinal Wiseman. He also wrote the life of his father, W. G. Ward (1812–82), Catholic theologian and philosopher, who spent his last years at Freshwater, Isle of Wight, where he was a neighbour and close friend of Tennyson.

1. Thomas Henry Huxley (1825–95), scientist and controversialist.

2. Edward Lear (1812–88), artist and poet. Tennyson's 'To E. L., on his Travels in Greece' (Ricks, 301) is addressed to him.

3. Richard Claverhouse Jebb (1841–1905), classical scholar; Professor of Greek at Glasgow 1875–89 and subsequently at Cambridge.

4. Douglas Jerrold (1803–57), journalist, editor and humorist. Browning's notoriously baffling *Sordello* had been published in 1840.

5. 'A talent develops in stillness'.

6. Arthur Hugh Clough (1819–61) had resigned his fellowship at Oriel College, Oxford, on account of religious scruples. His poems were published posthumously, with a memoir by F. T. Palgrave.

7. Macaulay compares Jane Austen with Shakespeare in an article in the *Edinburgh Review*, LXXVI (1843) 561.

8. François Guizot (1787–1874), French historian and statesman, spent various periods in England.

9. See p. 12.

10. See p. 12.

11. From 'To E. FitzGerald' (Ricks, 398); see also p. 7.

12. Frederick Denison Maurice (1805–72), theologian; Professor of Moral Philosophy at Cambridge, 1866–72. He was godfather to Hallam Tennyson. The reference is to Tennyson's poem 'To the Rev. F. D. Maurice', written in 1854 (Ricks, 312).

13. According to an unsigned review of *Tiresias and Other Poems* in the *Edinburgh Review*, cccxxxiii (1886) 489, 'the dedicatory lines to the late Mr FitzGerald scarcely pretend to be more than rhymed prose'.

14. 'Good Homer nods for a moment' (Latin)—usually quoted as 'Homer nods'. The quotation is taken from Horace's *Ars Poetica*.

15. See p. 176.

16. Immanuel Kant (1724–1804), German philosopher; George Berkeley (1685–1753), Irish philosopher; Nicholas de Malebranche (1638–1715), French philosopher.

17. Sir Robert Ball (1840–1913) published many popular works on astronomy.

18. 'Locksley Hall Sixty Years After' (Ricks, 417), written in 1886.

19. Lao-Tze, Chinese philosopher born c. 600 BC. Tennyson's poem 'The Ancient Sage' (Ricks, 415) was 'written after reading his life and maxims'.

20. Edmund Lushington married Tennyson's youngest sister, Cecilia. See his brief contribution to *Memoir*, I, pp. 201–3.

21. Alfred Wallace (1823–1913), biologist, arrived independently at a theory of natural selection and communicated it to Darwin in 1858. He published widely on scientific topics. The book referred to is *Darwinism*.

'Memories of Tennyson'*

BLANCHE WARRE-CORNISH

Farringford in its wooded seclusion is always beautiful, winter or summer. I saw it first on a bleak winter day. The great drawing-room, with the French windows opening on the lawn, and high trees, with a view of the lovely sweep of the bay, was occupied by a small party. I seem to remember Tennyson entering silently and moving slowly and remaining rather silent among his guests through luncheon. Lady Tennyson's perfection of reception, her touching beauty which wakened the heart and really warmed it as chiselled beauty so seldom does, dispelled shyness at the first meeting. I can

* *London Mercury*, v (1921–2) 147–8, 150–1, 153–5, 266–8, 271–3.

recall the whole far-off look of the poet as he came down from his morning's work. He moved slowly, as I have said, and looked sad; he wore grey tweed, with deep linen collar close up to the chin and deep shirt-cuffs turned back over the sleeves after a fashion not uncommon in the days of lavish laundry. As for the wearer, it is difficult to make a pen-and-ink portrait from a reminiscence of first meeting, but I should say that the consummate beauty of Tennyson's pose of head and of the shapely nose always impressed the beholder at first sight, though a short black beard marred the fine moulding of mouth and chin, and strong glasses, necessary to his sight, sealed up the light that was so often in his eyes. There were hard lines, too, near the mouth, which, like his grave motion, marked him as a man of sorrows.

Towards luncheon's end there was some conversation at the poet's side of the table about the Crimean War. I caught the story of a book of his in the breast-pocket of an officer who wrote to tell him that it had been pierced by a bullet and saved his life under fire. What struck my imagination as I sat by Mrs Tennyson was the talk about the Crimea. When did I ever hear it discussed? Here it was as if the war was yesterday. Every subject of the day was, of course, debated at Farringford, but it was my first impression of the way England's wars and affairs blended with its personal life. To-day and to-morrow came into the poet's life. The frame of it all was old-fashioned. There was something robust and old-world even about the luncheon. The roast which was carved upon the table and the four side-dishes placed, as Miss Thackeray once described, north, south, east, and west of the centre, and then the simplicity of the household, the modest-sized dining-room, the quiet service of a demure parlour-maid—all belonged to an old-fashioned 'haunt of ancient peace'.

This impressed a Parisian servant of ours who stayed once in the house. When asked about Farringford, she said, 'Oh, Madame, c'est la paix.'

At coming away the host led us kindly to the hall-door, where it was his wont to let his short-sighted eyes make closer acquaintance with his guests. He asked me if I knew Magdalene Brookfield. He heard that she was coming to stay at Freshwater, and he had learnt that she had grown up. 'She is the daughter of my old friend Brookfield.'[1] He pronounced the name like Maud and as Magdalen College is pronounced at Oxford. The Lincolnshire accent was more marked in Alfred Tennyson's speech than his younger brother Horatio's. It is to be remembered that the Somersby home broke up when the last-born Tennyson was a boy.

Presently, when she reached Freshwater, twenty, and lovely in mind and person, Magdalene Brookfield was told of the Laureate's respectful enquiries, and she replied, 'Of course.' Soon she was to accompany us to Farringford for a promised evening reading of 'The Holy Grail'.

As I have said, the house is always beautiful. By night it has a charming welcome secluded in the starlit park, with firelit book-walls within and the mask of Dante presiding over those in the great drawing-room. It was the old-fashioned after dinner tea-time. Life was early at Farringford. The pleasant order of its evenings has often been described, but I will depict it here because it belongs to an old world at peace, and we shall not recover that former stable and fixed existence. Winter and summer the dinner-hour was at half-past six and dessert was served in the drawing-room; after the wine the master of the house and the gentlemen—if any with him—mounted the winding stair to the study in a turret, and, except for an hour's smoke, the evening hours after tea would run till near midnight, while the poet sat on with his family—and guests, if there were any. As we entered we found the ladies only in the drawing-room. The candles on the centre table lit the stately room, the tea which had succeeded the dessert was prepared and the chairs ranged round the table according to the ritual of the night at Farringford. Presently Tennyson came in and, as at luncheon, greeted us rather dreamily and took his place in the high chair at the table. As he sat there in the candle-light, with vast breadth of white evening linen, I was better able than before to judge of the great *carrure* of his shoulders, the tall forehead shaped so like the forehead in the busts of Shakespeare, and the finely-shaped hands. Dean Bradley[2] and Dr Butler,[3] Master of Trinity, both then headmasters, had come in with him; their wives, Mrs Tennyson and her sister, Mrs Weld,[4] and her daughter, Agnes Weld, were present, and the sons of the house, Hallam and Lionel, appeared for the reading from belated schoolboy adventures in the bay.

It was a bass voice, deeper than Horatio's, that now began the dialogue in the cloister; it was varied in many tones but sustained like a chant. Tennyson's reading was full of his theory of sound, and the reading of blank verse was part of his lifelong devotion to the blank verse line. It was not enough with him to write it well, you must read it well.

'Many a man can write a poem, but very few can read one', she said to us once later on. . . .

Tennyson's talk ranged over every possible subject, from the most trivial thing of the passing moment, to which he somehow gave raciness and importance, to the greatest heights of thought and speculation. It is impossible to reproduce the intensity of conviction with which he uttered his graver thoughts, and they were never far off, but the following jottings chiefly describe and contribute to a personal life and its connection with the past.

Before 1876 when we had a home in North Devon we were often at Freshwater Bay and constantly welcomed at Farringford. One evening the poet spoke to me of Thackeray. Thackeray and Tennyson had been members of the same circle at Trinity College, Cambridge, but Thackeray was junior, and their intercourse was in London, chiefly at the house of the historian Hallam.[5] The following fragment of the poet's talk and reminiscence was written in a journal at the time.

'The whole lovableness of Thackeray's character came out in a letter he once sent me. I should like to think I had kept it, though I dislike the thought so much of letters of mine being kept. I don't generally care to keep any. This letter was written after we had been spending the evening together and had talked about Latin poetry. I had been praising Catullus's verse and saying that you couldn't go beyond him in perfection of form and tenderness of expression, and Thackeray had been declaring his opinion rather strongly that I overestimated him, that he could write as well himself, and I said nothing more. The next morning I received from him the humblest of apologies; he said he had begun looking at Catullus again as soon as he had got home, and immediately felt that he had known nothing of what he had been talking about, that every word I had said about him was true, and that he had been wholly in the wrong for speaking slightingly of him. It was impossible to have written a more beautiful letter, in a more generous spirit. The largeness of the man's mind came out in it. What do you think of it?'

'You had been having a very happy evening!'

'I always had a happy evening with him'—spoken in the tone of sadness of reminiscence of the dead.

Of *Vanity Fair* he once said, 'There is a passage in *Vanity Fair* that brings tears to my eyes. It is when the beginning of the battle of Waterloo is heard at Brussels whilst they are sitting at dinner, and the waiter puts down the dish he is handing and says, "C'est le feu."' . . .

My sister, Emily Ritchie, permits me to quote from memories of her many visits to the Tennysons at Farringford and at Aldworth, when she had the privilege of intimate intercourse spreading over twenty-four years.

I only once heard him talk much about Arthur Hallam, and that was one evening over his port wine when he dwelt on his intellectual power, on his geniality, on his courtesy, and ended by saying, 'How you would have loved him!'

Towards the close of his life it was given to me to hear Lord Tennyson read 'The Gleam' with the lines

> And last on the forehead of Arthur the blameless
> Rested the Gleam. . . .
> Arthur had vanished, I know not whither,
> The King who loved me and cannot die.

And he explained that he meant Arthur Hallam.

Music was a subject to which Tennyson gave his attention, with regret that he was by nature shut out from it. After hearing Joachim[6] play at his house: 'A great deal of the music means nothing at all to me, but I can feel the poetry of the bowing.' After my sister had played the Waldstein Sonata: 'I can feel the glory, though I can't follow the music. I know that I miss a great deal by not understanding it. It often seems to me that music must take expression up at the point where poetry leaves off, and expresses what can't be expressed in words.' When Sir Charles Stanford[7] first came to stay at Farringford he was greeted with, 'You are the man whose stomach is filled with minims and crotchets.' When Tennyson said of my husband's Scarlatti that it was 'a-sighing and a-longing.' he added that he had himself wanted some further expression, a passing into music, as he ended a poem.

But I must speak of the poem most identified with Freshwater. It was composed there on the downs, in the summer nights of 1854.

The hearing of *Maud* read by the poet whole at a sitting—that poetical adventure described by many—was mine once at Farringford. I was alone with the master of the house. It came about in this way. The Tennysons had lent us the Terrace—their house in the bay—where on our first visit we had found Horatio Tennyson. We were packing after a fortnight's Easter stay; a party of friends had just broken up. Mr Tennyson called upon us alone, for his usual companion, Hallam, had gone up to town. The poet took a fancy to the sight of Mudie books and magazines[8] about to be packed in my husband's book-box. He said he never saw any modern literature. He would like to read some. Could we lend him the contents of the book-box? But—tragically—how to return books? Hallam was away, paper and string, intolerable always. 'Stay two nights longer and I will read you *Maud*.'

My husband, alas! was obliged to depart, but he kindly urged me to stay. A Mudie novel or two went up to Farringford under the poet's big cloak for immediate study. The book-box was sent for. And the next evening I was admitted after the early dinner-hour, at Farringford.

To my surprise I was taken to the study and found the Bard alone. It was the new study, a spacious one built above the 'ballroom' in the wing of the house which came into existence as the boys grew up.

The cedar on the lawn outside spread its strong arms to the study windows. It was early twilight; thrushes and blackbirds were quieting down after the long day's vociferation; soon there would be the silence which precedes the night in the country—and *Maud* opened with a deep bell-note: 'I hate the dreadful hollow behind the little wood'. The familiar sequences of the narrative were read with the freshness of improvisation; the sorrowful retrospect of the crime committed in madness came in tones of infinite pathos—the murder of Maud's brother in the Hall garden. Other tones were delicate and tender, others passionate with mighty volume; the reading of *Maud* was delightful in variety and in calling forth every modulation. I saw the poet carried away by the spirit of his own creation and heard the splendid rhythm of 'come into the garden, Maud'. . . . All through the reading he constantly relied on the close verbal attention of the listener. He suddenly dropped his voice and asked after the line 'The dusky strand of Death', 'What is that strand?'

'Shore', was replied.

'You missed the word "inwoven"; it is the woven strand of a rope.'

With the second part of *Maud* another mood began, the mood of madness; the monologues of the lover reach fierce despair. It was night by this time, and candles had been lit in the study; they illuminated the fine face of the reader, who held the book up to his eyes, but darkness, within and without, seemed to the listener to enfold her. The horror when the lover fancies himself buried under the roadway and beneath the traffic of a city was comparable to Racine's 'l'horreur d'une profonde nuit'.

At length the reading ended in peace. There was some talk. The *trajet* from the large study to the pleasant lobby below, and garden door, was as usual full of kind, lingering good-nights. I only recall that in some connection with our talk Tennyson said, 'We have not done with prayer yet.'

His casual utterances on religion were more impressive than sermons.

Memory is inseparable from reflection, and remembering the reading of *Maud* I have often thought of Tennyson as a great poet of the 'Banner of Battle'.

The subject of war came up during the reading of *Maud*.

Whenever lines occurred about war, war the purifier, war the unifier, Tennyson stopped to say that the critics had misunderstood him. When had he been the champion of war? The poem was a dramatic monologue. The sentiments were in the mouth of a madman. He wished he had called the poem as first planned, *Maud or the Madness*. 'Anyone can see that the words about war represent a mood. But the critics are nothing.'

Again, in connection with the 'Ode on the Death of the Duke of

Wellington', Tennyson asked at another time whether he had in that poem praised war? It was duty not glory which his lines exalted:

> Not once nor twice in our rough Island story,
> The path of duty was the path of glory.

But at the same time, he once boasted, 'I have three times been taken into battle', meaning his poems carried on the person of a soldier into action. . . .

In the early autumn of 1875 the Tennysons were at Freshwater, and the reading of the new play *Queen Mary*[9] is part of the recollection of a perfect holiday-time. The house was full of life from the presence of Hallam, who had just closed his undergraduate career at Trinity, Cambridge. The reading was among the pipes in the new Farringford study without any solemnity at all.

'Why do you all like Elizabeth?' he asked of us. 'Elizabeth was not a religious woman and Mary was.'

There was extraordinary pathos in the poet's impersonation of Mary. He loved her as an English queen, and his pity for her was tender. But the fundamental interest of the drama was in Mary's religious passion. . . .

That sunny autumn of which I write saw the rise of lawn tennis in England. A beautiful clearing in the high wood at Farringford was now the tennis court, reached by a glade from the garden-door of the house, and there the poet followed his sons. The play had great attraction for him. Tennyson's extraordinary eyesight, which required the strongest lenses and made it necessary for him to go close up to a man or woman before he could see them, enabled him not only to watch the game and admire the athletic skill of men and maidens, but occasionally to take a racket and hit a ball.

'I like the play, but hate the game', he said. Fifteen love, thirty love, deuce. . . . I never could count. Despairing tones. Seated on a stone bench in that pleasant glade one day watching tennis, he spoke of the death of Mrs Carlyle. The poet's thought dwelt with horror on the letters of condolence Carlyle had received. Letters of condolence were intolerable. 'An old aunt of mine in Lincolnshire said when she lost her husband, "I get so many letters I can't eat my dinner in peace" '. More about the wretchedness of loss, the isolation of it. 'When my wife dies I want no letters.'

The tones of Tennyson's voice were admirably suited to expressing vague dismay. When one of the players suggested that tea should come out to the tennis ground, he appeared in his dining-room and announced, 'One of the ladies has asked me for fifteen cups of tea.' He could be a delightful child. 'Visitors all coming at once remind me of flies on a dungheap—all coming together and all going together', he was heard to say. He had a refreshing hatred of the commonplaces of intercourse, and a mistrust of what he called the humbug of society, but to visitors in his own house he showed ideal hospitality, bestowing *himself* upon them in a way which the most genial of the earth alone understand.

Tennyson's bluntness was always accompanied by goodwill. Here is an instance of a rough double compliment. Mrs Tennyson, in taking leave of Mrs Oliphant,[10] who had come up from Windsor to lunch with the poet in Eaton Square, said, 'How kind of you, Mrs Oliphant, to come to see us here!', and Mrs Oliphant had replied, 'But indeed it is very kind of you to have done me this honour.'

'What hypocrites you women are!' said the poet, standing over the two beautiful ladies.

A very famous outburst in South Kensington was in my sister Mrs Douglas Freshfield's house. Looking out of the window at the square, he said, 'I suppose this is South Kensington; it looks like a cold hell.' Douglas Freshfield and his wife were enjoying their guest in excellent vein at luncheon in their house and were delighted, but the story went forth and was repeated with strange variations.

Certain unspeakable 'Cockneys' at Freshwater, their incursions by the Farringford lane into 'Maidencroft', with a good look in at the summerhouse where the poet wrote, and up to the very windows of his house, brought forth many grumblings.

The following words about publicity are notable.

The amount of newspaper attention poets get nowadays would be enough to prevent me from putting forward any poetry at all if I were beginning now. I used always to think the ideal of happiness lay in the circumstances of a country squireen who lived on about eight hundred pounds a year quietly, with his wife and family, attracting no attention, and here I am *deluged* with public notice. I am being driven mad by the way people publish all manner of things about me that haven't the very faintest foundation. I am told by a gentleman who goes into Lincolnshire to take photographs of the scenes of my youth that this mill was the original of the mill in the 'Miller's Daughter' and that oak was the 'Talking Oak'. Never anything of the sort. Why do they give me no credit for any imagination? The power of poetical creation seems totally ignored now. All this modern realism is hateful; there seems nothing but vulgarity everywhere. No man with imagination can be tied down to any one thing for his ideas. Turner was an imaginative painter, and how absurd it would be to *account* for all his works! There *may* be special suggestions.

Why does one want to know about a poet's life? The less you

know the better; he gives you his best in his writings. I thank God, day and night, that we know so little about Shakespeare.

Farringford was never forsaken, but as early as 1870 the Tennysons retired before the summer invasion of Freshwater to their new solitude on Blackdown. Beautiful Aldworth, built in a clearing of the wooded hillside, approached by a rough sandy road from a vast heath-common above the house one mile off, remains secluded even now. The post-office was three miles distant. The terraces overlooked the wooded champaign of Surrey and Sussex, 400 feet below. Here Mrs Tennyson, with the consummate art of silent housewifery, made another home. . . .

'My husband must have quiet for his work', she would say half apologetically about the seclusion of Freshwater in the early days. But at Aldworth she welcomed the nearer access to old friends in London. And soon she hailed the rise of the dramatic phase of Tennyson's creation. There was a yearly season in town, and a house taken in London for about two months of earliest spring, and, to quote Aubrey de Vere,[11] 'The men the most noted of their time, year after year, statesmen, warriors, men of letters, science, and art, some of royal race, some famous in far lands, but none more welcome to him than the friends of his youth, met and listened to the music of Tennyson's talk and reading.' This was both in London and at Aldworth.

On this hierarchy reminiscence hardly dares to dwell, but a few impressions gather about the events of this period. There was in '74 a theatrical visit with Annie Thackeray and the boys to see *Hamlet* played by Irving at the Lyceum.[12] There was a visit of Irving to the box after the performance and a conversation about the acting. 'You are a good actor lost', Irving said to Tennyson, as she reported. . . .

[Tennyson] condemned 'Zolaism'. In talks he quoted Walt Whitman as showing an opposite spirit to Zola[13] in spite of his 'nakedness of expression'. 'There is no immorality in Walt Whitman. The most indecent things are those where there is only insinuation of indecency. As in painting or sculpture, the wholly nude need suggest no impropriety at all. The suggestion of impropriety is the really vicious thing. But the British working-man doesn't understand the nude as the ancient Greeks did, and it may be a mistake to exhibit it on the walls of the Academy.'

Tennyson could be very open in talk with men. Earlier in his career he took an optimistic view of the powers of progress of mankind. The procreation of children was a subject, he held, to which sufficient importance and attention had not been given. But, needless to say, in sexual matters his conclusions were that higher ideals, fewer suggestions of base instincts, were wanted.

'More harm can be done through bad literature than through anything else; the terrible thing is that man, being higher than the beast, can, through the fact of his intellect, make himself infinitely lower than the beast.' . . .

Tennyson at all times delighted in his Catholic friends. To Sir John Simeon,[14] of Swainston, in the Isle of Wight, he opened the recesses of his heart; to Sir John's daughter, Mrs Richard Ward, constantly at Farringford, I have heard him put terrific questionings of the faith to receive her breathless answer—for instance, about the Incarnation—'It does indeed seem wonderful, but I believe it.' Wilfrid Ward,[15] at the time of which I write, was the only young man with whom Tennyson could talk metaphysics; he mourned that even at Cambridge metaphysics were out of fashion. With all these friends he took the unorthodox line. But it was another friend in the Isle of Wight, the frequent companion of his thoughts in later years, who bore witness to an opposite mood. He never allowed her to be sceptical! He was like Dr Johnson on orthodoxy with his friend Mary Brotherton,[16] the novelist. She said he never let a doubting word pass from her lips without rebuke! Tennyson was subject from time to time to moods that trouble the mind, not temperamentally, merely, but intellectually. Under the cloud, no authority, no pleading could help him, only his own thought brought relief. Such thought finds utterance in reflections scattered up and down the *Memoir*, an inexhaustible and living store. Memory of friends can only confirm that the cardinal point of Tennyson's philosophy and religion was survival after death. Of such survival he had even a definite word: 'My idea of Heaven is the perpetual ministry of one soul to another.'

Tennyson's kindness in illness was full of thought; he brought Mary Anderson[17] to see me, a gladdening visit, as he intended. But it was from Mrs Brotherton that I heard most of his growing thoughtfulness for friends, and also of many of his communings at this time.

Mary Brotherton's door at Freshwater Gate never failed to admit the poet on his return from London or Aldworth, whatever the changes in his life and the ups and downs of his spirit. It was the door of a low farm-house with one attic storey above a long, low-raftered sitting-room. She and Mr Brotherton, an artist, settled here after life in Italy. They had known Frederick Tennyson, at Florence, and the Brownings. A reminiscence of Mrs Browning was in the round table and the custom of moving it mesmerically and listening for its knockings when a sympathetic friend or two came to the cottage. Horatio Tennyson when in the island questioned the Brothertons'

table. And on more than one occasion Alfred hovered rather
wistfully, waiting for results which never came. Once it was after the
sudden death of Matthew Arnold. The blow had fallen sadly on
Tennyson, for he had looked to Arnold as his successor in the
Laureateship. The natural man craved for a message from the dead
in the cottage of his friend, where it would be safe from reporters.
Mrs Brotherton was one of the best of letter-writers; her health
permitted her no other writing, her income allowed her no
travelling or change: it was this quiet life which Tennyson cheered
by his friendship. The poet once appeared alone on his return from
Aldworth with a query, 'What do you think they are going to do to
me?' His friends from his tone hardly knew whether the answer was
to be a condolence or not. 'They are going to make me a lord.' He
went on and enumerated his reasons for refusing the honour at first.
'Is it not like putting a coronet on the head of a skull?' 'My sisters say I
shall have to pay more for my wine.' The poet was right in the
resistance he offered Mr Gladstone's wish. In those days a Laureate
was looked upon as the people's possession. The Radicals did not like
his peerage. Tennyson received anonymous letters and said to Mrs
Brotherton, 'I seem to live in an atmosphere of hate.' His old
shepherd on the farm and downs at Freshwater expressed his
satisfaction to Mrs Brotherton with these words: 'What a headpiece
that man has got! What do he not know? And he don't *look* it neither.
He don't seem to have no pride.'

NOTES

Mrs Warre-Cornish was a daughter of the Hon. William Ritchie (a cousin of
Thackeray) and a sister of Richmond Ritchie, who married Thackeray's
daughter (see p. 31). Her husband was Francis Warre-Cornish, author and
bibliophile, who became vice-provost and librarian at Eton College.

1. See p. 12.
2. See p. 50.
3. See p. 50.
4. See p. 35.
5. Henry Hallam (1777–1859), historian and father of Arthur Hallam.
6. See p. 20.
7. See p. 130.
8. Mudie's circulating library supplied books by post to provincial
subscribers.
9. Historical drama by Tennyson written in 1874–5 and published in
1875.
10. Margaret Oliphant (1828–97), prolific novelist and reviewer.
11. See p. 15.
12. Henry (later Sir Henry) Irving (1838–1905), actor associated with the

Lyceum Theatre. Nearly twenty years later, his performance in Tennyson's *Becket* was a notable success.

13. Émile Zola (1840–1902), French novelist, whose work became synonymous in England with coarse and even pornographic realism.

14. See p. 39.

15. See p. 109.

16. Mary Brotherton (1820–1910) published novels and poems.

17. See p. 197.

Aldworth*

LADY RITCHIE

Aldworth was built some twenty years ago, when Lady Tennyson had been ordered change, and Freshwater was found to be unbearable and overcrowded during the summer months. It must be borne in mind that to hospitable people there are dangers from friendly inroads as well as from the attacks of enemies. The new house, where for many years past the family has spent its summers, stands on the summit of a high, lonely hill in Surrey[sic], and yet it is not quite out of reach of London life. It is a white stone house with many broad windows facing a great view and a long terrace, like some one of those at Siena or Perugia, with a low parapet of stone, where ivies and roses are trained, making a foreground to the lovely haze of the distance. Sometimes at Aldworth, when the summer days are at their brightest, and Blackdown top has been well warmed and sunned, I have seen a little procession coming along the terrace walk, and proceeding by its green boundary into a garden, where the sun shines its hottest, upon a sheltered lawn, and where standard rose-trees burn their flames: Lord Tennyson, in his cloak, going first, perhaps dragging the garden chair in which Lady Tennyson was lying; Hallam Tennyson following, with rugs and cushions for the rest of the party. If the little grandsons and their mother, in her white dress and broad, shady hat, and Lionel Tennyson's boys, absorbed in their books of adventure, are there, the family group is complete. One special day I remember when we all sat for an hour round about the homely chair and its gentle occupant. It seemed not unlike a realisation of some Italian picture that I had somewhere seen: the tranquil eyes, the peaceful heights, the glorious summer day, some sense of lasting calm, of beauty beyond the present hour.

Records of Tennyson, Ruskin and Browning, pp. 55–6.

Lord Tennyson works alone in the early hours of the morning, and comes down long after his own frugal meal is over to find his guests assembling round the social breakfast-table. He generally goes out for a walk before luncheon, with his son and a friend, perhaps, and followed by a couple of dogs. Most of us know the look of the stately figure, the hanging cloak, and broad felt hat.

There used to be one little ceremony peculiar to the Tennyson family, and reminding one of some college custom which continued, that when dinner was over the guests used to be brought away into a second room, where stood a white table, upon which fruit and wine were set, and a fire burned bright, and a pleasant hour went by, while the master of the house sat in his carved chair and discoursed upon any topic suggested by his guests, or brought forth reminiscences of early Lincolnshire days, or from facts remembered out of the lives of past men who have been his friends. There was Rogers,[1] among the rest, for whom he had a great affection, with whom he constantly lived during that lonely time in London. 'I have dined alone with him,' I heard Lord Tennyson say, 'and we have talked about death till the tears rolled down his face.'

NOTES

On lady Ritchie, see p. 31. Aldworth is in Sussex, a few miles south of Haslemere and near the top of Blackdown. Tennyson laid the foundation-stone of the house on 23 April (Shakespeare's birthday) 1868. After the move there the Tennysons continued to winter at Farringford.

1. Samuel Rogers (1763–1855), veteran poet, declined the Laureateship in 1850. For Tennyson's comments on Rogers, see *Memoir*, ii, p. 72.

At Dickens's Funeral*

ANON.

I remember, when he went with me to Westminster Abbey to hear Dean Stanley[1] preach Dickens's funeral sermon, we sat within the rails of the Sacrarium so as to be near the pulpit, and when we came away he told me the story of the Oriental traveller who mistook the organ for the church's god. He was very fond of the story, and often

* *Tennyson and his Friends*, pp. 253–4.

repeated it. As he told it, the traveller was made to say, 'We went into one of their temples to see their worship. The temple is only opened sometimes, and they keep their god shut up in a great gold box at one end of it. When we passed inside the doors we heard him grumbling and growling as if out of humour at being disturbed in his solitude, and as the worshippers came in they knelt down and seemed to supplicate him and try to propitiate him. He became quieter for a while, only now and then grumbling for a few moments, but then he got louder again and the whole body of the people stood up and cried to him together, and after a while persuaded him to be still. Presently he began once more and then, after praying all together several times, they deputed one of their number to stand up alone and address him earnestly on their behalf, deprecating his anger. He spoke so long without an interruption that it seemed the god had either fallen asleep or been finally persuaded into a better temper; but suddenly at last he broke out into a greater passion than ever, and with such tremendous noise and roarings that all the worshippers rose from their seats in fright and ran out of the temple.'

There was an immense congregation that day in the Abbey—and when the service was over—we stood up waiting a long time to pass out through the rails. But instead of dispersing by the outer door the people all turned eastward and flocked towards the altar, pressing closer and closer up to the Sacrarium. The chances of getting out became less and less, and I turned to Tennyson and said, 'I don't know what all this means, but we seem so hemmed in that it is useless to move as yet.' Then a man, standing close by me whispered, 'I don't think they will go, sir, so long as your friend stands there.' Of course I saw at once what was happening—it had got to be known that Tennyson was present, and the solid throng was bent on seeing him. Such a popularity had never occurred to me or to him, and justified his nervous unwillingness to be seen in crowded places. I was obliged to tell him what was going on, upon which he urgently insisted on being let out some quiet way and putting an end to the dilemma.

NOTES

Dickens was buried on 14 June 1870. Tennyson had heard him read *A Christmas Carol* at Manchester in 1857.

1. Arthur Stanley (1815–81), Dean of Westminster from 1864 to 1881.

'A First Sight of Tennyson'*

EDMUND GOSSE

It was the early summer of 1871, and I was palely baking, like a crumpet, in a singularly horrible underground cage, made of steel bars, called the Den. This was a place such as no responsible being is allowed to live in nowadays, where the transcribers on the British Museum staff were immured in a half-light. . . . I was dolefully engaged here, being then one of the humblest of mankind, a Junior Assistant in the Printed Books Department of the British Museum, on some squalid task, in what was afterwards described by a witness as an atmosphere 'scented with rotten morocco, and an indescribable odour familiar in foreign barracks', when a Senior Assistant, one of the rare just spirits in that academical Dotheboys Hall, W. R. S. Ralston,[1] came dashing down the flights of curling steel staircase, to the danger of his six feet six of height, and of the beard that waved down to his waist. Over me he bent, and in a whisper (we were forbidden to speak out loud in the Den) he said, 'Come up stairs at once and be presented to Mr Tennyson!'

Proud young spirits of the present day, for whom life opens in adulation, will find it scarcely possible to realise what such a summons meant to me. As we climbed those steep and spiral staircases towards light and day, my heart pounded in my chest with agitation. The feeling of excitement was almost overwhelming: it was not peculiar to myself; such ardours were common in those years. Some day a philosopher must analyse it—that enthusiasm of the 1870s, that intoxicating belief in 'the might of poesy'. Tennyson was scarcely a human being to us, he was the God of the Golden Bow; I approached him now like a blank idiot about to be slain, 'or was I a worm, too low-crawling for death, O Delphic Apollo?' It is not merely that no person living now calls forth that kind of devotion, but the sentiment of mystery has disappeared. Not genius itself could survive the Kodak snapshots and the halfpenny newspapers.

It must, I suppose, have been one of those days on which the public was then excluded, since we found Tennyson, with a single companion, alone in what was then the long First Sculpture Gallery. His friend was James Spedding,[2] at whom in other conditions I

* *Selected Essays: First Series* (London: Heinemann, 1928) pp. 114–18.

should have gazed with interest, but in the Delphic presence he was not visible to my dazzled eyes. Mr Thornycroft's statue of the poet, now placed in Trinity College, gives an admirable impression of him at a slightly later date than 1871, if (that is) it is translated out of terms of white into terms of black. Tennyson, at that time, was still one of the darkest of men, as he is familiarly seen in all his earlier portraits. But those portraits do not give, although Mr Thornycroft has suggested, the singular majesty of his figure, standing in repose. Ralston, for all his six feet six, seemed to dwindle before this magnificent presence, while Tennyson stood, bare-headed among the Roman emperors, every inch as imperial-looking as the best of them. He stood there as we approached him, very still, with slightly dropping eyelids, and made no movement, no gesture of approach. When I had been presented, and had shaken his hand, he continued to consider me in a silence which would have been deeply disconcerting if it had not, somehow, seemed kindly, and even, absurd as it sounds, rather shy.

The stillness was broken by Ralston's irrelevantly mentioning that I was presently to start for Norway. The bard then began to talk about that country, which I was surprised to find he had visited some dozen years before. Ralston kindly engaged Spedding in conversation, so that Tennyson might now apply himself to me; with infinite goodness he did so, even 'making conversation', for I was hopelessly tongue-tied, and must, in fact, have cut a very poor figure. Tennyson, it miraculously appeared, had read some of my stammering verses,[3] and was vaguely gracious about them. He seemed to accept me as a sheep in the fold of which he was, so magnificently, the shepherd. This completed my undoing, but he did not demand from me speech. He returned to the subject of Norway, and said it was not the country for him to travel in, since you could only travel in it in funny little round carts, called *karjols*, which you must drive yourself, and that he was far too near-sighted for that. (I had instantly wondered at his double glasses, of a kind I had never seen before.)

Then somebody suggested that we should examine the works of art, which, in that solitude, we could delightfully do. Tennyson led us, and we stopped at any sculpture which attracted his notice. But the only remark which my memory has retained was made before the famous black bust of Antinous. Tennyson bent forward a little, and said, in his deep slow voice, 'Ah! this is the inscrutable Bithynian!' There was a pause, and then he added, gazing into the eyes of the bust: 'If we knew what he knew, we should understand the ancient world.' If I live to be a hundred years old, I shall still hear his rich tones as he said this, without emphasis, without affectation, as though he were speaking to himself. And soon after, the gates of heaven were closed, and I went down three flights of stairs to my hell of rotten morocco.

NOTES

Edmund Gosse (1849–1928), later well-known as a critic, had entered the British Museum in 1867.
1. W. R. Shedden-Ralston (1828–89), Slavonic scholar, worked at the British Museum (1853–75).
2. See p. 7.
3. Gosse was joint author of *Madrigals, Songs and Sonnets*, published the previous year.

Last Meeting*

EDWARD FITZGERALD

To Fanny Kemble from Woodbridge, 21 September 1876

Now too one's garden begins to be haunted by that spirit which Tennyson says is heard talking to himself among the flower-borders.[1] Do you remember him?

And now—who should send in his card to me last week—but the old poet himself—he and his elder son Hallam passing through Woodbridge from a tour in Norfolk. 'Dear old Fitz,' ran the card in pencil, 'We are passing thro'.' I had not seen him for twenty years—he looked much the same, except for his fallen locks; and what really surprised me was, that we fell at once into the old humour, as if we had only been parted twenty days instead of so many years. I suppose this is a sign of age—not altogether desirable. But so it was. He stayed two days, and we went over the same old grounds of debate, told some of the old stories, and all was well. I suppose I may never see him again: and so I suppose we both thought as the rail carried him off: and each returned to his ways as if scarcely diverted from them.

NOTES

On FitzGerald, see p. 7. For Hallam Tennyson's account of the visit, see *Memoir*, II, pp. 213–14. The reunion is recalled in Tennyson's superb

* *FitzGerald: Selected Works*, p. 692.

verse-epistle 'To E. FitzGerald' (Ricks, 398), written at about the time of his friend's death in June 1883.

1. The reference is to the opening lines of Tennyson's early 'Song' (Ricks, 86).

A Composer Remembers*

SIR CHARLES VILLIERS STANFORD

My first personal acquaintance with Lord Tennyson dates from Christmas 1879, when I spent a short time at Freshwater. Previously, however, in 1875, I had had experience of his thoughtful kindness. He had chosen me, an unknown and untried composer, to write the incidental music to his tragedy of *Queen Mary* for its production at the Lyceum Theatre, then under the management of Mrs Bateman. Many difficulties were put in the way of the performance of the music, into the causes for which I had neither the wish nor the means to penetrate. Finally, however, the management gave as an explanation that the music could not be performed, as the number of orchestral players required for its proper presentment would necessitate the sacrifice of two rows of stalls. To my young and disappointed soul came the news of a generous action which would have been a source of pride to many a composer of assured position and fame. The poet had offered, unknown to me, to bear the expense of the sacrificed seats for many nights, in order to allow my small share of the work to be heard. The offer was refused, but the generous action remains, one amongst the thousands of such quiet and stealthy kindnesses which came as second nature to him, and were probably as speedily forgotten by himself as they were lastingly remembered by their recipients.

My memories of Farringford are for the most part too sacred for print. Moreover, I shall never cease to be influenced by his own keen dislike of any public intrusion into his private life. I shall, therefore, only mention a few of the outer impressions which the house and its master made so indelibly upon me. The house essentially of a poet, but of one who, himself secluded, had the life of all contemporary humanity consistently and unbrokenly before him: a house which gave a sense of restfulness from the moment its threshold was

* *Studies and Memories* (London: Constable, 1908) pp. 90–5, 97–8. (The chapter on Tennyson is reprinted from the *Cambridge Review* for 15 Oct 1892).

crossed: full of memories of great minds both in picture and in book: a thoroughly English hearth which was so homely that the veriest stranger at once felt himself insensibly to be part of the household. There were many little customs which endeared it to men of different stamp and pursuit. To a university man, for instance, it seemed only surprisingly natural to find that, after dinner was over, dessert was laid on the bare mahogany in another room after the fashion of a college combination room. Tennyson's life was one of the most wholesome regularity. The daily walk from 11 to 1 and the shorter stroll in the afternoon were timed to the moment. Sometimes on returning from his morning walk he would find that he had taken five minutes less than his fixed two hours, and would insist upon finishing the allotted period by pacing up and down in front of the door. These two hours were the delight of those privileged to be his companions; an unceasing flow of reminiscences, of humorous stories and of wise sayings made the time pass with much begrudged rapidity. His favourite walks were along the Downs to the Beacon and back by the foot of the hill, and to Totland Bay through the grounds of 'ideal' Ward[1]—'Most generous of Ultramontanes—Ward'.

His sight though very short was most extraordinarily keen for small objects, and for microscopically tiny details which would escape the notice of men with apparently four times his power of vision. It was easy after one of these walks to understand what made him the greatest English landscape painter of the day. His memory was startling. Only a year and a half ago (when he was eighty-one), sitting in the conservatory beside Mr Ward's house, the conversation turned on Andrew Marvell. My companion, Mr Arthur Coleridge,[2] and I were amazed to hear him suddenly roll out some thirty lines of his poetry without a hesitation or halt, as an illustration of his criticism.

His manner of reading poetry has often been described. It was a chant rather than a declamation. A voice of deep and penetrating power, varied only by alteration of note and by intensity of quality. The notes were few, and he rarely read on more than two, except at the cadence of a passage, when the voice would slightly fall. He often accompanied his reading by gentle rippling gestures with his fingers. As a rule he adhered more to the quantity of a line than the ordinary reciter, for he had the rare gift of making the accent felt, without perceptibly altering the prosody. Without being a musician, he had a great appreciation of the fitness of music to its subjects, and was an unfailing judge of musical declamation. As he expressed it himself, he disliked music which went up when it ought to go down, and went down when it ought to go up. I never knew him wrong in his suggestions on this point. The most vivid instance I can recall was about a line in 'The Revenge'—'Was he devil or man? He was devil for aught they knew.' When I played him my setting, the word 'devil' was set to a higher note in the question than it was in the answer; and the penultimate word 'they' was unaccented. He at once corrected me, saying that the second word 'devil' must be higher and stronger than the first, and the 'they' must be marked. He was perfectly right, and I altered it accordingly. It was apparently a small point, but it was this insisting on perfection of detail which made him the most valuable teacher of accurate declamation that it was possible for a composer to learn from. Of all his poems which I heard him read, those he made most impressive were 'The Revenge', and the 'Ode on the Duke of Wellington'. It may be interesting to record a point in the latter which, he said, was often misread. The line 'Let the bell be toll'd', he read with strong emphasis upon the first as well as the third and fifth words, ‿‿‿ not ‿‿‿‿. He said it wanted three strokes of the bell, not two. *Maud* he also read with a most extraordinary warmth and charm, particularly the climax of 'Come into the garden' and still more the stanza about the shell (part II) which he gave in a peculiarly thin and ghostly tone of voice, a quality he also used with great mastery in the Choric Song of 'The Lotos Eaters'. Nor was he less impressive when reciting Greek or German. Greek he vastly preferred as pronounced in the English fashion. He said it lost all its sonority and grandeur if modernised; and indeed to hear his illustration was in itself sufficient to convince. German he pronounced with a strong English accent, and yet I feel sure that Goethe himself would have acknowledged his reading of 'Kennst du das Land' to be a masterpiece. He was a great admirer of Goethe, and especially of this poem. He once read to me from his works for nearly half an hour.

The secret of the harmony of his verse lay in his incomparable ear for the juxtaposition of vowels and the exact suitability of each consonant. This makes it difficult to set his poems adequately to music. The music is so inborn in the poetry itself that it does not ask for notes to make incompleteness complete, and music is set to it rather for additional illustration than from inherent necessity. In discussing the sound of perfect lines, he told me that he considered the best line he ever wrote to be 'The mellow ouzel fluted in the elm' ('The Gardener's Daughter').

He had an inexhaustible fund of anecdote, at times serious, at times humorous. He would often light up a point with a turn of expression which showed the inward fire of poetry which permeated him; such as when describing his visit to Valentia in 1848, 'I looked out over the ocean with all the revolutions in Europe behind me.' . . .

He had to the end of his life raven-black hair without a streak of grey; I well remember his playful imitation of anger when some versifier sent him an autograph poem, closing with a prayer to be allowed to 'lay this wreath upon the poet's silvery locks'. This he tossed across the sofa with the words, 'And I never had a grey hair in my head in my life.' But perhaps what was most remarkable about him was his hand. Massive and large, with long broad fingers square to the tips, and a softness of the palm which was always a surprise. It felt like a cushion of soft velvet, which fitted itself to every cranny of the hand it pressed. It always seemed to me the outward and visible sign of his noble nature. Strength, greatness, and grasp unmistakable, with an immense fund of tenderness which seemed to make itself felt without necessity of show. The intellect of a giant with the heart of a child. So great a power of sympathy, that to men of all ages he seemed a contemporary. Nothing in him grew old save his bodily frame; up to his death he lived not in the past but in the present with that rare prophetic instinct which kept him looking forward to the future.

NOTES

Charles Villiers Stanford (1852–1924), composer, educated at Trinity College, Cambridge, and for nearly forty years Professor of Music at Cambridge; knighted in 1901. He was only twenty-four when Tennyson asked him to write the incidental music for *Queen Mary*; later he wrote the music for *Becket*.

1. See p. 109.
2. A legal official whose grandfather was an elder brother of Samuel Taylor Coleridge. In 1890, when Tennyson was nearly eighty-one, his wife wrote in a letter to Palgrave, 'He has walked an hour and a half or two hours before luncheon, many days, between Mr Arthur Coleridge and Dr Stanford, all three telling merry stories' (*Memoir*, ii, p. 369).

Visits to Aldworth*

WILLIAM ALLINGHAM

Thursday, 5 August 1880. Haslemere—very fine; Helen and I started about 3.30 to walk to Tennyson's, as invited. In the shady lane the carriage overtook us, T. had kindly called for us. He was in the carriage with his little grandson, Alfred, in his nurse's lap, and Mr Fields, an American guest. Little Alfred, aged three, had on the great Alfred's black sombrero, and the child's straw hat with a blue

* *William Allingham: a Diary,*, pp. 286–304, 320, 323–40, 344–5.

ribbon was stuck on the top of the poet's huge head, and so they drove gravely along. I followed on foot along the heath-fringed road on Blackdown, overlooking the vast expanses of light and shadow, golden cornfields, blue distances, from Leith Hill to Chanctonbury Ring. Walked through the house, long hall open at each end, and found tea on the further lawn, smooth, shut in with shrubs. The view of the lower windows of the house is now shut out by the growth of twigs and leaves. A. T. in sombrero and grey suit, broad-shouldered. He has been at Venice, Cadore, etc., with Hallam.

T. took me to a top room and out on the balcony to see 'the enormous view'. 'I sometimes see a spire out yonder (due east), but I don't know what it is.' Horsham I suggest, adding, 'Field Place is near it, Shelley's birthplace.' Below, H. sketched Don, the handsome old setter, Hallam keeping him quiet.

T.—'I gave Irving my *Thomas à Becket*. He said it was magnificent, but it would cost £3000 to mount it,—*he* couldn't afford the risk.[1] If well put on the stage, it would act for a time, and it would bring me credit—but it wouldn't pay. The success of a piece doesn't depend on its literary merit or even on its stage effect, but on its *hitting* somehow. Miss Terry said "we act mechanically after a long run—but on a first night nobody suspects how we have our hearts in our mouths!" '

T. did not much approve Irving's *Shylock*. 'He made you pity Shylock too much. I told Miss Terry she ought, as advocate, to stand on the steps to gain advantage, instead of standing on the level— a little female thing—and looking up at him. The worst of writing for the stage is you must keep some actor always in your mind.'

Sunday, 8 August 1880. Helen and I walked up—reached the house about 4. Tennyson on the front terrace with his two dogs, Don and Grig. He asked Helen had she brought her paints to finish Don's portrait. 'No—why not? Sunday? No one with wits in their brain would object. It's as allowable as lawn-tennis. Boys play cricket now on a Sunday. It's High Church to play cricket.'

Lord Lytton's return from India.[2] T. spoke in his favour. I object—the Afghan War, etc.

T.—'How can we know the rights and wrongs?'

W. A.—'An intelligent man has both the means and the right to form an opinion on public affairs now-a-days. The main particulars are soon published.'

T.—'I was arguing with the Duke of Argyll[3] about Romania and Turkey, and said to him, Why don't you answer me? He said, "You haven't read the Blue Books." '

Matthew Arnold—' "Something outside of us that makes for

righteousness"[4]—ugh!' (This is a sort of grunt of disgust very usual with T.)

'I was asked by some one in London, "Shall I ask M. A.?" I said I didn't much like dining with gods!'

T. praised in a general way 'Thyrsis' and 'The Scholar-Gipsy'.[5] ' "Thyrsis" very artificial', I thought.

'So is "Lycidas",' he said.

'But "Lycidas" came first and was in the spirit of its age.'

I brought in my hand Ferguson's *Poems*,[6] the volume published in May. T. looked into it but soon put it down. He read 'The Widow's Cloak'—'I don't much care for it; I can't read anything, much less poetry. On account of my eyes—yes—the doctor says I must only read for half an hour at a time. I shouldn't like both eyes to go. Everything now looks as in a very dusky twilight.'

He asked had I read Browning's new volume?[7] ' "Clive" is the best.' . . .

At dinner—the account in a New York paper (*The Tribune*) of Lionel's wedding—'the Poet Laureate, bent figure and tottering gait'.

'Why, there were five steps to come down,—no one had told me of them; I was looking for them in the obscurity, lest I should tumble on my nose.'

Then T. spoke of satire in general. 'It's quite dreadful to think of how satire will endure, no matter how unfair, if well written. Look at Pope—

> Now night descending, the proud scene was o'er,
> But liv'd in Settle's numbers one day more.[8]

The perfection of that brings tears into one's eyes—and it pillories Settle for ever! Everything will be in the British Museum—even the newspapers.'

We agreed on the absurdity of accumulating newspapers there, too many books even. But how select?—Who is to be empowered to do it?

A.—'Carlyle declares his father was the strongest-minded man he knew, yet he would admit no poetry into his house.'

T.—'He was right.'

A.—'Nor fiction of any sort.'

T.—'There he was wrong. But I suppose he was an old Puritan.'

T. denounced vivisection most fiercely: declared he would not owe his own life to a cruel experiment on a dog.

He made Helen taste his wine (Vouvray) from his own glass, and took her into the drawing-room.

'If the pronunciation of the English language were forgotten,

Browning would be held the greatest of modern poets, having treated the greatest variety of subjects in a powerful manner.'

Friday, 13 August 1880. Helen and I with the babes to Tennyson's. He sits on chair beside us. Two Miss ——s call (very old family). Tennyson tells us afterwards 'A former Lord H——, queer old fellow—was found on his knees near the kitchen one day riddling the cinders—he looked up and said, "Dick never riddles 'em right." He kept his two daughters in the nursery till they were thirty, and then they climbed over the garden wall and ran away. The young ladies today would have my autograph—ugh! I said, "The glory of your presence has got it. I would never have sent it if you had asked by letter." '

Fair and dark people—dark people are thinner skinned.

T.—'I am. A countryman in the North said, "A wouldn't be as black as him for summat!" At Dieppe the touter appealed to me as French, Spanish, Italian—and at last said in astonishment "Vous êtes anglais!" But my brother Frederick, a white and rosy man, got much more admiration when we travelled together—he was adored by all the landladies and chambermaids.'

'The New Forest is the finest thing in England, the most peculiar. There are mountains elsewhere, and cliffs, and lakes. When Palgrave and I came back from Spain we went to the New Forest, and as we lay under great trees with a green heaven above our heads I said, "We saw nothing so fine as this in Spain," and he said, "No." '

Friday, 20 August 1880. Helen and I walk to T.'s. Blackdown now purple with ling and heather. Lawn: Mrs Tennyson in invalid chair.

Mr Edward Lear coming on Monday—one of twenty children—drew birds at fourteen to help his family. Improvises on pianoforte.

A. T. and Hallam—Browning's *Dramatic Idyls*.

T.—'I wish he hadn't taken my word "idyll". I said the other day and you took it as a jest, but I meant it seriously, "if the pronunciation of the English language were lost, Browning would be considered the greatest of modern poets".'

W. A.—'A basis of good sense is often wanting in him.'

T.—'I don't perceive that.'

W. A.—'What do you make of *Fifine*?'[9]

T.—'I couldn't make anything of it. I tried it several times, and took it in my pocket on a walk—that's the best way to try.'

Sunday, 29 August 1880. Hallam calls. Helen and I walk up to Aldworth. Find A. T. on seat at end of lower terrace, reading a large type New Testament. We sit beside him.

Tennyson shows me a paper by Mr Crookes (Royal Society) on

'Four Kinds of Matter', solid, liquid, gaseous, and another which is imperceptible to the senses (sometimes called 'ether'). Molecules and atoms.

T. said (or something like this)—'I believe we never see matter: what we count the material world is only an appearance.'

Huxley's question, 'Has a frog a soul?'

W. A.—'I should first ask, "What do you mean by Soul?" But Huxley says questions about "soul" and "the future" don't interest him.'

T.—'Then, surely, that shows defect in him! Tyndall's metaphysics are very shaky, I think. They don't see that they are destroying their country.

'Old Sedgwick[10] told me he visited Laplace[11] in his last days and the old astronomer said to him, "You are an Englishman, suffer me to say to you a word or two on politics. Never emancipate the Catholics, and never tamper with your glorious constitution." '

Tennyson dislikes our quitting Afghanistan—'The want of continuity in our policy is the curse of our country; I believe Parliaments will be its ruin. We might have ruled the Afghans and made them good subjects, like the Sikhs.'[12]

I said England had no business in Afghanistan. Lord Beaconsfield's[13] policy was disapproved by Lord Lawrence, Lord Northbrook, and a majority of the Council of India. T. stuck to his own views. I told him, 'you always declare England to be right, whatever she does.'

T.—'I think she's often shockingly wrong. In this case it's unsafe to draw back.'

Speaking of the Irish agitator who said, 'I think their cattle will not much prosper'—a speech followed by the maiming of many animals—he exclaimed, 'How I hate that man—Ireland's a dreadful country! I heartily wish it was in the middle of the Atlantic.'

'Below the surface?' I asked.

'No, no, a thousand miles away from England. I like the Irish —I admit the charm of their manners—but they're a fearful nuisance.'

'Very troublesome,' I admitted, 'but there's some truth in the popular Irish notion that nothing can be got from England except by agitation.'

T. is a constant novel reader. 'What I dislike is beginning a new novel. I should like to have a novel to read in a million volumes, to last me my life.'

Thursday, 2 September 1880.   Drove up to Tennyson's to dinner. H. and I., Aubrey de Vere,[14] Dr Bradley,[15] Mrs and Miss Bradley.

A. T., Aubrey de Vere and I talk of poetry.

T. and I agree on the odiousness of various readings inserted on a poet's page—and of critical notes.

De Vere blames Ruskin for his recent remarks on Wordsworth—'a Westmorland peasant, etc.'.[16]

De V. wishes Wordsworth had written his *magnum opus*, of which *The Prelude* was the beginning.

T.—'His small things are the best. Even his "Tintern Abbey", fine as it is, should have been much compressed.'

De V.—'But if it pleased the artistic sense more, might it not appeal less to the sympathies?'

T.—'A great deal might be left out.'

W. A.—'One could turn the largest part of *The Excursion* into prose, very seldom altering a word, merely re-arranging. Here and there a line or a passage of poetry would be left, like a quotation. It is much easier to write bad blank verse than good prose.'

T.—'And it is much easier to write rhyme than good blank verse. I should not be sorry to lose anything from a poet which is not beautiful poetry. One plods over Wordsworth's long dreary plains of prose—one knows there's a mountain somewhere, and now and again you come to astonishing things. In old times, when copying was costly, Catullus, Horace, and the others gave only their best.'

De V.—'Wordsworth ought to have done great and perfect things, one fancies. He lived a poetic life, he devoted himself to poetry,—How was it?'

W. A.—'For many years he never read any poetry but his own. His mind became monotonous.'

De V.—'I believe that is true. And he was continually touching and altering, and sometimes injuring what he had written.'

W. A.—'His experience of real life was neither wide nor various. His material ran short.'

De V.—'And yet, if he gives us a good deal of dullness, might not the same be said of Homer and of Milton?'

T. (grunts)—'No, no!'

De V.—'Well, I find a great deal of Homer very dull—and surely the last six books of *Paradise Lost* are much below the first six?'

T.—'Possibly—but there's the charm of Milton's style. He invented his verse—just as much as Virgil invented his.'

De V.—'I read to Wordsworth your "Of old sat Freedom on the heights", and "You ask me, why, tho' ill at ease", and he said, "Fine poetry and very stately diction."'

T. said 'H'm!' contentedly.

W. A.—'Coleridge was more essentially a poet than Wordworth.'

T.—'I don't know that.'

De V.—'I think so. But how melancholy to think that all his finest

poems were produced in one single year of his life. Then he went to
Germany and took to metaphysics—such a pity!'

T.—'But the man I count greater than them all—Wordsworth,
Coleridge, Byron, Shelley, every one of 'em—is Keats, who died at
twenty-five—thousands of faults! (twiddling the fingers of one hand
in the air)—but he's wonderful!'

De V.—'He doesn't pall upon you?'

T.—'No.'

De V.—'Shelley used to be a great idol of yours.'

T.—'O yes. We lived near the most prosaic village in the world, a
little beast! where they had never heard of anything. One day we
went there to meet my brother Frederick, who was coming back
from somewhere, and as we were driving home he whispered, "I've
got a poet who's much grander than Byron", and repeated one line,
"Waterfalls leap among wild islands green", which I thought
delicious.

'Alastor was the first poem of his I read. I said, "This is what I
want!"—and still I like it the best, though one can't tell how much
these first loves are to be trusted. The Revolt of Islam is splendid but
gives me a headache—it's fatiguing—all mountain tops and glories.'

De V. agreed, and named as his favourites 'The Ode to the West
Wind'—'Ode to Naples'—(of which he recited some lines, and
another piece).

Tennyson quoted a passage from Shelley and said, 'What can you
do with a man who has such command of language? But Keats was
not wild and wilful, he had always an intention. At the same time he
was daimonisch—he had a touch (he was a livery-stable keeper's
son—I don't know where he got it from, unless from Heaven).

> Perhaps the self-same song that found a path
>   Through the sad heart of Ruth when, sick for home,
>   She stood in tears amid the alien corn;
>   The same that oft-times hath
>   Charm'd magic casements opening on the foam
>   Of perilous seas, in faery lands forlorn.

'What can be lovelier? (He said the last two lines again.) I once saw it
printed "In fairyland forlorn", which totally ruined it—one doesn't
know why.'

W. A.—' "Fairyland" has been much used.'

When I shook hands with him he said, 'Good-night, Statuette!' I
laughed and said, 'I know what you mean.' (A little poem in my
Songs, Ballads and Stories, a volume Hallam borrowed of me yesterday
and which T. had not seen before.)

T.—'It's modest—and it may be quite true. No one can in the least tell who will survive.'

We went out to the porch, T., Hallam, De Vere, Helen and I, with lantern—brilliant starry night.

T.—'Millions upon millions of suns.'

W. A.—'And Whewell[17] argues that the earth is probably the only seat of conscious life. Suppose one looking from a distance at the Earth, a dot among other dots.'

T.—'That's just what I said at the time.'

We parted, and H. and I followed our lantern-gleam on the heath and down the shady lane to Haslemere.

Sunday, 19 September 1880. Rain—clears. H. and I walk to Aldworth—glorious prospects, breadth of sunshine and shadow— green woodlands, bounding hills, blue distances—sweet cool air. Mrs Tennyson very friendly.

T.—'A lady the other day here—a very nice woman (I don't altogether like the word, but I want it), was praising a friend of yours. "Nice" is objectionable, but it is useful—a "nice" person is one that you're satisfied with.'

W. A.—'It used to mean fastidious,—discriminative, but there's not much harm in its being turned about and applied to the object.'

T.—'No: it's something or somebody that satisfies your nice-ness.' . . .

Dinner, pleasant and lively talk.

T.—'A Russian noble, who spoke English well, said one morning to an English guest, "I've shot two peasants this morning."—"Pardon me, you mean pheasants." "No, indeed, two men—they were insolent and I shot them." '

W. A.—'In Ireland it's the other way.'

T.—'Couldn't they blow up that horrible island with dynamite and carry it off in pieces—a long way off?

W. A.—'Why did the English go there?'

T.—'Why did the Normans come to England? The Normans came over here and seized the country, and in a hundred years the English had forgotten all about it, and they were all living together on good terms.'

(I demurred: T. went on, raising his voice).—'The same Normans went to Ireland, and the Irish with their damned, unreasonableness are raging and foaming to this hour!'

W. A.—'The Norman Duke had a claim on the crown of England.'

T.—'No rightful claim.'

W. A.—'But suppose all these to be bygones. You speak of a century, a short time in history—think what Ireland had to complain of only in the last century—the penal laws, and the deliberate destruction of their growing industry by the English Government: what do you say to that?'

T.—'That was brutal! Our ancestors *were* horrible brutes! And the celts are very charming and sweet and poetic. I love their Ossians and their Finns and so forth—but they are most damnably unreasonable!'

W. A.—'They are most unfortunate.'

Hallam.—'What would you do?'

W. A.—'This last phase of discontent is perhaps the worst—flavoured with Americanism and general irreverence; but what I would have done long ago I would try still—encourage peasant proprietorship to the utmost possible.'

Hallam.—'Get rid of all the landlords and give the land to the people?'

W. A.—'Not at all. There are many good Irish landlords, and they usually get on well with their tenants. The peasant proprietors would have to be made gradually, and on business principles.'

T.—'What is the difference between an English landlord and an Irish landlord?'

W. A.—'Is it a conundrum?'

T.—'Not at all.'

(I tried to explain some great differences. T. came back to his old point.)

T.—'The Celts are so utterly unreasonable! The stupid clumsy Englishman—knock him down, kick him under the tail, kick him under the chin, do anything to him, he gets on his legs again and goes on; the Celt rages and shrieks and tears everything to pieces!'

Tennyson spoke of the 'sea of silver mist' seen at early morning from his windows at this season—also of the effect of mist spread over the wide green woodland and the sun shining on it—'incredible! Turner[18] would have tried it.'

Mrs T. thought it a great pity that the French Government was interfering with the Religious Orders—even those that nursed the sick. I said they were dealing with the Church of Rome as a great political power, known to be adverse to the Republic.

T. spoke of Venice. 'We stayed too short a time—the Giant's Stairs are very fine. Milan Cathedral struck me far more than St Mark's.'

I quoted, 'A mount of marble! a hundred spires!'

T.—'Well, that's what it seemed like. Plenty to object to, no doubt—but the great coloured windows are wonderful Putting together the little I have seen of Italy, this time and the first time, I think the great charm is the number of old cities, so various, each with a character of its own.'

We talked of London. T. has a vague notion that he would like to live there. 'Chelsea Embankment is a charming place—I could live there all the year.' Hallam (*sotto voce*).—'He always get tired of London in a fortnight.'

I referred to Emerson's essay (in *Society and Solitude*), that the feeling of Age is often less in ourselves than in our consciousness of being looked upon as old by others.

T. (partly agreeing).—'Yes; I feel younger in some ways than when I was fifty.'

In talking of London, we spoke of old nooks and corners, old taverns, 'Bertolini's', off Leicester Square, now shut up; old Mr Seymour—who dined there fifty years, etc.; 'The Cock'—'Dick's'.

T.—'I had a room at "Dick's" once—I often dined at "The Rainbow".'

He has, amid his ruralism, longings now and again for the humours of London streets; but alas he cannot easily go about without provoking notice. An Irish flower girl said to T. in Regent St, 'Ah, sure now, Misther Tinnison, ye'll buy this little nosegay!'

Thursday, 23 September 1880. H. and I walked up to Aldworth to dinner.

Dr Johnson.—T.: 'I don't think I should have liked his company, but like Boswell's book.'

Byron.—T.: 'When a boy I used to worship him. But I do think Byron great. His *Vision of Judgement* is the most wonderful thing in the world.' Then T. quoted for *Don Juan*—'Then rose from sea to sky the wild farewell', etc.

I said 'The Shipwreck' as a whole was not good.

T.—'The famous lines about the sea in *Childe Harold* are abominably bad.'

We examined them. I suggested 'Thy waters washèd them while they were free' as possible, but T. truly thought 'washed' was not like Byron; he was more likely to write 'washed', sense or no sense.

Ruskin's criticisms on Byron in the *Nineteenth Century*. 'After reading them I read "The Island" through the other night.'

'Well, did you find much in it?

'No.'

'And what Ruskin calls the finest line ever written by an Englishman about the sea—

> the swell
> Of Ocean's Alpine azure rose and fell.

T.—'The open vowels are good. I don't know what is meant by "Alpine azure". And certainly that about the rivulet falling from the cliff being like a goat's eye is very bad.'

W. A.—'What did you think of Ruskin's article altogether?'

T.—'I thought his remarks on the passage in Shakespeare very good—on the fitness of the placing of words.'

Tennyson drives into Haslemere; he sits in our garden and looks at newspaper—admires the uphill garden and fir trees: 'it is like one at Florence. The south of England is like Italy. When I came back this summer and looked from the terrace at Blackdown, I thought it was exactly like Italy.'

[*In the evening at Aldworth*.] T. read us the 'Bugle song'. I said 'That's Killarney.'

T.—'Yes, it was Killarney suggested it. The bugle echoes were wonderful—nine times—at last like a chant of angels in the sky. But when I was there afterwards I could only hear two echoes—from the state of the air. I complained of this and said, "when I was here before I heard nine". "Oh!" says the bugler, "then you're the gintleman that's brought so much money to the place!" ' (The 'Bugle song' increased the number of tourists to Killarney.)

He said an Irish lady asked him how he liked the scenery—'Too much bog,' he thought, 'black and dismal.' 'O then, where,' she retorted in tones of indignation—'where would you have the poor people cut their turf?'

Afterwards Tennyson read to us from his new unpublished volume,[19] 'The Cobbler with his Gin Bottle', 'The Entail or the Village Wife'—'one of those gossiping beasts!' he said.

Wednesday, 13 October 1880.   Tennyson and I drive in his carriage up Hindhead as far as the Huts, to look for gypsies, but find none.

T.—'Old Hallam used to say the longer one lived the higher one rated Dryden as a poet.'

W. A.—'I should say that to rate Dryden very high is proof of a non-poetic mind.'

Helen, at his wish, made a sketch of the landscape as seen through one of the arches of the porch. T., looking over her, said, 'I suppose I owe you £20 for this?' H. said the payment would be to give her a sitting or two, and he gave in rather grumblingly; hitherto he had refused, and said one day, 'I'll go out of the room if you look at me!'

H. had two or three short sittings in his study, with fading light, and made a couple of beginnings. He promised to sit again when we next met. I talked to him while he sat, and tried to keep him from looking unhappy. He gave Helen a copy of the collected edition of his brother Charles's sonnets,[20] about to be published, and one day read several of them to her with great feeling and warm praise. He read the sonnet I said had impressed me a year ago. T. said; 'I know the place, the road, everything.'

He spoke of the objection that the sonnets were not in perfect sonnet form, and said, 'I never care to read a perfect sonnet. I look down the rhymes and that's enough. I thought the other day of writing a sonnet beginning, 'I hate the perfect Sonnet!' After going on for four lines I should say,

> And now there's "down" and "crown" and "frown" and "brown":
> I'll take the latter. Then there's "cheer" and "fear"—
> And several others,—

and so forth, would it be worth doing?'

T. often speaks of the absolute need of delicacy of elocution to give the true beauty of poetry.

T.—'Rogers[21] used to quote with approval the praise of good verse by some Frenchman who declared it to be *beau comme prose*, that is, as easy and natural.'

T.—'I'm seventy-*nine* (this was a joke), but I don't feel the weight of age on my shoulders. I can run uphill; I can waltz—but when I said this to Fanny Kemble[22] she replied in a ghastly voice, "I hope I shall never see you do it!" '

He read us very powerfully the poem of the mother and the gibbet. I objected to the title of 'Rizpah' (in private life he called it 'Bones'), and also to an explanatory note (now omitted) prefixed to the piece. The lady who gave him the story called it 'The Modern Rizpah'. She gave it as true, the scene near Brighthelmstown, but dates and other particulars vague.[23]—

Thursday, 21 October 1880. Haslemere. Our last visit (this time) to Aldworth. Snow on the ground. We all drive up.

The Wordsworth Society.—T. entirely objects to it. 'They'll give one a disgust for Wordsworth. Why can't people be quiet? Ugh!

'Reading magazines breaks one's mind all to bits. One ought to leave off newspapers.

'A servant woman that left us told somebody in her next place: "She is an *angel*, but he—why he's only a public writer." ' (T. often says English people have no respect for poets.)

Looking at the chimney-piece, T. said, 'When I began to read Italian, I wrote down every word that puzzled me on the sides and front of the chimney-piece where I lodged—painted white—and made a kind of dictionary for myself. I went away for two or three days and when I came back it was all washed off. "Thought it was dirt", the woman said.

'Worse than that—when I was twenty-two I wrote a beautiful poem on Poland, hundreds of lines long, and the housemaid lit the fire with it. I never could recover it.'

Tennyson repeated some lines of his own from an old idyll never published, they were something like this:

> The rich wed richer, and the poor the poor,
> The mount of gold accumulating still,
> The gulf of want enlarging, deepening, till
> The one into the other sink at last
> With all confusion.

'That's not quite the thing—"all confusion". Oh, I've written thousands of lines that went up the chimney.'

After dinner Tennyson called on Hallam to sing 'John Brown', which he accordingly began in a strong bass voice, T. joining in (the first time I ever heard him try any musical performance), and sometimes thumping with his fists on the table—

> John Brown's body lies mouldering in the grave,
> But his soul is marching on!

He urged Hallam to go on, saying, 'I like it, I like it', but Hallam thought the noise too great, and drew off. The soul marching on delighted Tennyson.

In the evening he read us in the drawing-room 'The Voyage of Maeldune' (from Joyce's *Old Celtic Romances*).[24]

T.—'At first I made half the men kill the other half in every fray, and Maeldune himself return *alone*.'

I said the Irish were fond of extravagant stories, somewhat in the manner of Rabelais, and told him of another, where the hero travelled by land. We talked of subjects for poems, and T. said 'I want something quite mad.'

After eleven we went home in T.'s carriage, happy with the good company and friendly kindness.

1883.   He spoke of Edward FitzGerald—had not seen him for years before his death; FitzGerald could not be got to visit.[25]

'But no sort of quarrel?'

'O no! fancy my quarrelling with dear old Fitz!'

We talked a little about the steam voyage with Gladstone.[26]

'Why did you read "The Grandmother" to the great folk?'

T.—'The Princess of Wales asked for it; she had heard Mrs Greville read it. I read it in a cabin on deck; the Princess sat close to me on one side and a young lady whom I didn't know on the other. The wind came through an open window and the Princess whispered "Put on your hat"—but I said I ought if possible to make myself balder than ever before so many Royalties! She said again, "Oh put it on!" so I did, and I heard afterwards that the King of Denmark's court-fool who was in the background (they really keep a court-fool) remarked, "He may be Laureate, but he has not learnt court manners."

'When I was done the ladies praised me, and I patted the unknown one on the back by way of reply, and presently I found out she was the Empress of Russia.'

'Had you any talk with the Czar?'

'Hardly any—he said he couldn't speak English. Perhaps he was disgusted at my patting his wife on the back. His head was up in the cabin ceiling as he walked about below.'

Saturday, 26 July 1884. Witley. After much urging from H. (I have always a rooted belief that people don't really want to see me) I went to Haslemere today: cool with showers: and walked up to Aldworth, arriving about 3 p.m. Found an arch in Avenue, 'Welcome Home'— so the bride and bridegroom are back. 'Lady Tennyson'—'Yes sir'—on her sofa, sweet, pale and friendly.

Enter Hallam, looking stouter and face broadened. He tries his Father's door. 'Come in', and there was T., just wakened from his usual nap—glad to see me, and says, 'I've done an Irish poem and I want you to help me with the brogue. But you're from the North.'

I told him I knew various Irish brogues—had he chosen any one in particular?

'No.'

He took up Carleton's *Traits and Stories*, which he was reading for the first time (to get up the brogue), and was delighted with, all the more for its caricature. Then he produced the MS of 'Molly Maghee'[27] (I asked him to strike out the 'h'), and we spent about an hour over it. First Tennyson read the piece to me, I commenting on it; then I read it to him, he looking over my arm the while. Aubrey de Vere gave him the subject, as a fact—the body of a man drowned in a bog-hole found undecayed after forty years or so. His old sweetheart recognises him and drops down 'dead on the dead'. The same incident is told of a Cornish miner, and I published a prose story upon it in Leigh Hunt's journal.[28] Hamilton Aïdé[29] has a poem on the same subject. I suggested many corrections in the brogue, and some in other points. I told T. the Irish would not like it, but he didn't see why not.

I am pressed to stay for dinner, and then to stay the night— consent, and send telegram to Helen. Then T. and I, in rain, make a little run in the copses to a new summer-house with a writing-table and pens, and a vista cut in front to see the vast view of the weald, etc. Dinner at 6.30. Stay a little with Lady T. and Hallam: then drawing-room, where T. at table close to window with Mrs Hallam—wine and strawberries.

He thinks England is entering on gloomy times—perhaps coming to the end of her grandeur and glory. 'Goschen feels the same—is much depressed about it, the Lord Chancellor too. I voted for the franchise to avoid worse things.'

I said I wished he had voted against pigeon torture.

Hallam.—'So do I.'

T. said nothing, but I stuck to the subject.

'Hope you'll vote for the Bill next time.'

'Don't think I'll ever go into the House again.'

'Well, you can pair.'

'Lecky says the Irish want a despot', and T. agrees.

'The English are not poetical or musical or clever—they're very stupid and heavy—but they are for reasonable and constitutional liberty, that a man should have his own opinion without being knocked on the head for it. In Ireland, if I don't agree with a man, he shoots me or knocks my brains out! I never knew a rational Irishman in my life! except you' (this *sounded* very parenthetical), 'and you don't care a pin for the grand Empire of England. You ought to be proud surely to be part of it. There you are, with an English name, English in every way, but you happened to be born in Ireland, therefore you are for it.'

I pleaded that I was more impartial than most people; 'if I were Nationalist I might be popular in Ireland and perhaps get into Parliament if I liked. My brother was offered a seat for Waterford free of cost.'

T.—'I hate to think of Ireland. Here they are, after 700 years raging and roaring.'

W. A.—'A most unlucky country!' (to which Hallam agreed). 'Suppose England tried leaving them to themselves.'

T.—'Civil war!'

W. A.—'Then let them settle it. England would be able to take care of herself.'

T.—'Ireland might join with France against England.'

W. A.—'Another plan: take away all franchise and representation from Ireland for seven years, letting her manage her local affairs as she pleases.'

T.—'They would roar incessantly. I hate speaking of it!' (*da capo*).

T. was shocked to hear of William Morris's Democratic Socialism, and asked to see a copy of *Justice*.[30] (Morris's *Justice*, I partly agree with and partly detest. It is incendiary and atheistic, and would upset everything. How about America, which started a hundred years ago as a democracy with almost ideal advantages? I want reforms and thorough-going ones, but not by the hands of atheists and anarchists.)

Sunday, 27 July 1881.   Aldworth. About eleven T. and I came out to walk, first to the stables, where he unchained a deerhound, a black setter and two smaller dogs, then with these on Blackdown—along road, returning by Chase Farm uphill through plantations.

Poetry—Browning: 'one is constantly aware of the greatness of the man, yet somehow baulked of satisfaction.

'He offered me the subject of *The Ring and the Book*. "My Last Duchess" is very fine.'

As he stood looking at the pond by Chase Farm, I spoke of Ruskin's essay on versification, and his selection of Coleridge as the exemplar of a bad versifier, and of these lines from 'Christabel' as an example of bad verse:

> But vainly thou warrest,
>   For this is alone in
> Thy power to declare,
>   That in the dim forest
> Thou heard'st a low moaning,
> And found'st a bright lady, surpassingly fair;
> And did'st bring her home with thee in love and in charity,
> To shield her and shelter her from the damp air.

'Nobody,' I said, 'but a true and heaven-born metrist could have written that—'twas like a legato passage on the violin, flowing through from beginning to end with one bow.' T. did not entirely agree. He objected to 'Did'st bring her home with thee in love and in charity'.

I said the whole passage had an air of spontaneousness, of naïvety, and this to me was the last perfection of poetry.

T.—'The last perfection is the wild and wonderful

> Charm'd magic casements, opening on the foam
>   Of perilous seas, in faery lands forlorn.'

W. A.—'Coleridge was a great poet—Well, he was an endless talker, but not a bothering one; 'twas like a fountain running, you went away from it when you pleased. He did not care about convincing or converting or convicting you.'

T.—'Ruskin's dictum is not to be relied on.'

W. A.—'Especially on poetry. He printed a volume of poems of his own; but that (he wrote to me once) is "the disgrace of whatever faculty I possess".—Recently he has republished his Oxford Prize Poem on the "Caves of Elephanta"—entirely worthless.'

When on the upper road, looking over the gate where you see the Valewood ponds below, we still spoke of poetry.

'One believes in a poet', I said, 'whose lines are perpetually coming into one's mind. Yours do with me.'

T.—'Repeat a line.'

W. A.—'Dozens, if you like.'

T.—'I was praising one of Rogers's poems to him once and he said, "Repeat a passage—ha, you can't", and I couldn't at the moment.' . . .

As we turned down Pack Horse Lane, T. spoke of eternal punishment as an obsolete belief.

I said, 'At Witley Station hangs on the wall a large book of Bible texts, one page for each day of the month. Today I read, "All the dead shall arise, the righteous to eternal life, the wicked to everlasting damnation." '

T.—'It's not a right translation.'

W. A.—'But it's the authoritative teaching of the Church.'

T.—'Have you read Farrar's book?'[31]

W. A.—'I never read such books.'

T.—'Oh, but here he proves from original sources that no such doctrine existed in the early days of Christianity.'

I told T. that Bishop Wilberforce[32] was very proud of having saved the Athanasian Creed when the Archbishop of Canterbury was for giving it up, which interested him.

'Did he? My father (I think it was his father) would never read the Athanasian Creed.'

As we entered the back wicket and went along the shady little walk to the house T. said, 'You're not orthodox, and I can't call myself orthodox. Two things however I have always been firmly convinced of,—God,—and that death will not end my existence.'

W. A.—'So I believe.'

T. (stopping and turning round)—'Do you hold these?'

W. A.—'I do.'

Thursday, 7 August 1884.   A hot day. Helen and I all the afternoon at Aldworth. Various visitors and callers, so I had little talk with T.

Some numbers of *Justice*—Democrat Socialist paper which I lent him—made him 'vomit mentally', he said. He would agree to the heavy taxing of large incomes if it could be done. I told him about Alfred Wallace,[33] whom we visited last Saturday, and spiritualism. Wallace a thorough-going believer—but has had *no* experiences himself. Also, he never visualises his thoughts. I suggested that to such a man the mere visualising power of some other minds might appear supernatural, he having nothing like it in his experience.

T.—'I said long ago, "A poet never sees a ghost".'

Still, he is most anxious to believe in ghosts.

'As to visualising,' he said, 'I often see the most magnificent landscapes.'

'In dreams?'

'Yes, and on closing my eyes. Today when I lay down I saw a line of huge wonderful cliffs rising out of a great sweep of forest—finer than anything in nature.'

Other gifts he has, but T. is especially and pre-eminently a landscape painter in words, a colourist, rich, full and subtle.

He has, lately, a very practical side to his character, and in using this his profound quietude of temperament and manner helps immensely.

We talked of Carlyle. T. said, 'He used to tell me, "You must do this—You mustn't do that"—but I never minded him in the least. I repeated some of Marvell's lines about Holland to Carlyle—'They with mad labour fished the land to shore'—but he saw no humour in them, and said it was wrong to ridicule a serious diligent Nation.'

Mem.—Tennyson read Baudelaire's *Fleurs du Mal*,[34] and thought him 'a kind of moralist', though his subjects, he allowed, are shocking. I could not agree (and had, I think, studied Baudelaire more closely); he seems to me to take pleasure in seeing evil committed, and also in seeing evil-doers punished—a devil rather than a moralist.

Monday, 8 September 1884. H. and I to Aldworth. In the drawing-room we find Lady Tennyson—then T. comes in. His two little grandsons run in. Tennyson went to his bedroom and returned with a soap-dish and piece of soap, which he rubbed into a lather, and proceeded to blow bubbles, himself much delighted with the little crystal worlds and their prismatic tints—'Never was anything seen so beautiful! You artists (to H.) can't get such colours as these.'

The children jumped and laughed, and we fanned the bubbles to the ceiling and watched them burst in various parts of the room. Then T., inverting his pipe, blew up a magic cluster of diamond domes on the saucer, which rolled over and wetted his knees, till we put a newspaper to save him. Next he took his trusty tobacco pipe, lighted it and blew opaque bubbles which burst with a tiny puff of smoke, like shells over a besieged fortress.

Thursday, 6 November 1884. At luncheon, talk about the tropic woods: Wallace said you would find one kind of tree in flower for about a week, and at another time another kind of tree in flower for a short time, but you might come again and again and find no flowers at all; there were never in the tropics such masses of floral colour as in an English spring.

T. was disappointed at this, and asked about the trailing plants. W. called them 'glorious', but more for the rich drapery than the colours. The palm-tops are mostly a grayish green.

We digressed to novels. Mr W. (rather to my surprise) reads 'a good many in the course of the year', but does not hurry over them. He and Hallam exchanged names of novels to be ordered from the circulating library, Lord Tennyson being an incessant novel-reader. While we were speaking of woods etc. T. said, 'Bayard Taylor, who has been everywhere, said the most beautiful sight he ever saw was a wood in Lapland covered with frozen rain and the sun shining on it.'

Also, 'Sir Robert Kane[35] said the most awful thing he ever experienced was the absolute silence of an Arctic winter.'

Mr Wallace, Hallam and I went round the grounds, looking at various conifers.

To the study. W. gave details of table-rapping, table-prancing, and so forth, his own experiences and other people's. He never doubts any statement whatever in favour of 'spiritualism', and has an answer to every objection. 'Maskelyne and Cooke[36] do wonderful things.'—'Yes, partly by the help of mediumship.'

'The "spirits" often give foolish and misleading answers.'—'Yes, as might be expected; that only proves them to be human beings.'

'Why noises and motions of tables? Why these particular "mediums"?'—'Such are the conditions; why, we do not know.'

W. said it was absurd to suppose that matter could move itself. I ventured to remark that matter, so far as we can penetrate, does move itself, indeed is perpetually in motion.

He rejoined that in table-rapping etc. the phenomena were manifestly governed by an intelligence like our own. The means of communication between the Unseen World and ours were few and difficult.

Here Tennyson said, 'A great ocean pressing round us on every side, and only leaking in by a few chinks?'—of which Wallace took no notice, but went on to describe instances of spirit-writing on slates, by Slade[37] and others.

(I fear my tone all through was hardly respectful to the spirits.)

Somehow or other a sudden digression was made to politics, and W. came out with a strong opinion of the worthlessness of the House of Lords and the absurdity of the hereditary principle.

T. said, 'I think I respect it more than the other House.'

W.—'The other House wants reforming very badly, no doubt.'

The Duke of Marlborough was mentioned. Wallace denounced the purchase of his Raphael with the public money as 'scandalous'—would not buy any pictures or works of art with the taxpayers' money—'Let wealthy men buy and present them to the nation if they think fit.'

Egypt somehow came in, and Wallace thought we ought to leave the Mahdi alone. He is perhaps a great man, and at all events we know no harm of him.

T.—'I know no good of him.'

W. A.—'Would you not like to see the Nile?'

T.—'I'd much rather see tropical nature, but now I never shall.'
And then he questioned W. again about tropical scenery, producing a poem in MS, from which he read two or three lines about palms and purple seas. He wanted to know if the palm-trees could be seen rising distinct above the rest of the forest.

W.—'Yes, on a hillside.'

'What colour are they?'

'Rather light—grey-green.'

'Is an expanse of tropical forest *dark*, seen from above?'

'Not particularly; less so than an English woodland.'

T.—'Then I must change the word "dark".'

He writes his poetry now in trim small quarto books, in limp covers, the writing as neat as ever, though sometimes a little shaky. He keeps these books handy and takes them up very often, both at set times and odd moments, considering and correcting, and frequently reading new poems aloud from them, first to his family and afterwards to visitors. After the compositions are put into type he usually keeps them by him in proof for a long time, months or even years, reconsidering and perfecting every part.

T. referred with praise to Wallace's book, *Tropical Nature*,[38] and remarked, 'You have said something very bold about matter? I think matter more mysterious than spirit. I can conceive, in a way, what spirit is, but not matter.'

W.—'I conceive matter not as a substance at all, but as *points of energy*, and that if these were withdrawn matter would disappear.'

T. said this was something like his own notion.

W.—'So far from a material atom being indestructible, I believe that all the matter in existence might be immediately destroyed by the withdrawal of the sustaining Force.' . . .

In the evening Tennyson questioned me again about Irish brogue, 'How do they pronounce "door"?'

I answer, like 'boor': 'floor' sometimes thus, and sometimes with a sharper *u*—like 'flute'.

T. has rhymed 'door' to 'ashore' in his Irish poem, and is uneasy in his mind about it, notwithstanding Aubrey de Vere's thinking it all right.

In 'Mary Donnelly' I have

When she stood up for dancing her steps were so complete
The music nearly killed itself to listen to her feet

but I avoid writing brogue, and leave it to the speaker or singer. An Irishman could read these lines without a jar in the rhymes and at the same time without saying 'complate' in a broadly vulgar manner.

But T. insists on the brogue all through his piece; it's a brogue poem, and the rhymes ought to help emphatically.

Hallam showed me his father's lines in the *St James's Gazette* about the cataract.[39] T. coming to us, said it was a cataract like those on the Nile (not precipitous), the river is supposed to divide round an island. The first word, printed 'statesman', he has altered into 'steersman'.

We spoke of Gladstone's oratory: I said I thought Brougham's (whom I heard two or three times) the most like it in practised verbosity and the long sentences out of which the speaker wound himself at last without a break—few memorable passages in either case.

Tennyson is very fond of Gladstone as a private friend.

Then spoke of Carlyle: Froude's[40] quotation of the bitterness against Gladstone. I told Carlyle's saying about Dizzy[41]. 'I wonder how long John Bull will allow this Jew to dance on his belly!' which amused Tennyson.

T. or Hallam said that Gladstone (his own account) gave Carlyle offence at Rogers's table by refusing to agree in Carlyle's estimate of Goethe, and C. never forgave him. Gladstone laughed at the description of himself as 'the contemptiblest man'.

T. thinks Byron's morals ought not to be considered in judging his poetry. 'Unless they come into his poetry' (I maintain), and they certainly do. But it is less as voluptuary than as sneerer that I can't bear Lord Byron. T. thinks he was perhaps the cleverest man of his time. The more shame for him to be what he was.

Byron was just before T.'s time, so there are no personal feelings one way or other such as are almost inevitably mixed with contemporary estimates.

W. A.—'Did you ever meet Coleridge?'

T.—'No, I was asked to visit him, but I wouldn't.'

W. A.—'Coleridge was a "noticeable man, with large grey eyes".'

T.—'Oh yes.'

We talked a good deal about metres—nothing new. T. brought on again the question of the rhymes in his Irish piece.

I said, 'Have Maria (an Irish housemaid here) and try her with them.'

T. on this told us a little story—'A Suffolk vicar going into a parishioner's cottage found a Catholic engraving on the wall, the Virgin with St Joseph on one side and St Somebody else on the other. The woman of the house had got it by some chance.'

'Did she know what it meant?'

'Well, yes, she'd made it out: "There's the young woman, and two men making up to her, and the one man he says to t'other at last, "Ave Maria!' That's what's wrote up, you see, sir." '

Miss Ritchie played us some Beethoven finely. At Hallam's request she tried Edward FitzGerald's music (MS) to 'Locksley Hall', but found it amateurish in structure.

Next day, wonderfully fine, T. started at his usual time (11.30) for a walk, Miss Ritchie,[42] Hallam and I with him, and two dogs. We went by Chase Farm, fine yellow russets still on the woods. T. stopped us to see the white doves on the outhouse. Then on the western ridge of Blackdown, looking over Valewood, Lynchmere, etc., mistily rich, hills folded on hills. In the foreground some bushes of gorse in good bloom. T. went up to one taller than himself, covered with new golden blossoms, and stood looking at it: I have the picture in my mind.

Speaking of the new Franchise Bill, Miss R. said, 'I suppose there's no country where the people care so much for politics as in England?'

T.—'I hate politics! I'm for the *Empire*, but I hate politics. The Queen said to me, "*I* hate politics", and no wonder she does. As to this Bill, I don't believe the people care anything about it.'

In the evening Miss Tennyson reminded Alfred of the stories he used to tell his brothers and sisters. One called 'The Old Horse' lasted for months. . . .

We spoke of William Morris (from whom I had just had a long letter).

T. said, 'He has gone crazy.' I said I agreed with many of Morris's notions. Labour does not get its fair share.

T.—'There's brain labour as well as hand labour.'

W. A.—'And there are many who get money without any labour. The question, how to hinder money from accumulating into lumps, is a puzzling one.'

T.—'You must let a man leave money to his children. I was once in a coffee-shop in the Westminster Road at four o'clock in the morning. A man was raging "Why has So-and-So a hundred pounds, and I haven't a shilling?" I said to him, "If your father had left you £100 you wouldn't give it away to somebody else." He hadn't a word to answer. I knew he hadn't.'

T. said, 'It's very strange thing that, according to Wallace, none of the spirits that communicate with men ever mention God, or Christ.'

I said I always felt that the Deity was *infinitely* above us. Another step will bring us no nearer.

T.—'Wallace says the system he believes in is a far finer one than Christianity: it is Eternal Progress—I have always felt that there must be somewhere *Someone who knows*—that is, *God*. But I am in hopes that I shall find something human in Him too.' . . .

Lady Tennyson came down to dinner, very pale—spoke and was

spoken to little, went upstairs again, almost carried by Hallam. A dear, almost angelic woman.

We were quoting odd and rough verses when the pony-carriage came—and William drove us rapidly to the station, feeling happy with our friendly visit. . . .

[On a later visit, Tennyson], once more spoke a good deal about the want of some fixed standard of English pronunciation, or even some fixed way of indicating a poet's intention as to the pronunciation of his verses. 'It doesn't matter so much (he said) in poetry written for the intellect—as much of Browning's is, perhaps; but in mine it's necessary to know how to sound it properly.'

I suggested that he might put on record a code for pronouncing his own poetry, with symbolised examples, and he seemed to think this might be done.

After tea he turned over the leaves of the new volume, I looking over his arm. Put last now (it was first) is a sonnet against raking together and publishing the fragments of a deceased poet.[43] This is to 'swamp the poets with themselves' (a favourite turn of phrase with T). Then he turned to a longish poem called 'The Flight' and said, 'This was written fifty years ago.' I asked him to read it: he said, 'Oh, it isn't worth reading'—but he read it. It is not very notable among his varied riches, but simpler and more straightforward in style than some of his later pieces. I said I liked it, and he said he was glad of that. (I had read 'Vastness' in *Macmillan's Magazine* without any sense of gain.)

Saturday, 7 November 1884. Aldworth, 8.15—misty. Walked with T. down the lane to Lythe Hill and back. I asked him what he had seen of Gordon. Saw him once only: he came to luncheon one day to T.'s, in London. He was shy and rather silent, but he had a pleasant look.

W. A.—'Have you read Gordon's *Journals*?'[44]

T.—'No. The Queen told me I ought to read them.'

W. A.—'You ought indeed.' Then I rapidly but at some length gave him a sketch of the contents of that curious book, and of Gordon's character—man of great powers, immense wilfulness, whence followed a great catastrophe. T. listened much more patiently than I expected, and laughed at G.'s entry 'I am insubordinate, incorrigible; if I were my own superior I would certainly never employ myself!'

He told a droll thing about Lord F. at a farmers' dinner at Exeter the other day. Speaking to some toast, his lordship had occasion to name one of the most important farmers present, and alluded with sympathy to 'a recent family affliction' which had befallen him—the man's wife having died a short time before. The farmer, having to speak by and by, thanked his lordship very kindly for the way he had spoken of him, but 'as for my old woman' (he went on) 'she were a teasy twoad, and the Lord's welcome to her!'

We talked of Rabelais. T. made light of his stercoraceous qualities, and said he used to read him aloud at Cambridge to some of his friends and they all nearly tumbled off their chairs with laughing. The foulness was but a mask to hide his free-thinking. But, I said, he evidently enjoyed it, revelled in it.

NOTES

On Allingham, see p. 30.

1. According to *Memoir*, ii, pp. 195–6, Henry Irving refused Tennyson's play *Becket* in 1879; he produced it (in his own adaptation) at the Lyceum Theatre in 1891 and told Hallam Tennyson that it was 'one of the three most successful plays produced by him' there.

2. Lytton had been Viceroy of India, 1876: 'at home especially his administration was regarded as a failure' (*Dictionary of National Biography*), largely thanks to Britain's involvement in the Afghan War (1879).

3. See p. 20.

4. Quoted, not quite accurately, from Arnold's *Literature and Dogma* (1873).

5. Poems by Arnold published in 1867 and 1853, respectively.

6. Sir Samuel Ferguson (1810–86), whose *Poems* had been published in Dublin in 1880.

7. *Dramatic Idyls: Second Series* (1880).

8. *The Dunciad*, i. 89.

9. *Fifine at the Fair*, a poem by Browning published in 1872.

10. Adam Sedgwick (1785–1873), Professor of Geology at Cambridge and Fellow of Trinity College.

11. Marquis de Laplace (1749–1827), French mathematician and astronomer.

12. See n. 2 above.

13. Lord Beaconsfield (Disraeli) was Prime Minister from 1874 to 1880.

14. See p. 15.

15. See p. 50.

16. In his article 'Fiction, Fair and Foul: II' in *Nineteenth Century*, viii (1880) 205, Ruskin had written, 'Wordsworth is simply a Westmoreland peasant'.

17. See p. 51.

18. J. M. W. Turner (1775–1851), English painter.

19. Published as *Ballads and Other Poems* in December 1880. The poems referred to are 'The Northern Cobbler' (Ricks, 376) and 'The Village Wife' (Ricks, 180).

20. *Collected Sonnets, Old and New* (1880), by Charles Tennyson Turner. Tennyson contributed a prefatory poem to the volume (Ricks, 377).

21. Samuel Rogers: see p. 122.

22. See p. 5.

23. The lady was Mary Brotherton: see p. 121 and *Memoir*, ii, p. 249. 'Brighthelmstown' is the old name of Brighton.

24. By P. W. Joyce, published in 1879.
25. On FitzGerald and on Tennyson's last meeting with him, see pp. 7, 126.
26. See p. 161.
27. Later published as 'Tomorrow' (Ricks, 404).
28. Leigh Hunt edited various journals at different times; the reference may be to *The Examiner* (flourished 1808–80), of which he was joint founder.
29. Hamilton Aïdé (1810–1906), poet and novelist.
30. William Morris (1834–96), poet, artist and socialist, was associated with the Social Democratic Federation, which launched its weekly paper *Justice* in January 1884.
31. Probably *The Life of Christ* (1874 and many subsequent editions) by Frederic William Farrar.
32. Samuel Wilberforce (1805–73), bishop successively of Oxford and Winchester.
33. See p. 110.
34. Published in 1857.
35. Sir Robert Kane (1809–90), Irish scientist and writer on scientific topics.
36. A famous partnership of professional magicians.
37. A few years earlier Dr Henry Slade had been convicted of fraudulent spiritualistic practices.
38. Published in 1878.
39. 'Compromise' (Ricks, 406).
40. J. A. Froude's biography of Carlyle appeared in 1882.
41. Disraeli.
42. Miss Emily Ritchie, daughter of Richmond and Anne Ritchie (see p. 31); her recollections of Farringford are printed in *Memoir*, II, pp. 85–7.
43. 'Poets and their Bibliographies' (Ricks, 399).
44. General Charles George Gordon had been killed at Khartoum on 26 January 1885 and before the end of the year several volumes of his journals had appeared in response to the enormous public interest: *General Gordon's Private Diary of his Exploits in China*, *The Journals of Gordon at Khartoum*, *General Gordon's Last Journal*. Tennyson's 'Epitaph on General Gordon' (Ricks, 411) was published on 7 May 1885.

Centennial Recollections*

T. H. WARREN

First of all, he was throughout his life a splendid specimen of the human race. 'As a young man he was singularly fine looking, a sort of

* *The Centenary of Tennyson, 1809–1909* (Oxford: Clarendon Press, 1909) pp. 17–22, 25–6.

Hyperion,' said his contemporary FitzGerald: 'Apollo and Hercules in one', as he wrote elsewhere, tall, six feet in height, broad-chested, strong-limbed, large-handed, with waving hair, dark, like one of southern race, of great physical strength. I myself only knew him when he was quite old. I well remember, I shall never forget, the first impression he made on me. *Qualis artifex!*[1] were the words which rose to my lips, 'a great poet is a great artist'. Sensitiveness, imagination, discrimination, the critical, the creative spirit, seemed to breathe from his mien and face. Something of the same impression I received when I first saw Watts,[2] and indeed they had not a little in common, these two friends and brother artists. It was only later that I came to see how strong he was, even in his extreme old age; how magnificently strong he must have been in his prime. This union of strength and sensitiveness must always have been his. You see it in the portraits. Some of them show the one quality more than the other. The best show both. Samuel Laurence's[3] noble portrait of him as a young man shows, I think, both. The sensitive and the intellectual perhaps predominate in the very interesting early drawing, the earliest known portrait, that by Mrs Weld. Woolner's two busts display more of the strength. It is perhaps more natural for sculpture to do so, but in the beardless one the sensitiveness is not wanting. Of Watts's fine portraits, some I think give less than the strength. The sensitiveness amounts to a troubled, almost vacillating sensitiveness. This may have been true in certain epochs, or at certain moments, of his life. Palgrave writes of his first impressions in 1849: 'He had the look of one who had suffered greatly: strength and sensitiveness blended.' The last portraits by Watts—the Trinity, Cambridge, portrait, for instance—seem to me truer to the poet's noble yet sensitive strength. For this was the man. He could not have been either the man he was, or the poet he was, without both. His friends found his portrait in the lines meant to be a prologue to 'The Gardener's Daughter', but his son tells us it was not his intention that they should give such a portrait, and though they have some general characteristics of his, they do not satisfy me as individual enough. 'Tall and broad-shouldered as a son of Anak, with hair, beard, and eyes of southern darkness; something in the lofty brow and aquiline nose suggests Dante, but such a deep, mellow, chest voice never could have come from Italian lungs', so Bayard Taylor[4] described him in 1857.

Carlyle's somewhat earlier descriptions are well known. 'A Lifeguardsman spoiled by writing poetry.' 'One of the finest-looking men in the world; a great shock of rough, dark, hair; bright, laughing, hazel eyes; a massive, aquiline face, most massive yet most delicate'; 'bronzed'; 'almost Indian looking'; 'his voice musical, metallic, fit for loud laughter and piercing wail, and all that may lie between'. Such are some of the touches by which at different times he described him about 1840.

His old friend Professor Cowell[5] (who taught FitzGerald to read Omar) wrote in a letter to Dr Rouse, 'He was, as you say, a really great man. He looked one and he was one.'

Sydney Dobell[6] said finely: 'If you had been told that that man had written the *Iliad* you would not have been surprised'; while Henry Reeve,[7] who had known him from youth, spoke of his 'imposing appearance', when he was nearly seventy, at his son Lionel's wedding in Westminster Abbey: 'He looked round the Abbey as if he felt the Immortals were his compeers.'

Perhaps after his early sorrows and anxieties had passed away, after he had married, and 'the peace of God had passed into his heart', the troubled expression may also have passed, but the same combination of strength and sensitiveness, the 'most massive yet most delicate' of Carlyle, I think always remained, and I think too it was characteristic of the man. Independent, standing in his own strength, fearless, candid as a child, he was yet, as he said himself, 'a shy beast loving his own burrow', and sensitive. Long after his worldwide fame had been firmly established he was still sensitive to criticism, even when he knew it was wrong. I remember one of his own characteristic utterances in which he put this himself in his own way. We had walked out from Farringford in the direction of the Needles. On our outward journey we had talked of fame, and I remember thinking how strange it was to be thus walking and talking with one whose thoughts and words would affect the world and whose memory would be preserved like the memory of the great of old, like that of Sophocles or Virgil, perhaps many thousand years hence. It was like being in a little boat towed for a short time by a great ship that is about to sail to the ends of the world. As we turned back in our walk our converse fell upon Plato and the tenth book of *The Republic*, of which he was very fond, with the 'metempsychosis' as it is called, that famous idea that the souls of the dead, when their time comes to return from the other world to a renewed life in this, are allowed to choose what lives they will have, and how men then chose the lives of beasts and birds, while birds and beasts chose the lives of men; how the King Agamemnon chose the life of an eagle; and Ajax, the strong hero, the life of a lion; and the scurrilous jester, Thersites, the life of a monkey; and the shrewd, world-worn, famous Ulysses, the life of a private man with no cares.

'If I had to choose life over again,' said Tennyson, in his deep voice, half humorously, 'I wouldn't be a poet, I'd be a pachyderm.' Then, seeing me smiling, 'I don't mean a hippopotamus,' he went on, 'I mean I'd choose to be a thick-skinned fellow with no nerves.' A few years later I was reminded of this when another great artist and man of letters, George Meredith, was talking to me of Tennyson and his relations with him in his own younger days. I had strolled down Box Hill, on the top of which I was staying, one sunny Sunday afternoon in September, about fifteen years ago, to see the old novelist. I found him lurching round and round his garden in the sun. The paralytic lameness which later on crippled him so sadly had already begun, but there was no lameness in his mind. He talked with the most delightful brilliancy on a number of subjects. We touched for a few minutes on Tennyson. He told me that when he was a young man he had a great admiration for the early poems of Tennyson, and he sent him, in some trepidation, his first volume.

This came out, it may be remembered, in the year 1851. Tennyson wrote back a very pretty letter, saying that there was one poem in the book which he had been going up and down stairs repeating, and that he had told his wife he wished he had written it. This, I gathered, from something Tennyson had told me, was 'Love in the Valley'.

Tennyson then asked him to come and stay the night with him at Twickenham, where he was living at that time. Next morning, as they walked out towards the Thames, Tennyson began, 'Apollodorus says I am not a great poet.' Apollodorus was the 'gifted Gilfillan', as he was called, a Scotch Minister and critic, author of *A Gallery of Literary Portraits* published in 1845, who took himself, and was taken in those days, with a seriousness now forgotten. 'I said,' quoth Meredith, 'Why should you mind what such a man says?' To which Tennyson replied, 'I mind what *everybody* says.' Swinburne told him, Meredith went on, that Tennyson once said to him that a review in a halfpenny newspaper had caused him a sleepless night. . . .

My first talk with him, I remember, was about criticism. He came into the room with the *Spectator* in his hand; the organ in those days of his friend and one of his best critics, as he himself thought, the late Mr R. H. Hutton. He began saying something about criticism. I mentioned the name of the late Mr John Addington Symonds, who had encouraged me to write to him. He said, 'Do you think Symonds a good critic?' I replied that in many ways I did, but that I would rather hear whom he thought a good critic than suggest any myself. He replied, 'I don't know. I sometimes think a good critic's very rare, rarer than a good poet. I used to think that Goethe was one of the best critics. He always tried to see all the good he could in a man.' Something of these ideas he embodies in the little poem entitled 'Poets and Critics', when written I know not, but first published in his last volume, in 1892. It always seems to me in tone and form very like Goethe. How good and kindly his criticisms were may be seen from those scattered up and down throughout his son's Life, specially concentrated in certain chapters. He was aided by an admirable memory which enabled him to illustrate his judgements most delightfully. . . .

There are many legends current about the poet's 'roughness and gruffness', as it is called. There always are such legends about the personal peculiarities of genius. Some are mere gossip, some amusing and harmless, whether true or not, some not overkind nor overtrue. 'There never yet,' as he sang himself, 'Was noble man, but made ignoble talk.'. . .

Again, you will hear it said that his son's Life gives too flattering and smooth a picture, that the 'seamy side' is not shown. There was none to show, no side that by any stretch deserves to be called 'seamy'.

> And was the day of my delight
> As pure and perfect as I say?
> The very source and fount of Day
> Is dash'd with wandering isles of night.

Foibles even the best have, of course. If the picture is a bright one, after all that is as it should be. His was an heroic and a glorious figure.

All I can say is that I found him consistently most kind, and when I got over the first shyness, most genial and cordial. His playfulness, his humour, were as remarkable as his profundity and his sublimity. But perhaps what struck me most was his transparent candour. 'A terrible sagacity,' as poor Cowper says, 'informs the poet's heart.' It was so with Tennyson. He saw through the shams, the conceit, the personal motives of so many who came to him with some axe or some penknife to grind, and he could not help showing that he saw through them, and sometimes telling them so.

NOTES

Thomas Herbert Warren (1853–1930), classical scholar, President of Magdalen College, Oxford, from 1885 to 1928, and Professor of Poetry at Oxford, 1911–16. The pamphlet from which these extracts are taken reprints a lecture given at Oxford on 6 August 1909.

1. 'What an artist!' (quoted from '*qualis artifex pereo*' which according to Suetonius were the dying words of the emperor Nero).
2. George Frederick Watts (1817–1904), painter and sculptor.
3. Samuel Laurence (1812–84), portrait painter.
4. Bayard Taylor (1825–78), American traveller and writer.
5. Edward Cowell (1826–1903), Sanskrit scholar.
6. Sydney Dobell (1824–74), poet of the 'Spasmodic School'.
7. Henry Reeve (1813–95), journalist and man of letters; he edited the *Edinburgh Review* from 1855 to 1895.

Conversations at Aldworth*

W. G. McCABE

The first time I ever met him he railed against personalities touching men of genius as only Tennyson could rail when deeply stirred.

I had just come to the Tennysons from a visit to my old friend Mrs Richmond Ritchie,[1] Thackeray's daughter, who at the time was sorely perplexed as to what should be done in the matter of a biography of her illustrious father, inasmuch as so many apocryphal stories of his private life were finding their way into the London journals.

Just before the great novelist died, he was reading one day some fulsome biography of a certain man of letters whom he had known and on her entering the room, he had held up the book, and said with unwonted vehemence: 'Remember, Annie, when *I* am gone, there is to be nothing of this sort about me.'

This she regarded in the light of a dying injunction, and has ever since so held it. But these apocryphal stories greatly distressed her, and, in her perplexity, she had talked the matter over with me and done me the honour to ask my advice.

I unhesitatingly advised her to write her father's life, for she was not only his daughter, but his closest friend, and, as we all know, possesses the practised hand. Conditions had arisen, I said, which he had not thought of, and I believed he would approve the step could he know all.

On my first visit to Aldworth, I mentioned this conversation to Tennyson (for Mrs Ritchie was one of his closest friends) and the reasons for my emphatic counsel to her. But he would none of it.

'I thank God we know nothing of Shakespeare more than we do,' he growled out. 'Why can't people be satisfied with a man's books?'

I differed with him promptly, and then began one of the many friendly and delightful 'disputations' I was destined to have with the old poet.

He was very vehement in his anathemas, but I stood my ground, inexorable as a Greek chorus. I told him plainly that a Life of himself was inevitable when he should have passed away, and that, if he wanted the truth told about him, instead of a 'pack of lies' (a

* 'Personal Recollections of Tennyson', *Century Illustrated Monthly Magazine*, n. s., XLI (1902) 723, 725–7, 736–7.

favourite phrase of his), the most sensible thing to do was to entrust the work to someone who could speak with authority, and thus forestall the 'free-lances', whose apocryphal stories were sure to be of such startling and 'infinite variety' as would make him turn over in his grave.

I shall never forget the way in which he boomed out his reply: 'I don't want to be ripped up like a hog when I'm dead.'

The truth is that the man was by nature so thoroughly a recluse, shrinking instinctively from publicity of every kind, and that his privacy had been so outrageously invaded by utter strangers, that he had become morbid on the subject. . . .

Every little scrap of information touching him personally, or in regard to his forthcoming books, was eagerly caught up by the London press and expanded with a fertility of imagination that made him fairly rage. . . .

Of all the talkers I have ever met he was, 'taking him all round', as we say, the most interesting, when 'I' the vein', which was commonly near midnight, in his den and over a pipe. Swinburne (*tantum ridi*, I may say) is a more brilliant talker, especially when moved by a subject he loves and knows well, such as the early English dramatists. Browning (who, to use an expression which Tennyson detested, was 'awfully kind' and hospitable to me) just won your heart, and your brain too, by the simple honesty, the infectious boyishness of his talk. Matthew Arnold, too, was always to me, whether in the whirl of London society, or in a quiet corner at the Athenaeum, or in his modest Surrey home at Cobham, one of the most delightful of men to listen to. He was so cordial, so full of kindly simplicity, that I never once detected in the genial flow of his conversation that academic note which some have objected to.

But delightful as were all these, Tennyson's talk was far and away the best and the most enjoyable I have ever listened to, with its dry humour, shading off suddenly into vehement earnestness; its felicity of epithet, that at times flashed out like a searchlight, and lighted up the whole subject of discussion; its underlying vein of robust common-sense; its wealth of apt quotation and charming reminiscence. . . .

There was one salient characteristic of Tennyson that must have struck the most unobservant, and that was his direct honesty and simplicity in things small and great. On the pavement of the entrance-hall at Aldworth is the Welsh motto in encaustic tiles, 'The Truth against the World'. It was not idly placed there. Such was, indeed, the spirit that informed every act and utterance of the master of Aldworth. He hated shams of every sort; and that is, in great measure, as Mr Knowles[2] has observed, the key to his detestation of what we call 'society'. Its 'small insincerities', without which it could not exist, repelled and disgusted him. He had a quick, almost an imperious way of flashing round on one with a sudden question, somewhat embarrassing to shy folk.

A downright answer, or downright confession of ignorance, would win him to most delightful and instructive talk, but pinchbeck omniscience he would exploit relentlessly. As all lovers of his poetry know, that passion for truth and fidelity of detail underlies all his poetic art.

Whether describing the shifting aspects of nature in her varying moods, from storm to sunshine, on land or sea, whether depicting almost at a stroke with winged epithet some flashing insect or 'skimming swallow' his touch is always the sure touch of trained observation, and over all this minute knowledge of the specialist is cast the glamour of genius.

Once we were talking of battle lyrics, and I was praising Campbell's stirring 'Battle of the Baltic'.

'Yes,' he said, ''tis fine. But you remember the lines

> By thy wild and stormy *steep*,
> Elsinore!

Now, there's no "steep" at Elsinore; the coast there is as flat as your hand.'

And as I had just come back from Denmark I had to confess, with a laugh, that he was right. . . .

His defective eyesight was ever an acute annoyance to him, and added greatly to his innate shyness of meeting strangers and going into society. He constantly referred to it, and once said to me, 'It led to rather an amusing incident a few years ago. Hallam and I went with Mr Gladstone as Sir Donald Currie's guests on a cruise in the *Pembroke Castle* among the Hebrides and thence on to Denmark.[3] While lying in the harbour of Copenhagen we were invited to dine at Fredensborg with the King and Queen of Denmark, and the next day the whole royal party came on board to luncheon. There were the King and Queen, "the Princess", the Czar and Czarina, and their attendant ladies and gentlemen. After luncheon "the Princess" asked me to read one of my poems, and someone fetched the book. I sat on a sofa in the smoking-room next "the Princess", and another lady came and sat beside me on the other side. The Czar stood up just in front of me. When I finished reading, this lady said something very civil, and I thought she was Andrew Clark's daughter, so I patted her on the shoulder very affectionately, and said, "My dear girl, that's very kind of you, very kind." I heard the Czar chuckling mightily to himself, so I looked more nearly at her, and, God bless me! 't was the Czarina herself.' I fancy that it was the first time that august lady had been patted on the back and called a 'dear girl' since she had left the nursery.

But with all his dislike of society, and despite his grim exterior, he was possessed of that genuine spirit of courtesy which can come only from a thoroughly kind heart. I was strolling slowly with him once on the terrace at Aldworth, during one of my earlier visits, when the first gong sounded for dinner.

'I'm off,' I cried, 'to get into my clothes.'

He detained me a moment, saying kindly, 'You must excuse my not dressing for dinner. I never dress for anybody. My old friend Argyll[4] was here last week, and I said to him, "Argyll, I can't dress for you, for I never dress for any one, and if I made an exception and dressed for a duke, my butler would set me down as a snob." We must keep well with our butlers, you know', he laughed, as I sped away to change.

At another time a dog-cart and single groom had been sent to meet me at the station, instead of the carriage with its array of footmen, and he fussed and fumed about it when he found it out, and grumbled at Hallam's explanation that one of the coach-horses had gone lame. Had I been a great nobleman or some famous man, he wouldn't have 'cared tuppence'. Much cheap republicanism has been aired in this country about his having accepted a peerage, and I have heard a well-known American, who (as I happen to know) 'dearly loves a lord' in his secret heart, declare that he had lost much of his admiration for Tennyson 'since he had condescended to take a title'. The fact is, as I heard from Tennyson's own lips, that when a peerage was first offered him, he was strongly opposed to accepting it, having thrice before declined a baronetcy, and told Mr Gladstone that he preferred to remain a simple commoner. But the veteran Prime Minister urged that, as such a signal honour had never before been actually conferred for distinction in literature pure and simple (for Grote[5] had declined the overture, and Macaulay's[6] case was not identical), he owed it to the literary guild to accept this recognition, on the part of the Queen and her ministers, of the dignity and worth of letters. When put to him in that light he felt it his duty to his craft to accept.

NOTES

W. G. McCabe was headmaster of a school in Petersburg, Virginia; he visited Tennyson at Aldworth during the 1880s.

1. See p. 31.
2. See p. 97.
3. For Hallam Tennyson's account of this voyage in September 1883, see *Memoir*, II, pp. 278–84. Some further details are provided by Sir Algernon

West, who had been Gladstone's private secretary and was another member of the party. In his *Recollections 1832 to 1886* (1899) II, p. 160, he writes:

> Sir William [Harcourt] directly after dinner proposed to smoke, saying he was sure the Poet Laureate, who had sung of 'The earliest pipe of half-awakened birds', would not object. Mr Tennyson, who had given one the impression of being somewhat *farouche* and rough at first, had soon softened down. We had many pleasant conversations together, and he had begun reading to our small party at the instigation of Miss Tennant in the smoking-room in the mornings and evenings. He was very much offended on one occasion by detecting Mr Gladstone apparently asleep during his reading; oddly enough he preferred his dramas to his other poems, though he was fond of reading *Maud* and 'The Grandmother'.

Sir Algernon West also records that Tennyson read to the assembled crowned heads 'with his great wideawake on his head'.

4. See p. 20.

5. George Grote (1794–1871), author of a monumental *History of Greece*, declined a peerage in 1869.

6. Macaulay accepted a peerage in 1857; in addition to his writings he was a notable politician and administrator.

Memories of my Grandfather*

SIR CHARLES TENNYSON

I suppose I'm the last person alive who had any at all intimate connection with Tennyson. It's nearly seventy-seven years since he died at the age of eighty-three. I was approaching the end of my thirteenth year, so I was quite old enough to have a fairly strong impression of him. I was his grandson, and though I was the son of his second son, for the first ten years of my life I and my brothers were the only grandchildren. Then my father died, at the age of just over thirty-one, when I was six, and that perhaps intensified the interest which my grandparents took in my brothers and myself. Tennyson didn't like London, and he had two country houses. One was on the Isle of Wight, which he bought in 1855, and which he retained for the rest of his life. In 1867 he built a new house in Sussex, and the reason for this is interesting. After the publication of

* 'Sir Charles Tennyson Remembers his Grandfather', *The Listener*, LXXXII (1969) 548–50.

Enoch Arden in 1864, he became so fantastically popular that the tourists used absolutely to besiege him on the Isle of Wight: people used to climb the trees in his garden to watch for him coming out, and press their noses against the panes of the dining-room window in order to watch him having his lunch. He was a very shy man, and very averse to publicity of all forms, and so he decided to build another house in Sussex, and in as remote a place as he could find. The house, which is still standing, is at Aldworth near Haslemere. He used to stay on the Isle of Wight until the spring flowers were over. The spring flowers in the west end of the island are very beautiful and he liked to get the full benefit of them; then he would come up to Sussex at the beginning of June and would stay there until the autumn leaves fell in November. It was a very beautifully wooded hillside and he liked to see the autumn leaves reach their full beauty. We were a good deal with him in both those houses, but more in Sussex because he was there when we had our long school holidays.

Now seventy-seven years is a very long time and my memories are necessarily rather blurred, and confined to the last years of his life. In the winter of 1888–9 he had a very bad illness from which his doctors thought he would never recover, but he was a man of tremendous will-power and he did recover, with his mental ability almost unimpaired, and a great deal of his physical ability. But he was, during the last three years of his life, rather a broken man, and my grandmother, who looked after him with the greatest attention and devotion, felt that he ought to be protected from irritations and interruptions of all kinds. Small boys are apt to be a little bit tiresome. So we didn't see, perhaps, quite as much of him in those last three years as we had done before, and unfortunately the earlier times I don't remember. Nevertheless, my memories of him are extremely vivid, because he was the most extraordinary personality: in a very long life his is by far the most impressive and singular personality that I've ever come across.

He was very tall, well over six foot high. Very broad, very powerfully made. He had large hands, with curiously square finger tips. Somebody once said that they looked fit for kneading clay or dough. He had a very tall head, which rose to an egg-shaped type of crown, rather bald, and fringed by untidy dark hair. His hair changed colour hardly at all, and he had in his old age, as everyone knows, rather a long grizzled beard. He was dark and swarthy, much more like a Spaniard than an Englishman. He had very dark eyes, with heavy lids, and he was terribly short-sighted. He always said that he was the second most short-sighted man in England. Who the first was I don't remember. This gave his eyes a piercing and rather remote sort of look. He was very aquiline in features, and one thing which added greatly to the singularity of his appearance was the clothes which he always wore. Until the end of his life he always wore the same style of clothes—I very nearly said 'the same clothes', which might not have been far from the truth—that he wore in the reign of King William I V when he was a young man with his brothers and his university friends: a long, sleeveless sort of Spanish cloak with a velvet collar, dark blue or black, and a large black wideawake felt hat with a very broad brim. He nearly always wore a sort of a poacher's John Bull frock-coat, halfway between a tail-coat and a frock-coat, with big poacher's pockets at the sides and rather baggy trousers, which, in old age, made his legs look rather like the hind legs of an elephant.

Many people thought it was an affectation that he wore this kind of clothes, but I'm quite sure it wasn't, for two reasons. First of all, he was always phenomenally untidy from his youth up, and there's very good evidence of that in a cloak and hat of his which were left to me by my mother's father, Frederick Locker, and which I have now given to the Tennyson Research Centre at Lincoln. The story of this hat and cloak was as follows. My grandfather had gone abroad with Mr Locker for a week's holiday—in Paris, I think—and coming back, when they went to Mr Locker's flat in Victoria Street, he suddenly discovered that he'd left his hat and cloak in the train. Mr Locker said: 'You needn't worry about that. All you've got to do is to go back and pay sixpence and they'll give you the cloak and hat.' 'Well,' said my grandfather, 'I'm not going to pay sixpence for that cloak and hat. If you'd like to go and pay sixpence you can get them and keep them'—which Mr Locker, being a great collector, immediately did. Now the interesting thing is that although this was in 1871, the cloak has a little label inside saying it was made for Tennyson in 1840, so he'd been wearing it for thirty-one years, and the hat, from its appearance, I should say about as long.

The other reason I have for saying that the clothes he wore were not an affectation was a story which was told me by the widow of Kenneth Grahame, the author of The Wind in the Willows. Her family were very friendly with Tennyson at the end of the 1860s, or in the early 1870s, and when he came to London, he used to like to call on them and to take her out for a walk. She was a little girl then of about eight years old, and they used to go walking through the streets together. He would be striding along in his great black cloak and his great wide hat, with the little girl trotting along beside him. People always stared at them but he never seemed to notice this until one day they were almost mobbed in the street. He was very much taken aback, and he stopped, looked down at the little girl and said, 'My child, you should get your mother to dress you less conspicuously. People are staring at us.'

He was a tremendous walker. He didn't play any games and he hated blood sports, but he walked, morning and afternoon, right up to the end of his life. As he walked, he ceaselessly observed—he was a great naturalist and a keen student of geology, astronomy and the various forms of natural science. He also composed, I feel sure, a great deal at that time. If he was working on a long poem, he would turn it over in his mind and when he got back, he jotted down in notebooks the lines which he'd made, or the half-lines or the phrases. He had a curious gait as a walker: a sort of gliding or shuffling step. An American poet who saw him in England said it reminded him of a Red Indian. It was rather furtive and, at the same time, very decided. Another thing was that he always liked to have great big dogs with him. The one I remember particularly is, I think, the one commemorated in the famous Watts statue in Lincoln—a Siberian wolf-hound which we called Karenina. I think we should have called it Karenina. but we didn't know any better. I have one very, very clear recollection of him preparing to go out for his walk with Karenina. He was standing on the lawn in front of the house, which looked right over the Sussex Weald. He'd got on his big black hat Karenina was running round and round, pretending to bite him, and he was throwing his cloak over her and prodding at her with his big holly stick.

I also have a very clear recollection of him right at the end of his life, coming downstairs before his walk. He always breakfasted alone, and nobody was ever allowed to disturb him for at least an hour and a half after his breakfast because he said it was then that his best ideas came to him. He would come down and put on his hat and cloak and go out for a walk. And very often my brother and I would be in the broad corridor at Aldworth when he was coming down the stairs, rather heavily, leaning on the banisters. It was a regular ritual that he would hold out his great brown hand, rather trembling, rather shaking, and we would kiss it. That was always our morning greeting. Although he always breakfasted alone, he liked to have his other meals with company, and he was very fond of his food. That was an unexpected trait, perhaps. He also had some rather singular habits in the way of food. He always had an apple pie at his side on the dumb-waiter for lunch, and I believe for dinner too.

One very characteristic incident I remember connected with lunch at Aldworth: the incident of the fungi. As I say, he was a great naturalist and he'd been out walking one morning and he came back with the great wideawake hat full of the most terrible-looking fungi, which he brought into the drawing-room where I happened to be with my grandmother. He showed her his hat full of these objects and said: 'Emily, will you please have these cooked for luncheon?' My grandmother was absolutely horrified: 'My dear Ally'—she always called him Ally—'you couldn't possibly eat those. I'm sure they're most unsafe and poisonous.' He said: 'Emily, I know quite well what they are. They're very good to eat and I should like to have them cooked for luncheon.' I think my grandmother, although she was said to influence his poetry unduly, always knew when she was beaten, so she rang the bell and gave the hat full of mushrooms to the butler, who carried them off and had them cooked. At luncheon they appeared on a large dish, and they were handed all round the table, and everybody refused them until they got to him—he was, of course, last on the circuit—and rather aggressively he took the whole contents of the dish and ate them all with everybody glaring anxiously at him, thinking that he would probably fall down dead.

Although he lived surrounded by people who were thinking in a concentrated way about him, and doing their utmost to make life easier for him, I have the impression of a very solitary person, living very much alone, very much turned in upon himself. Although with his friends and congenial people he was extremely good company and fond of society, he was very shy with strangers. He was very fearful of meeting uncongenial people.

My grandmother tried to protect him from strangers. He'd built his Sussex house on a flat site on the face of a hill about 1000 feet high, and the site was cleared out of a dense copse and woodland. He left these copses coming as close as he could to the actual site on which the house was built, and he had a series of connected lawns, with green corridors cut through the copse woods, and it was always said that towards the end of his life, perhaps when he couldn't walk in the afternoon, he used to go and smoke his pipe and read on one of these lawns. My grandmother would have her long chair brought to the far end of the corridor leading to the little lawn where he was reading, and there she would lie to prevent anybody interrupting him.

He was a tremendous smoker. He always smoked clay pipes and in early life he smoked a very strong shag tobacco which many of his friends said smelt appalling. In latter years I think he smoked something lighter, a sort of Bird's Eye, and he always cleaned out his pipes, or had them cleaned out, with eau-de-cologne. Ellen Terry used to say that one of the things that she'd enjoyed doing for him when she was a girl was cleaning out his pipes with eau-de-cologne. He would never have smoked in my grandmother's drawing-room, but he would retire after lunch and dinner and smoke endless clay pipes up in his big library. After dinner there was always a singular ritual, which may have dated back to his Cambridge days. He liked to have his dessert in a separate room from his dinner, so he and his guests would move across to this other room and there they would have their dessert, and with it he always had one pint of port. And it was none of your tawny stuff—it was a good strong vintage port. He seemed to need both the port and the tobacco as sedatives and stimulants to his imagination. When people criticised him or laughed at him for being excessively interested in his food, he used to say, 'All fine-natured men are greedy', which is a good excuse. And then there was a very nice story about a literary lady who had been longing to meet him. At last she succeeded in getting invited to lunch and in getting put next to him. Unfortunately, the only thing that he said during the whole of lunch was when a plate of mutton was put before him: 'Mutton should be cut in wedges.'

My last recollection of him was at Aldworth a few weeks before his death. He was a good deal weakened, but he'd been quite active, and I remember that he'd taken to wearing a black skull-cap to keep off the draughts. His great library at Aldworth was on the left-hand side of the landing at the top of the front stairs, and the door of his library was open. There I saw him sitting in front of his desk in the embrasure of the big bow window and, with his tremendous aquiline profile in silhouette against the light of the window, looking, as I now realise, very much like the self-portrait of the aged Titian.

NOTE

Sir Charles Tennyson (1879–1977) was the son of Lionel Tennyson (younger son of the poet) and Eleanor Locker. He published various works on his grandfather, including a biography (see p. xiv).

Notes on Tennyson's Conversation (1835–53)*

EDWARD FITZGERALD

1835.   Resting on our oars one calm day on Windermere, whither we had gone for a week from dear Spedding's Mirehouse[1] at the end of May 1835,—resting on our oars, and looking into the lake quite unruffled and clear, he quoted from the lines he had lately read us from the MS of 'Morte d'Arthur' about the lonely Lady of the Lake and Excalibur.

* From 'Some Recollections of Tennyson's Talk from 1835 to 1853', in Hallam Tennyson (ed.), *Tennyson and his Friends*, pp. 142–6.

Nine days she wrought it, sitting all alone
Upon the hidden bases of the Hills.[2]

'Not bad that, Fitz, is it?'

(One summer day looking from Richmond 'Star and Garter'.)
'I love those woods that go triumphing down to the river.'
'Somehow water is the element which I love best of all the four.'
(He was passionately fond of the sea and of babbling brooks.[3])
'Some one says that nothing strikes one more on returning from the Continent than the look of our English country towns. Houses not so big, nor such rows of them as abroad; but each house, little or big, distinct from one another, each man's castle, built according to his own means and fancy, and so indicating the Englishman's individual humour.

'I have been two days abroad—no further than Boulogne this time, but I am struck as always on returning from France with the look of good sense in the London people.'

(Standing before a Madonna, by Murillo, at the Dulwich Gallery— her eyes fixed on you.)
'Yes—but they seem to look at something beyond—beyond the Actual into Abstraction. I have seen that in a human face.' (I, E. F. G., have seen it in *his*. Some American spoke of the same in Wordsworth. I suppose it may be so with all *poets*.)

1850. 'When I was sitting by the banks of Doon—I don't know why—I wasn't in the least spoony—not thinking of Burns (but of the lapsing of the ages)—when all of a sudden I gave way to a passion of tears.'

'I one day hurled a great iron bar over a haystack. Two bumpkins who stood by said there was no one in the two parishes who could do it. I was then about twenty-five.' (He could carry his mother's pony round the dinner-table.—E. F. G.)

'The sea at Mablethorpe[4] is the grandest I know, except perhaps at Land's End.' (That is as he afterwards explained to me in a letter.)

'Thackeray is the better artist, Dickens the [more affluent] Genius. He, like Hogarth, has the moral sublime sometimes: but not the ideal sublime. Perhaps I seem talking nonsense; I mean Hogarth could not conceive an Apollo or a Jupiter.' (Or Sigismunda[5]— E. F. G.) 'I think Hogarth greater than Dickens.'

(Looking at an engraving of the Sistine Madonna in which only she and the Child, I think, were represented.)

'Perhaps finer than the whole composition in so far as one's eyes
are more concentrated on the subject. The Child seems to me the
furthest result of human art. His attitude is that of a man—his
countenance a Jupiter's—perhaps rather too much so.'
(He afterwards said (1852) that his own little boy, Hallam,
explained the expression of Raphael's. He said he thought he had
known Raphael before he went to Italy— but not Michaelangelo—
not only statues and frescoes, but some picture (I think) of a
Madonna 'dragging a ton of a Child over her shoulder'.)

Seaford: 27–28 December 1852.   'Babies delight in being moved to
and from anything: that is amusement to them. What a life of
wonder—every object new. This morning he (his own little boy)
worshipp'd the bed-post when a gleam of sunshine lighted on it.'[6]
'I am afraid of him. It is a man. Babes have an expression of
grandeur that children lose. I used to think that the old painters
overdid the expression and dignity of their infant Christs: but I see
they did not.'
'I was struck at the Duke's (Wellington's) Funeral with the look of
sober manhood and humanity in the British soldiers.'

Brighton and elsewhere, 1852–3.   'The finest sea I have seen is at
Valentia (Ireland), without any wind and seemingly without a wave,
but with the momentum of the Atlantic behind it, it dashes up into
foam—blue diamond it looked like—all along the rocks—like
ghosts playing at hide and seek.'
(At some other time on the same subject.) 'When I was in Cornwall
it had blown a storm of wind and rain for days—all of a sudden fell
into perfect calm; I was a little inland of the cliffs, when, after a space
of perfect silence, a long roll of thunder—from some wave rushing
into a cavern, I suppose—came up from the distance and died away.
I never *felt* silence like that.'
'*This*' (looking from Brighton Pier) 'is not a grand sea: only an
angry curt sea. It seems to *shriek* as it recoils with its pebbles along
the beach.'
'The Earth has light of her own—so has Venus—perhaps all the
other planets—electrical light, or what we call Aurora. The light
edge of the dark hemisphere of the moon—the "old Moon in the
new Moon's arms".'
'Nay, they say she has no atmosphere at all.'
(I do not remember when this was said, nor whether I have exactly
set it down; therefore must not make A. T. answerable for what he

did not say, or for what after-discovery may have caused him to unsay. He had a powerful brain for physics as for the ideal. I remember his noticing that the forward-bending horns of some built-up mammal in the British Museum would never force its way through jungle, etc., and I observed on an after-visit that they had been altered accordingly.)

'Sometimes I think Shakespeare's sonnets finer than his plays—which is of course absurd. For it is the knowledge of the plays that makes the sonnets so fine.'

'Do you think the artist ever feels satisfied with his song? Not with the whole, I think; but perhaps the expression of parts.'

Standing one day with him looking at two busts—one of Dante, the other of Goethe, in a London shop, I asked, 'What is wanting to make Goethe's as fine as the other's?'

'The Divine.'

(Taking up and reading some number of *Pendennis*[7] at my lodging.) 'It's delicious—it's so mature.'

(Of Richardson's *Clarissa*, etc.) 'I love those Great, still books.'

'What is it in Dryden? I always feel that he is greater than his works.' (Though he thought much of 'Theodore and Honoria',[8] and quoted emphatically, ('More than a mile *immerst* within the wood.')

'Two of the finest similes in poetry are Milton's—that of the fleet hanging in the air (*Paradise Lost*), and the gunpowder-like "So started up in his foul shape the Fiend".' (Which latter A. T. used to enact with grim humour, from the crouching of the toad to the explosion.) 'Say what you please, I feel certain that Milton after death shot up into some grim archangel.' (*NB*. He used in earlier days to do the sun coming out from a cloud, and returning into one again, with a gradual opening and shutting of eyes and lips, etc. And, with a great fluffing up of his hair into full wig, and elevation of cravat and collar, George the Fourth in as comical and wonderful a way.)

NOTES

On FitzGerald, see p. 7.

1. On Spedding, see p. 7. His home, Mirehouse, was at Bassenthwaite Lake in the Lake District.

2. 'Morte d' Arthur' (Ricks, 226) ll. 105–6 (but FitzGerald quotes very inaccurately). The poem was written in 1833–4.

3. Note added by Hallam Tennyson.

4. Near Tennyson's boyhood home in Lincolnshire.

5. Tragic lover in Boccaccio's *Decameron*.

6. FitzGerald gives another version of this and the following paragraph in a letter to W. F. Pollock (22 September 1875):

I daresay I may have told you what Tennyson said of the Sistine Child, which he then knew only by Engraving. He first thought the Expression of his Face (as also the Attitude) almost too solemn, even for the Christ within. But some time after, when A. T. was married and had a Son, he told me that Raffaelle was all right: that no Man's face was so solemn as a Child's, full of Wonder. He said one morning that he watched his Babe 'worshipping the Sunbeam on the Bedpost and Curtain'. (*Selected Works*, p. 692)

Raphael's painting of the Sistine Madonna is at Dresden.
    7. Thakeray's novel had been published serially in 1848–50.
    8. One of Dryden's *Fables* (1699), a retelling in verse of a story by Boccaccio.

Notes on Tennyson's Conversation*

ARTHUR COLERIDGE

I believe that in the early days of our acquaintance the poet, seeing me with what appeared to be a notebook under my arm, suspected me of Boswellising,[1] but I was duly warned and reassured him of my innocence. I simply recorded very briefly in my diary a few of his 'dicta' which I wished to have for the benefit of my children, one of whom was a frequent and delighted listener to the Laureate's reading of his own poems. Mary Coleridge, at that time a shy, timid girl, was more than once asked to dictate the particular poems she wanted him to recite. I can hear him saying, 'Give me my seven-and-sixpenny' (meaning the single volume edition), and then we listened to the 'high Orphic chant', rather than the conventional reading of many of our favourite poems. I often asked for the 'Ode on the Duke of Wellington', and on one occasion, in the presence of Sir Charles Stanford[2]—then organist of Trinity College, Cambridge—the poet, lowering his voice at the words, 'God accept him, Christ receive him', added, 'It's a mighty anthem, that's what it is.' Stanford's music to 'The Voyage of Maeldune' was written at Freshwater, and four of us visitors sang a lovely quartet in that work for the first time in the

* 'Fragmentary Notes of Tennyson's Talk', *Tennyson and his Friends*, pp. 256–7, 259, 262–9.

poet's presence. It was rather nervous work, for the composer and ourselves were anxious to satisfy the poet in a work intended as a novelty for the Leeds Festival. The verdict was rather enigmatical: 'I like the ripple of your music.' . . .

It was my daily habit during the Easter holidays for three years to call at Farringford at 10.30, and present myself in the poet's sanctum, where I found him at his desk in the very act of hatching a poem or amending an old one. He would greet me with 'Here comes my daily bread.' Then I read the newspaper or a book until we started for our morning walk. The dialogue would begin abruptly, starting from some impressions left by our musical rehearsals on the previous day. 'Why is Stanford unable to set to music the word "cosmopolite"?' . . .

T.—'You cannot wonder at my horror of all the libels and slanders; people began to slander me in early days. For example, after my marriage we spent the honeymoon on Coniston Lake in a cottage lent to me by James Marshall.[3] Shortly after this, a paragraph appeared in an American newspaper to the following effect: "We hope, now that Mr Tennyson is married and has returned to his native lakes, that he will give up opium." The penny-a-liners evidently confounded your uncle, S. T. Coleridge, with myself— anyhow, if he wasn't quite certain, he gave your relative the benefit of the doubt.

'Again, I was once persuaded by an adventuress (who wrought upon me by her tale of hopeless poverty) to hear her read in my own drawing-room. She was in my house for exactly half an hour, and profited by her experience in telling her audiences that she had seen me thrashing my wife, and carried away drunk by two men-servants to my bedroom.' . . .

Miss L——, Doctor Johnson's godchild, used to tell a disagreeable story about him. Tennyson said about this, 'One should not lay stress on these oddities and angularities of great men. They should never be hawked about.'

T.—'"Break, break" was made one early summer morning, in a Lincolnshire lane. "Crossing the Bar" cost me five minutes one day last November.'

'At ten years of age I wrote an epic poem of great length—it was in the *Marmion* style. I used to rush about the fields, with a stick for a sword, and fancied myself a conqueror advancing upon an enemy's country.' . . .

T.—'Edward FitzGerald and I used to weary of the hopelessly prosaic lines in some books of *The Excursion*, and we had a contest, the prize for which was to be for the weakest line by mutual consent that we could either of us invent. FitzGerald declared the line was his—it really was mine—"A Mr Wilkinson, a clergyman".' I wish I could have told him of Jem Stephen's commentary on 'Heaven lies about us in our infancy', 'That is no reason why we should lie about Heaven in our old age.' Among other passages he quotes with admiration Wordsworth's lines on the Simplon Pass.

T.—'I am sorry that I am turned into a school-book at Harrow; the boys will say of me, "That horrible Tennyson". The cheapness of English classics makes the plan acceptable to schoolmasters and parents.'

He quoted with approval Byron's line 'Then farewell, Horace, whom I hated so'. 'He was quite right. I, too, was so overdosed with Horace as a boy, that I don't do him justice now I am old. I suppose Horace was the most popular poet that ever lived?' . . .

T.—'*The Tempest* has been dreadfully damaged by scenes intercalated by some common stage-adapter. At one time of my life I thought the sonnets greater than the plays. Some of the noblest things are in *Troilus and Cressida*. "Perseverance, dear my Lord, keeps 'honour bright", etc.' . . .

'I doubt that fine poem 'Kubla Khan' having been written in sleep; I have often imagined new poems in my sleep, but I couldn't remember them in the morning. Your uncle's words "Tennyson has no sense of rhythm and scansion" have been constantly quoted against me.[4] The truth is that in my youth I used no hyphens in writing composite words, and a reader might fancy that from this omission I had no knowledge of the length and measure of words and expressions.' . . .

Great sailors and soldiers were very favourite subjects. The Poet had personally known well one naval officer who had served with Nelson.

T.—'Among many odd letters I have received, an American curate wrote to me that he made a sudden resolution one Sunday that he would read "The Charge of the Light Brigade" instead of his ordinary sermon. An old Dorsetshire soldier who had fought at Balaclava, happened to be in the congregation, though the preacher was unaware of the fact. The verses had the happy result of the soldier giving up a bad, reckless life, and completely reforming. My poem was never meant to convey any spiritual lesson, but the very curious fact of the chance soldier and the parson's sudden resolution has often set me thinking.'

NOTES

On Arthur Coleridge, see p. 130.

1. Taking notes of conversations whilst they are in progress for use in a biography, as James Boswell did with Dr Johnson.

2. See p. 130.

3. Mrs James Marshall was a sister of Stephen Spring-Rice, one of Tennyson's friends at Trinity College. The house was Tent Lodge.

4. The passage referred to occurs in *Specimens of the Table Talk of the Late Samuel Taylor Coleridge* (1835) II, p. 164:

> I have not read through all Mr Tennyson's poems, which have been sent to me; but I think there are some things of a good deal of beauty in what I have seen. The misfortune is, that he has begun to write verses without very well understanding what metre is . . . .

(S. T. Coleridge was actually the great-uncle of Arthur Coleridge.)

Tennyson on the Romantic Poets*

FREDERICK LOCKER-LAMPSON

We talked of Byron and Wordsworth. 'Of course,' said Tennyson, 'Byron's merits are on the surface. This is not the case with Wordsworth. You must love Wordsworth ere he will seem worthy of your love. As a boy I was an enormous admirer of Byron, so much so that I got a surfeit of him, and now I cannot read him as I should like to do. I was fourteen when I heard of his death. It seemed an awful calamity; I remember I rushed out of doors, sat down by myself, shouted aloud, and wrote on the sandstone, *"Byron is dead!"* '[1]

He said that as a boy he had 'delighted in Pope's *Homer*', but he added, though 'Pope is a consummate artist, in the lower sense of the term', he could not now read him. I suppose he meant 'lower' as compared with the supreme power and sublime music of *Paradise Lost*, about which. I have often heard him quote Polixenes in *The Winter's Tale*.

> This is an art
> Which does mend nature, change it rather, but
> The art itself is nature.

* *Memoir*, II, pp. 69–70.

Tennyson went on to say that there was a great wind of words in a good deal of Shelley, but that as a writer of blank verse he was perhaps the most skilful of the moderns. He said, 'Nobody admires Shelley more than I once did, and I still admire him. I think I like his *Epipsychidion* as much as anything by him.' He said that Keats had 'a keen physical imagination; if he had been here (at Mürren) he would, in one line, have given us a picture of that mountain.' (The Mönch, etc. opposite.)

We often talked of Wordsworth. I remember his saying something to this effect: 'You must not think because I speak plainly of Wordsworth's defects as a poet that I have not a very high admiration of him. I shall never forget my deep emotion the first time I had speech with him. I have a profound admiration for "Tintern Abbey".' And yet even in that poem he considered the old poet had shown a want of literary instinct, or whatever it may be called. He thought it too long. He pointed out that the word 'again' occurs four times in the first fourteen lines, that the sixth and seventh lines[2] might have been more terse. 'Something like this', said he, extemporising on the spur of the moment: 'That makes a lone place lonelier'. He pencilled these and some other remarks in my volume of Wordsworth. Of course he greatly praised the famous line 'Whose dwelling is the light of setting suns'—'the permanent in the transitory';—he ended by saying, and saying emphatically, that, putting aside a great deal that Wordsworth had written which was not by any means first rate, he thought that 'Wordsworth's very best is the best in its way that has been sent out by the moderns.' I think that those were his exact words. I understood him to mean since Milton.

I spoke with admiration of his 'Ulysses'; he said, 'Yes, there is an echo of Dante in it.' He gave 'Tithonus' the same position as Ulysses. He said that if Arthur Hallam had lived he would have been 'one of the foremost men of his time, *but not as a poet*'.

NOTES

Frederick Locker (1821–95) (Locker-Lampson from 1885), minor poet. His daughter Eleanor married Lionel Tennyson, the poet's younger son. In 1869 Locker travelled with Tennyson in France and Switzerland; he later contributed his recollections of this tour, with some notes on Tennyson's conversation, to the *Memoir*. In his autobiography, *My Confidences* (London, 1896) pp. 358–9, he gives a brief account of Tennyson's relationship with Gladstone:

At that time Tennyson was a political admirer of Mr Gladstone; but even then he had a vague apprehension as to what the grand old man might possibly be going to do next.

Eleanor drove back to London with these two eminent personages, and on her arrival at home she gave an amusing account of the drive, and of the many searching inquiries that Tennyson had addressed to Mr Gladstone on the most delicate matters of Cabinet policy, questions civil and religious, domestic and foreign.

The child, seated in her dark corner, was greatly diverted with the simple and startlingly direct way in which Alfred put his questions, and the amiable and wary manner in which Mr Gladstone parried them.

1. 'Byron's death on 19 April 1824 was, as Tennyson remarked on another occasion, "a day when the whole world seemed to be darkened for me" ' (*Memoir*, I, p. 4).
2. 'That on a wild secluded scene impress/Thoughts of more deep seclusion'.

A Conversation with Tennyson (1870)*

WILLIAM KNIGHT

. . . Tennyson entered, and almost at once proposed that we should go out of doors. After a short stroll on the lawn under the cedars, we went into the 'careless ordered garden', walked round it, and then sat down in the small summer-house. It is a quaint rectangular garden, sloping to the west, where Nature and Art blend happily,— orchard trees, and old-fashioned flower-beds, with stately pines around, giving to it a sense of perfect rest. This garden is truly 'a haunt of ancient peace'. Left there alone with the bard for some time, I felt that I sat in the presence of one of the Kings of Men. His aged look impressed me. There was the keen eagle eye; and, although the glow of youth was gone, the strength of age was in its place. The lines of his face were like the furrows in the stem of a wrinkled oak-tree; but his whole bearing disclosed a latent strength and nobility, a reserve of power, combined with a most courteous grace of manner I was also struck by the *négligé* air of the man, so different from that of Browning or Arnold or Lowell.

He soon threw aside his picturesque cloak, and laid down his broad-brimmed hat upon the table. He asked me about my work at

* 'A Reminiscence of Tennyson', *Blackwood's Magazine*, CLXII (1897) 264–70.

St Andrews, and referred to that of his friend F. D Maurice[1] at Cambridge, asking if I knew his books. I gave my opinion of them, referring especially to the treatment of mediaevalism in Maurice's *History of Mental and Moral Philosophy*. I said I thought it the best discussion of mediaeval thought which we had in English; but I added that the man was greater than his philosophy. He answered, 'You are right. Maurice was one of the greatest and best of the men I have ever known.' I referred to what had struck myself so much, viz., the uplifting influence of his conversation and the magnetic effect of his mere presence—like that of Martineau[2] or Newman,[3] to take two very different cases. 'Ah!' he replied; 'far greater than Newman, really more spiritual, and profounder every way.'

We soon talked of the season, and of the poets. 'The Promise of May' was all around us, and he quoted, with a rich musical intoning of their words, passages from Milton, Virgil, and Lord Surrey. I forget the passages from the two former; but from Lord Surrey[4] it was part of his sonnet on spring.

> The soote season, that bud and bloom forth brings,
> With green hath clad the hill, and eke the vale.
> The nightingale with feathers new she sings;
> The turtle to her make hath told her tale.
> Summer is come, for every spray now springs,
> Winter is worn that was the flowers' bale.

I asked if he knew the 'Day's Estival', by our Scottish poet Alexander Hume,[5] and quoted a stanza from it on the effect of sunrise:

> For joy the birds with boulden throats
>   Against his visage sheen,
> Take up their kindly music-notes
>   In woods and gardens green.

He said he preferred Lord Surrey's way of putting it:

> The Sun, when he hath spread his rays,
> And shew'd his face ten thousand ways;
> Ten thousand things do then begin,
> To shew the life that they are in.

We talked much of the sonnet. He thought the best in the language were Milton's, Shakespeare's, and Wordsworth's; after these three those by his own brother Charles. He said, '*I* at least like my brother's next to those by "the three immortals".' 'The Sonnet arrests the free sweep of genius, and if poets were to keep to it, it would cripple them; but it is a fascinating kind of verse, and to excel in it is a rare distinction.' I ventured to refer to the metrical and structural necessity that its last line should form the climax,—both of thought and of expression,—in a sonnet; and that the whole should be like a wave breaking on the shore. He said, 'Not only so; the whole should show a continuous advance of thought and of movement, like a river fed by rillets; as every great poem, and all essays and treatises, should. Going back to Milton, he said that he had caught the spirit of his blank verse from Virgil, the long sonorous roll, of which he is such a master. He quoted two passages from each in illustration.

He had no great liking, he said, for arranging the poets in a hierarchy. He found so much that surpassed him in different ways in all the great ones; but he thought that Homer,-Aeschylus, Sophocles, Virgil, Dante, Shakespeare, and Goethe—these seven—were the greatest of the great, up to the year 1800. They are not all equal in rank; and, even in the work of that heptarchy of genius, there were trivial things to be found.

He spoke of the diseased craving to have all the trifles of a man of genius preserved, and of the positive crime of publishing what a poet had himself deliberately suppressed. If all the contents of a poet's waste-basket were taken out and printed, and issued in a volume, one result would be that the things which he had disowned would be read by many to whom the great things he had written would be unknown. He said that he himself had suffered in that way. I told him of a poem which Wordsworth wrote when he lived at Alfoxden—an unworthy record of a revolting crime—which he had the good sense never to publish. I had not seen the original, but only a copy, which I threw in the fire as soon as I had read it. Tennyson was greatly pleased, and said, 'It was the kindest thing you could have done.' He then spoke of the folly of fancying that all that a poet says in his verses must have some local meaning, or a personal reference. 'There are some curious creatures who go about fishing for the people, and searching for the places, which they fancy must have given rise to our poems. They don't understand, or believe, that we have any imagination of our own, so create the people or the places. Of course we often describe, but we generally let that be known easily enough.'

He quoted in this connection

> The seven elms, the poplars four
> That stand beside by father's door.

These things are returned to us by the 'great artist Memory', but when critics and commentators search for subterranean meanings they generally lose themselves in fancies.

We then went on—I do not remember what the link of connection was—to talk of spiritualism, and the Psychical Society,[6] in which he was much interested, and also of the problems of theism. He spoke of the great Realm of the Unknown which surrounds us as being *also known*, and having Intelligence at the heart of it; and he told more stories than one of spirit manifestations as authentic emanations from the unknown and as proof that out of darkness light could reach us.

Just at this stage of our talk Mrs Hallam Tennyson, Mrs Douglas Freshfield, and her daughter came up the garden-walk to the summer-house. Miss Freshfield wore a hat on which was an artificial flower, a lilac branch. It at once caught Tennyson's eye. There was a lilac tree in bloom close at hand, and he said, 'What is that you are wearing? It's a flowery lie, it's a speaking mendacity.' He asked how she could wear such a thing in the month of May! We rose from the bower, and all went down the garden-walk to see the fig-tree at the foot of it, and sundry other things at the western entrance-door, where Miss Kate Greenaway[7] was painting. We returned along a twisting alley under the rich green foliage of elms and ilexes. He spoke much of the ilex, a tree which he greatly admired. We heard both the cuckoo and the nightingale. 'Rosy plumelets' were on the larch. He said the finest larches he had ever seen were at Inveraray. 'What grand trees you have in Scotland! It's nonsense to complain, as some do, of the want of them. Dr Johnson was either very unfortunate, or very inaccurate, or incorrectly reported by Boswell on this point.'[8] I spoke of the vast destruction of our pine-forests, of noble birches and other trees, in our great gales. He lamented it, for, he said, 'Your Scotch fir is a magnificent tree, next to the oak in stateliness, and how glorious the colour!' He said he bewailed the loss of all old things—old trees, old historic places, the old creatures of the forest, and of the air. 'Aren't your eagles getting scarce? and I hear that even the kingfisher is less common than it was.' I replied that both eagle and kingfisher were becoming almost extinct.

Walking up the lane outside the grounds at the back of Farringford, he pointed out the view beyond Freshwater to the east, where, as he says in a well-known poem,

> The hoary channel
> Tumbles a breaker on chalk and sand.[9]

This led him to speak of prehistoric things, and of the wonders which geology had brought to light. He referred to the period of the Weald, when there was a mighty estuary, like that of the Ganges, where we then stood; and when gigantic lizards, the iguanodon, etc., were the chief of living things. As we afterwards walked to and fro on the lawn under the shade of the cedars, sheltered by the 'groves of pine' (to which he refers in his poem addressed to Maurice),[10] he told me—without the slightest touch of vanity—that, when he was between thirteen and fourteen years of age, he wrote an epic of several thousand lines. His father was proud of it, and said he thought 'the author would yet be one of the great in English literature' (good prophet of the future, thought I); 'but', he added, 'I burned it, when I read the earliest poems of Shelley'.

'I don't care a bit for various readings from the poets', he said, 'although I have changed my own text a good deal. I like to enjoy the book I am reading, and footnotes distract me. I like to read, and I just read straight on.'

'What do you do with the books which are sent to you?' he asked, 'and do you get many? I have several every day, chiefly books of poetry or rhyme. I wish they would rather send me prose. I calculate, by the number of verses which the books contain, that I get a verse for every three minutes of my life; and the worst of it is that nearly all the writers expect me to answer and acknowledge them!' He handed to me Dr Kynaston's[11] Latin version of 'Demeter', a copy of which, typewriten, he had received that morning. It was excellent, and he said he had thought of getting a typewriter to answer those correspondents who sent him their verses!

He then spoke of the labour necessary to produce the best things in poetry, and of the recasting of verses. He said he thought that almost every poet did this habitually. It was very rarely that the simplest song came into the writer's mind in a rush of melody all at once. He mentioned someone saying of a poet, 'Oh! *he* didn't revise his verses; his MSS are all unblotted.' 'How do you know?' I replied to him. '*No one knows* what the poets have done with their verses, as they revise them in their mind before they are written down.' He added that *his* chief work was done, not as Wordsworth's was in the open air, but in his library, in the evenings. It seemed as if he needed the quiet of the close of day, and the meditative reverie to which it led, to start him productively.

As we were going toward the house, a nightingale was singing loud and ceaselessly. He told me that, while sitting in a grove, on a still evening, one of these birds was close beside him. 'I was as near it as I am to you, and it did not cease to sing. We were so close that I felt the very air move by its wings (I thought it was by its voice), and it did not stop singing, or seem to notice me.'

Next day we walked along the 'ridge of the noble down' towards the Needles. To begin with, our talk was chiefly on the problems of philosophy, and his conversation on the great questions of belief was quite as significant as his remarks on poetry, or even as his poems themselves. We spoke of the 'Metaphysical Society', of which he was one of the original promoters, along with Dr Martineau, Dean Stanley, Huxley, and Dr Ward. He did not often attend, being seldom in London, but he thought their meetings very useful. For himself he did not get much good from debating problems, especially ultimate ones; but the confederacy, and the exchange of views which took place in such a society, was good for all its members.

He raised the question, How should philosophy be defined? The 'love of wisdom' was all very well, but to love it and seek it, and yet not find it, was mere vanity and vexation of spirit; and the question was, could we *find* it? I said that philosophy was both a search and a discovery; at once a process and a product. 'Yes,' he replied; 'but how is the product produced? and I want to know how we are to unite the One with the Many, and the Many with the All.' I said that was the great question of the ages, the radical problem of metaphysic, and that it was fundamentally an insoluble one. 'For my part,' he said, 'if I were an old Greek I should try to combine the doctrine of Parmenides with that of Heraclitus. I find that both of them are true in part; but does not all metaphysic seek that which underlies phenomena?' 'Yes; and what it finds it reaches intuitively, and at first-hand. The great beliefs are not conclusions deduced by logic, but premisses grasped by intuition. I think it is not analysis, with a view to new inductions, that we need nowadays, so much as a new philosophical synthesis.' 'Well,' he said, 'we must get to some height above phenomena. We must climb up, and we can't ascend a ladder without rungs. Isn't the ladder of analogy very useful in metaphysics?' 'It is, but why not dispense with a ladder altogether? It's chief use is to enable us to leap from it, and to reach the infinite, not by a tedious process of ascent, but by seeing it everywhere within the finite' 'Yes; I agree with that, and I have tried to show something like it in some of my poems; but the outward world, where the ladders and symbols are, is surely more of a veil which hides the Infinite than a mirror which reveals it.' 'Yes: and Browning put this well:

> Some say Creation's meant to shew Him forth;
> I say it's meant to hide Him all it can.[12]

He then spoke of Darwin, and of the great truth in evolution; but it was only one side of a truth that had two sides. 'All things are double one against another.' He also spoke of Bruno,[13] with whom he had much sympathy. From this we passed to the subject of immortality. I ventured to say that it was a more pressing problem in our time than even that of theism, and that agnosticism had undermined it in many quarters. He said he did not require argumentative proof of a future life, and referred me to *In*

Memoriam. He had nothing further to say; and, although his faith was not stated dogmatically in that poem, every one could see that he believed in the survival of the individual. 'Annihilation was impossible, and inconceivable. We are parts of the infinite whole; and when we die, and our souls touch the great *Anima Mundi*, who knows what new powers may spring to life within us, and old ones awaken from sleep, all due to that touch.'

The subject of free will was next talked of, and he referred to the way in which it had been discussed by Dr Ward, and in the columns of the *Spectator*. He said he liked the *Spectator*. He did not always agree with its literary articles, but its philosophy was good . Here the conversation turned to the newspaper press, and to politics. In politics, as elsewhere, he strove to shun 'the falsehood of extremes'. He was a Liberal Conservative, and a Conservative Liberal. He had written

> He is the true conservative
> Who lops the mouldered branch away.[14]

'But', said he, 'the branch must be a mouldered one, before we should venture to lop it off.'

Listening to the wind in the trees, and to the sound of running water—although it was the very tiniest of rillets—led us away from philosophy, and he talked of Sir Walter Scott, characterising him as the greatest novelist of all time. He said, 'What a gift it was that Scotland gave to the world in him. And your Burns! he is supreme amongst your poets.' He praised Lockhart's *Life of Scott*,[15] as one of the finest of biographies; and my happening to mention an anecdote of Scott from that book led to our spending the greater part of the rest of our walk in the telling of stories. Tennyson was an admirable storyteller. He asked me for some good Scotch anecdotes, and I gave him some, but he was able to cap each of them with a better one of his own—all of which he told with arch humour and simplicity.

He then told some anecdotes of a visit to Scotland. After he had left an inn in the island of Skye, the landlord was asked, 'Did he know who had been staying in his house? It was the poet Tennyson.' He replied, 'Lor'—to think o' that! and sure I thoucht he was a shentleman!' Near Stirling the same remark was made to the keeper of the hotel where he had stayed. 'Do you ken who you had wi' you t'other night?' 'Naa; but he was a pleesant shentleman.' 'It was Tennyson, the poet.' 'An' wha'may *he* be?' 'Oh, he is a writer of verses, sich as ye see i' the papers.' 'Noo, to think o' that! jeest a pooblic writer, an' I gied him ma best bedroom!' Of Mrs Tennyson, however, the landlord remarked, 'Oh! but *she* was an angel.'

I have said that the conversational power of Tennyson struck me quite as much as his poetry had done for forty years. To explain this I must compare it with that of some of his contemporaries. It was not like the meteoric flashes and fireworks of Carlyle's talk, which sometimes dazzled as much as it instructed; and it had not that torrent-rush in which Carlyle so often indulged. It was for more restrained. It had neither the continuousness nor the range of Browning's many-sided conversation; nor did it possess the charm of the ethereal visionariness of Newman's. It lacked the fullness and the consummate sweep of Mr Ruskin's talk; and it had neither the historic range and brilliance of Dean Stanley's, nor the fascinating subtlety—the elevation and the depth combined—of that of the late F. D. Maurice. *But* it was clear as crystal, and calm as well as clear. It was terse and exact, precise and luminous. Not a word was wasted, and every phrase was suggestive. Tennyson did not monopolise conversation. He wished to know what other people thought, and therefore to hear them state it, that he might understand their position and ideas. But in all his talk on great problems, he at once got to their essence, sounding their depths with ease; or, to change the illustration, he seized the kernel, and let the shell and its fragments alone. There was a wonderful simplicity allied to his clear vision and his strength. He was more child-like than the majority of his contemporaries; and, along with this, there was—what I have already mentioned—*a great reserve of power*. His appreciation of other workers belonging to his time was remarkable. Neither he nor Browning disparaged their contemporaries, as Carlyle so often did, when he spotted their weaknesses, and put them in the pillory. From first to last, Tennyson seemed to look sympathetically on all good work; and he had a special veneration for the strong silent thinkers and workers. He was an idealist at heart. Underneath the realism of his nature, this other feature rose above it. He was not so much of a Platonist as a Berkelean, but faith in the great Kantian triad (God, Duty, Immortality) dominated his life—God being to him both personal and impersonal, Duty being continuous unselfish devotion to the good of all, and Immortality the survival not only of the race, but of all the units in it.

NOTES

William Knight (1836–1916) was Professor of Moral Philosophy at St Andrews (1876–1902) and a prolific author.
    1. See p. 110.
    2. See p. 97.
    3. John Henry Newman (1801–90), influential writer who was converted to Roman Catholicism in 1845 and created Cardinal in 1879.
    4. Henry Howard, Earl of Surrey (died 1547), poet.

5. Alexander Hume (1560?–1609), Scottish poet.

6. Tennyson was one of the founder members of the Society for Psychical Research, established in 1882.

> [He] had begun his study of the subject with high hopes that it might provide the proof of spiritual survival which he so earnestly desired . . . but had become disillusioned and sceptical about the methods of his fellow-students, feeling that God and the ghosts of the departed would choose something better than the legs of tables through which to communicate with man, if they wished to do so.   (Sir Charles Tennyson, *Alfred Tennyson*, p. 499)

7. Kate Greenaway (1846–1901), artist and illustrator of children's books.

8. Johnson's remarks 'upon the nakedness of the country, from its being denuded of trees' when he toured Scotland in 1775 were widely repeated—*Boswell's Life of Johnson*, ed. G. B. Hill (Oxford: Clarendon Press 1934) II, p. 301.

9. 'To the Rev. F. D. Maurice' (Ricks, 312) ll. 23–4 (but Tennyson has *billow*, not *breaker*).

10. Ibid., l. 21.

11. Herbert Kynaston (1809–1878), scholar and teacher.

12. From Browning's poem 'Bishop Blougram's Apology' (but Browning has 'think', not 'say').

13. Giordano Bruno (d. 1600), Italian philosopher.

14. 'Hands All Round!' (Ricks, 307, 393), again slightly misquoted.

15. Published 1837–8.

Tennyson on Religion*

WILLIAM BOYD-CARPENTER

It fell out naturally when I met him that conversation turned on religion or theological subjects. His mind, courageous, inquiring, honest, sought truth beyond the forms of truth. On the occasion of my first visit to Aldworth, in the smoking-room we talked of the problem of pain, of determinism, of apparent contradictions of faith. That night, indeed, we seemed to talk. 'Of faith, free will, foreknowledge absolute'. But the impression left upon my mind was that we were engaged in no more scholastic discussion; it was no mere intellectually satisfactory creed which was sought: it was something

* 'Tennyson and his Talk on Some Religious Questions', *Tennyson and his Friends*, pp. 298–305.

186 TENNYSON: INTERVIEWS AND RECOLLECTIONS

deeper and more abiding than anything which may be modified in form from age to age; the soul needs an anchorage, and to find it there must be no ignoring of facts and no juggling with them once they are found. In illustration of this I may relate how once, when walking with him among the heather-clad heights round Aldworth, he spoke of the apparent dualism in Nature: the forces of darkness and light seemed to meet in conflict. 'If I were not a Christian,' he said, 'I should be perhaps a Parsee'.[1] He felt, however, that if once we accepted the view that this life was a time of education, then the dark things might be found to have a meaning and a value. In the retrospect hereafter the pain and suffering would seem trivial. . . . He once quoted to me Hinton's[2] view that we were not in a position to judge the full meaning of life; that we were in fact looking at the wrong side of things. We saw the work from the underside, and we could not judge of the pattern which was perhaps clear enough on the upper side.

Next day I was able to remind him that he had approved this view of life. He was not well, and I think that the darker aspects loomed larger in his mind; at any rate, he was speaking more gloomily than usual. When I remarked that God did not take away men till their work was done, he said, 'He does; look at the promising young fellows cut off.' Then I brought up Hinton's theory and illustration, and asked whether we could judge when a man had finished his appointed work. Immediately he acquiesced; the view evidently satisfied him.

He took a deep interest in those borderland questions which sometimes seem so near an answer and yet never are answered. At the hour of death what are the sights which rush upon the vision? Of these he would sometimes speak; he told me how William Alling ham,[3] when dying, said to his wife, 'I see things beyond your imagination to conceive.' Some vision seemed to come to such at death. One lady in the Isle of Wight exclaimed, as though she saw 'cherubim and seraphim'. But these incidents did not disturb the steady thought and trust which found its strength far deeper down than in any surface phenomena. He never shirked the hard and dismaying facts of life. Once he made me take to my room Winwood Reade's *Martyrdom of Man*.[4] There never was such a passionate philippic against Nature as this book contained. The universe was one vast scene of murder; the deep aspirations and noble visions of men were the follies of flies buzzing for a brief moment in the presence of inexorable destruction. Life was bottled sunshine; death the silent-footed butler who withdrew the cork. The book, with its fierce invective, had a strange rhapsodical charm. It put with irate and verbose extravagance the fact that sometimes

> Nature, red in tooth and claw,
> With ravin shrieked against his creed

but it failed to see any but one side of the question. The writer saw clearly enough what Tennyson saw, but Tennyson saw much more. He could not make his judgement blind against faith any more than he would make it blind against facts. He saw more clearly because he saw more largely. He distrusted narrow views from whatever side they were advanced. The same spirit which led him to see the danger of the dogmatic temper in so-called orthodox circles led him to distrust it when it came from other quarters. There was a wholesome balance about his mind . . . but we should be wholly wrong if we supposed that he did not realise the value of form. He knew that faith did not lie in the form, but he knew also the protective value of form to faith; the shell was not the kernel, but the kernel ripened all the better in the shelter of the shell. He realised how sacred was the flesh and blood to which truth divine might be linked, and he uttered the wise caution,

> Hold thou the good: defend it well
> For fear divine philosophy
> Should push beyond her mark and be
> Procuress to the lords of Hell.

In his view, as it seemed to me, there were two attitudes of mind towards dogmatic forms—the one impatient of form because form was never adequate to express the whole truth, the other impatient of form because impatient of the truth itself. These two attitudes of mind were poles asunder; they must never be confused together.

I may be allowed to illustrate this discriminating spirit by one or two reminiscences. I once asked him whether they were right who interpreted the three ladies who accompanied King Arthur on his last voyage as Faith, Hope, and Charity. He replied with a touch of (shall I call it?) intellectual impatience: 'They do and they do not. They are those graces, but they are much more than those. I hate to be tied down to say, "This means that", because the thought in the image is much more than the definition suggested or any specific interpretation advanced.' The truth was wider than the form, yet the form was a shelter for the truth. It meant this, but not this only; truth must be able to transcend any form in which it may be presented. . . .

I have already spoken of his recognition of the apparent dualism in Nature. His outlook on the universe could not ignore the dark and dismaying facts of existence, and his faith, which rose above the shriek of Nature, was not based upon arguments derived from any

survey of external, physical Nature. When he confined his outlook to
this, he could see power and mechanism, but he could not from these
derive faith. His vision must go beyond the mere physical universe;
he must see life and see it whole; he must include that which is
highest in Nature, even man, and only then could he find the
resting-place of faith. He thus summed up the matter once when we
had been walking up and down the 'ballroom' at Farringford: 'It is
hard,' he said, 'it is hard to believe in God; but it is harder not to
believe. I believe in God, not from what I see in Nature, but from
what I find in man.' I took him to mean that the witness of Nature
was only complete when it included all that was in Nature, and that
the effort to draw conclusions from Nature when man, the highest-
known factor in Nature, was excluded, could only lead to mistake. I
do not think he meant, however, that external Nature gave no hints
of a superintending wisdom or even love, for his own writings show,
I think, that such hints had been whispered to him by flower and
star; I think he meant that faith did not find her platform finally
secure beneath her feet till she had taken count of man. In short, he
seemd to me to be near to the position of Thomas Erskine of
Linlathen, who said that truth as soon as learned was felt to be held
on a much deeper and more unshakable ground than any authority
which appealed to mere intellect, namely, on its own discerned
truthfulness. The response to all that is highest in Nature is found in
the heart of man, and man cannot deny this highest, because it is
latent in himself already. But I must continue Tennyson's own
words: 'It is hard to believe in God, but it is harder not to believe in
Him. I don't believe in His goodness from what I see in Nature. In
Nature I see the mechanician; I believe in His goodness from what I
find in my own breast.' I said, 'Then you believe that Man is the
highest witness of God?' 'Certainly,' he replied. I said, 'Is not that
what Christ said and was? He was in man the highest witness of God
to man', and I quoted the recorded words, 'He that hath seen me
hath seen the Father.' He assented, but said that there were, of
course, difficulites in the idea of a Trinity—the Three. 'But mind,'
he said, 'Son of God is quite right—that he was.' He said that, of
course, we must have doctrine, and then he added, 'After all, the
greatest thing is Faith.'

He was alive to the movements of modern thought. He saw in
evolution, if not a fully proved law, yet a magnificent working
hypothesis; he could not regard it as a theory hostile to ultimate
faith; but far beyond the natural wish to reconcile faith and thought,
which he shared with all right-thinking men, was the conviction of
the changeless personal relationship between God and man. He
might find difficulties about faith and about certain dogmas of faith,
such as the Trinity. No doubt, however, the poet's conception

brought the divine into all human life; it showed God in touch with us at all epochs of our existence—in our origin, in our history, in our final self-realisation, for He is 'Our Father and our Brother and our God'.

NOTES

William Boyd-Carpenter (1841–1918), Bishop of Ripon from 1884, was well known as a writer and preacher.
1. An Indian follower of Zoroaster.
2. James Hinton (1822–75), surgeon and member of the Metaphysical Society, published several books on philosophy and religion.
3. See p. 30.
4. William Winwood Reade (1838–75), novelist and controversialist, travelled widely in Africa. Of his *Martyrdom of Man* (1872) the *Dictionary of National Biography* remarks that 'the author does not attempt to conceal his atheistical opinions'.

Tennyson on Free Will*

RODEN NOEL

It does not appear that Tennyson ever became less of a recluse. Of his alleged bearishness, however, I for my part saw nothing. He had no doubt an abrupt, growling, fragmentary way of talking, and was often silent. From what one hears, I suppose he could be disagreeable when he chose, or was much bored, and in the mood for it. But on the too rare occasions of my visiting him, at Aldworth, and in London years ago, I found him (although I did not know him enough to become intimate with him) more than courteous, kind and helpful in the most gracious manner, giving me, as a young man, warm encouragement and wise counsel concerning my own poetry.

On one occasion, as we walked in the terraced garden of beautiful Aldworth, enjoying the wonderful view, he recited, or rather chaunted, to me in his magnificent sonorous voice, those noble lines of Wordsworth describing the Pass of Gondo.[1]

One incident of my visit to Aldworth I remember as if it had happened yesterday. He went to the oriel window of his study, and looked out upon the distant view, so immense, so beautiful, so English. We had been talking about free will, and other metaphysical

* 'Lord Tennyson', *Atalanta* (1892) pp. 269–70.

puzzles; then he said, dreamily, 'I believe that everything which happens to us we remember; it is all stored up somewhere to come forth again upon occasion, though it may seem to be forgotten— even this movement to the window we shall remember.' But he added, 'perhaps not this, so trivial a circumstance!' And now how that very utterance has impressed this circumstance upon me!

Tennyson, as has been well observed by one who knew him, was simple as a child, transparent, said out what he felt, and would not conceal his feeling. But, indeed, that childlikeness is a characteristic of true greatness. He did not, for instance, pretend that he did not mind the neglect, or abuse even, of 'a thousand peering little-nesses'—why should he? Of neglect he certainly got little. But he did not like an unfavourable criticism to be left about for his servants to see, and his son carefully shielded him from the sight of these depreciations in later life. . . .

Lord Tennyson believed in 'free will'. When I urged the argument of Jonathan Edwards,[2] and other more modern arguments against the popular conception of it, he replied that free will, not being subject to the law of causation, was a *miracle*, no doubt; but that consciousness testifies to the fact.

NOTES

The Hon. Roden Berkeley Wriothesley Noel (1834–94), minor poet and critic. When he published an article on the *Idylls of the King* in the *Contemporary Review*, Tennyson wrote to him: 'You are wrong about the *Idylls of the King*, but wrong in a gracious and noble way, for which I am obliged to you' (*Memoir*, ii, p. 311).

1. In Book vi of *The Prelude*.

2. There were two eighteenth-century American theologians of this name; the reference is perhaps to the younger's *A Dissertation Concerning Liberty and Necessity* (1797).

Tennyson's Conversation: the Last Days*

T. H. WARREN

He began about Catullus: 'Catullus says that a poet's lines may be impure provided his life is pure. I don't agree with him: his verses fly

* *Memoir*, ii, pp. 400–1.

much further than he does. There is hardly any crime greater than for a man with genius to propagate vice by his written words. I have always admired him: "Acme and Septimius" is lovely. Then he has very pretty metres. "Collis O Heliconii" is in a beautiful metre. I wrote a great part of my Jubilee Ode in it. People didn't understand. They don't understand these things. They don't understand English scansion. In the line 'Dream not of where some sunny rose may linger' they said the first syllable of 'sunny' was long, whereas it evidently is short. Doubling the *n* in English makes the vowel before short.'

At his request Warren repeated some undergraduate lines about Jowett:

> What I know not is not knowledge:
> I am the Master of this college.

'Very unfair,' my father said, 'Jowett never set up to be omniscient. It might possibly have suited Whewell. Jowett got his pronunciation of "knowledge" from me (long o). "Free-will, fore-knowledge absolute." "Fore-knŏlledge" would be horrible there.'[1]

The talk turned on religion and 'God is Love', and he said that Jowett, who had liked the simple hymn for children in *The Promise of May*, III. i, wanted him to write another hymn, and he quoted a prayer by Jowett, praying that 'we might see ourselves as others see us.' 'I should not pray for that: others cannot see much of one's inner self.'

Warren (after a pause)—Is not the existence of evil (the 'mystery of iniquity') the great difficulty?

A. T.—Yes. I tried to bring that out in a poem that comes after the 'Charge of the Heavy Brigade'. That charge was a wonderful affair. An officer who was there, after they came out said it was the finest excitement ever known, that drink, gambling, and horse-racing were nothing to it.

Warren.—Will you write the hymn?

A. T.—A good hymn is the most difficult thing in the world to write. In a good hymn you have to be commonplace and poetical. The moment you cease to be commonplace and put in any expression at all out of the common, it ceases to be a hymn. Of hymns I like Heber's 'Holy, Holy, Holy' better than most, it is in a fine metre too. What will people come to in a hundred years? Do you think they will give up all religious forms and go and sit in silence in the churches listening to the organs?

NOTES

On T. H. Warren, see p. 158. He had 'two or three talks' with Tennyson in April 1892, within a few months of the latter's death.

1. Many other writers have commented on Tennyson's idiosyncratic pronunciation of certain words. Margaret L. Woods writes,

> Tennyson was, as might be expected, greatly interested in the pronunci-ation of English. He deplored the narrowing of our vowels and the general clipping of our words. The word 'shone', he rightly protested, should not be pronounced 'shonn' but with a broad 'o'. He instanced Shelley's use of 'glode' for glided. The word 'knowledge', he said, should not be pronounced 'knollege', but with the emphasis on the 'know'. ('My Recollections of Tennyson', *Poetry Review*, XXXIII (1942) 277)

'Notes on Characteristics of Tennyson'*

BENJAMIN JOWETT

Absolute truthfulness, absolutely himself, never played tricks.

Never got himself puffed in the newpapers.

A friend of liberty and truth.

Extraordinary vitality.

Great common-sense and a strong will.

The instinct of common-sense at the bottom of all he did.

Not a man of the world (in the ordinary sense) but a man who had the greatest insight into the world, and often in a word or a sentence would flash a light.

Intensely needed sympathy.

A great and deep strength.

He mastered circumstances, but he was also partly mastered by them, e.g. the old calamity of the disinheritance of his father and his treatment by rogues in the days of his youth.

Very fair towards other poets, including those who were not popular, such as Crabbe.

He had the high-bred manners not only of a gentleman but of a great man.

He would have wished that, like Shakespeare, his life might be unknown to posterity.

* *Tennyson and his Friends*, pp. 186–7.

Conversation

In the commonest conversation he showed himself a man of genius. He had abundance of fire, never talked poorly, never for effect. As Socrates described Plato, 'Like no one whom I ever knew before.'

The three subjects of which he most often spoke were 'God', 'free will', and 'immortality', yet always seeming to find an (apparent) contradiction between the 'imperfect world', and 'the perfect attributes of God'.

Great charm of his ordinary conversation, sitting by a very ordinary person and telling stories with the most high-bred courtesy, endless stories, not too high or too low for ordinary conversation.

The persons and incidents of his childhood very vivid to him, and the Lincolnshire dialect and the ways of life.

Loved telling a good story, which he did admirably, and also hearing one.

He told very accurately, almost in the same words, his old stories, though, having a powerful memory, he was impatient of a friend who told him a twice-repeated tale.

His jests were very amusing.

At good things he would sit laughing away—laughter often interrupted by fits of sadness.

His absolute sincerity, or habit of saying all things to all kinds of persons.

He ought always to have lived among gentlemen only.

Of his early friends (after Arthur Hallam) FitzGerald, Spedding, Sir John Simeon, Lushington—A. T. was enthusiastic about them.

NOTE

Benjamin Jowett (1817–93), Regius Professor of Greek at Oxford from 1855 and Master of Balliol College from 1870, was on terms of close friendship with Tennyson for 'nearly forty years', as he says in the reminiscences written at the very end of his life and included in the *Memoir*, ii, pp. 459–68. 'To the Master of Balliol' (Ricks, 440) is addressed to him.

The End*

HALLAM TENNYSON

On Saturday and Sunday he was very drowsy. . . .

On Sunday afternoon he was much worse, and his breathing terribly uneven.

On Monday morning at eight o'clock he sent me for his Shakespeare. I took him Steevens's edition, *Lear, Cymbeline*, and *Troilus and Cressida*, three plays which he loved dearly. . . .

On Wednesday [5 October 1892] he wanted to know whether his book had come, probably meaning the proofs of his new volume[1]. . . .

He had been talking to Dr Dabbs about death, and about 'What a shadow this life is, and how men cling to what is after all but a small part of the great world's life.' Then Dr Dabbs told him (for his interest was always keen 'in the lot of lowly men') of an incident that had lately happened. 'A villager, ninety years old, was dying, and had so much pined to see his old bedridden wife once more that they had carried her to where he lay. He pressed his shrunken hand upon her hand, and in a husky voice said to her, "Come soon", and soon after passed away himself.' My father murmured, 'True Faith': and the tears were in his voice. Suddenly he gathered himself together and spoke one word about himself to the doctor, 'Death?' Dr Dabbs bowed his head, and he said, 'That's well'.

His last food was taken at a quarter to four, and he tried to read, 'but could not. He exclaimed, 'I have opened it.' Whether this referred to the Shakespeare, opened by him at

> Hang there like fruit, my soul,
> Till the tree die![2]

which he always called among the tenderest lines in Shakespeare: or whether one of his last poems, of which he was fond, was running through his head I cannot tell:

> Fear not thou the hidden purpose of that Power which alone is
> great,
> Nor the myraid world, His shadow, nor the silent Opener of the
> Gate.[3]

* *Memoir*, ii, pp. 425, 427–9.

He then spoke his last words, a farewell blessing, to my mother and myself.

For the next hours the full moon flooded the room and the great landscape outside with light; and we watched in solemn stillness. His patience and quiet strength had power upon those who were nearest and dearest to him; we felt thankful for the love and utter peace of it all; and his own lines of comfort from *In Memoriam* were strongly borne in upon us. He was quite restful, holding my wife's hand, and, as he was passing away, I spoke over him his own prayer, 'God accept him! Christ receive him!'[4] because I knew that he would have wished it.

I give the medical bulletin published next day by Dr Dabbs:

The tendency to fatal syncope may be said to have really commenced about 10 a.m. on Wednesday, and on Thursday, 6 October, at 1.35 a.m., the great poet breathed his last. Nothing could have been more striking than the scene during the last few hours. On the bed a figure of breathing marble, flooded and bathed in the light of the full moon streaming through the oriel window; his hand clasping the Shakespeare which he had asked for but recently, and which he had kept by him to the end; the moonlight, the majestic figure as he lay there, 'drawing thicker breath',[5] irresistibly brought to our minds his own 'Passing of Arthur'.

Some friends and the servants came to see him. He looked very grand and peaceful with the deep furrows of thought almost smoothed away, and the old clergyman of Lurgashall stood by the bed with his hands raised, and said, 'Lord Tennyson, God has taken you, who made you a prince of men! Farewell!'

NOTES

Tennyson died at Aldworth on 6 October 1892 and was buried in Westminster Abbey six days later.

1. *The Death of Oenone, Akbar's Dream, and Other Poems* was published on 28 October.

2. *Cymbeline*, v. v. 264–5.

3. 'God and the Universe' (Ricks, 460), lines 5–6; the poem was written in 1892.

4. The last line of Tennyson's 'Ode on the Death of the Duke of Wellington' (Ricks, 309), written in 1852.

5. 'Morte d'Arthur', l. 148.

Tennyson's Funeral*

MARY ANDERSON DE NAVARRO

Morning, Wednesday, 12 October 1892. Tony and I went to Westminster Abbey to pay our last tribute to the poet. We arrived early, but already found a great crush for the funeral; and were relieved to hear the friendly voice of Alma-Tadema[1] calling to us over his shoulder to keep near him that we might sit together. We had special places, but were much jostled in trying to reach them. Jarring cries came to our cloister from the streets; shrill voices of vendors, ' "Crossing the Bar"—sixpence a copy', 'Here's the latest photograph of Lord Tennyson.' At last we entered the Abbey and escaped these out-of-tune noises. We were near the dark opening in the floor; a bust of Longfellow close by. The glow from a stained glass window threw a soft flush on the face of Evangeline's creator—the only fleck of colour I could see in that forest of grey stone and livid marble. At last the great bell boomed and the organ and choir softly sounded through the Abbey:

> Sunset and Evening Star,
>   And one clear call for me.
> And may there be no moaning at the bar,
>   When I put out to sea.

At the request of the Prince of Wales ([later] King Edward VII) a Union Jack covered the coffin, which was placed on a high catafalque. . . .
Among the pall-bearers were:

> Lord Salisbury,
> Lord Rosebery,
> The United States Ambassador,
> The Duke of Argyll,
> The Master of Trinity (Dr Butler),
> Lord Kelvin,
> Mr Froude.

And the men of Balaclava were there: the men of the Light Brigade, whose valour the poet has immortalised. The golden hair of

* *A Few More Memories* (London: Hutchinson, 1936) pp. 28–9.

Tennyson's grandson was in strong contrast to the silver hair of Dr Jowett, whose face was full of solicitude as he watched the stricken figure of Hallam, the poet's only remaining son. The funeral rite over, Lord Salisbury and the other coffin-bearers made way for the distinguished mourners to file past the open grave for a last look at the laurel-crowned pall: the organ, meanwhile, voicing the nation's grief in the solemn march from *Saul*.

NOTE

Mary Anderson (1859–1940) was an American actress who married Antony de Navarro and settled in England. She produced Tennyson's play *The Cup* and visited him at Aldworth. She published two volumes of memoirs, *A Few Memories* (1896) and *A Few More Memories* (1936).

1. Sir Lawrence Alma-Tadema (1836–1912), painter.

Index

202 *Index*